MARGARET CHASE SMITH

Margaret Chase Smith (1897–   ). Permission to reprint 1946 portrait of Margaret Chase Smith granted by the Margaret Chase Smith Library in Skowhegan, Maine. Photographer Chase Statler of Washington, D.C.

MARGARET CHASE SMITH

SMITH

Model Public Servant

&

Marlene Boyd Vallin

Foreword by Halford R. Ryan

Great American Orators, Number 27
Bernard K. Duffy and Halford R. Ryan, Series Advisors

GREENWOOD PRESS
Westport, Connecticut • London

Library of Congress Cataloging-in-Publication Data

Vallin, Marlene Boyd.
 Margaret Chase Smith : model public servant / Marlene Boyd Vallin.
  p. cm.—(Great American orators, ISSN 0898-8277 ; no. 27)
 Includes bibliographical references and index.
 ISBN 0-313-29163-2 (alk. paper)
 1. Smith, Margaret Chase, 1897- . 2. Women legislators—United
States—Biography. 3. Legislators—United States—Biography.
4. United States. Congress. Senate—Biography. I. Title.
II. Series.
E748.S667V35 1998
328.73′092—dc21   97-53290
[B]

British Library Cataloguing in Publication Data is available.

Library of Congress Catalog Card Number: 97-53290
ISBN: 0-313-29163-2
ISSN: 0898-8277

First published in 1998

Greenwood Press, 88 Post Road West, Westport, CT 06881
An imprint of Greenwood Publishing Group, Inc.

Printed in the United States of America

The paper used in this book complies with the
Permanent Paper Standard issued by the National
Information Standards Organization (Z39.48–1984).

10 9 8 7 6 5 4 3 2 1

Copyright Acknowledgments

The author and the publisher gratefully acknowledge permission for use of the following material:

Permission to reprint Senator Margaret Chase Smith's speeches granted by Margaret Chase Smith.
Senator Smith's speeches can be found at the Margaret Chase Smith Library in Skowhegan, Maine.

To the memory of my beloved parents

— John and Anna Boyd —

who taught me all about perseverance

Contents

Series Foreword *by Bernard K. Duffy and Halford R. Ryan*   ix
Foreword *by Halford R. Ryan*   xiii
Preface   xv

Part I: Critical Analysis

  1. Margaret Chase Smith: A Great American Orator   3
  2. "I Speak as an American"   13
  3. "I Speak as a United States Senator"   45
  4. "I Speak as a Woman"   73
  5. "I Speak as a Republican"   93
     Notes   115

Part II: Collected Speeches

"Women and Leadership"   127
"No Place for a Woman"   131
"Answer to a Smear"   136
"Election Eve Radio Speech"   143
"Women's Progress"   147
"Declaration of Conscience I"   153
"The Importance of Individual Thinking"   158
"Response to Professor Fullam's 'Are You Proud?' Speech"   163
"Celebrating the Fortieth Anniversary"   170
"Nuclear Credibility (1961)   175
"The Kennedy Twist"   184
"Nuclear Credibility" (1962)   195

"Nuclear Test Ban Treaty"   203
"Presidential Candidacy Announcement"   207
"Anti-ABM"   214
"Declaration of Conscience II"   219
"I Speak as a Woman"   223

Chronology of Significant Speaking Events   229
Bibliography   233
Index   239

Series Foreword

The idea for a series of books on great American orators grew out of the recognition that there is a paucity of book-length studies on individual orators and their speeches. Apart from a few notable exceptions, the study of American public address has been pursued in scores of articles published in professional journals. As helpful as these studies have been, none has or can provide a complete analysis of a speaker's rhetoric. Book-length studies, such as those in this series, will help fill the void that has existed in the study of American public address and its related disciplines of politics and history, theology and sociology, communication and law. In a book, the critic can explicate a broader range of a speaker's persuasive discourse than reasonably could be treated in an article. The comprehensive research and sustained reflection that books require will undoubtedly yield many original and enduring insights concerning the nation's most important voices.

Public address has been a fertile ground for scholarly investigation. No matter how insightful their intellectual forbears, each generation of scholars must reexamine its universe of discourse, while expanding the compass of its researches and redefining its purpose and methods. To avoid intellectual torpor new scholars cannot be content simply to see through the eyes of those who have come before them. We hope that this series of books will stimulate important new understandings of the nature of persuasive discourse and provide opportunities for scholarship in the history and criticism of American public address.

This series examines the role of rhetoric in the United States. American speakers shaped the destinies of the colonies, the young republic, and the mature nation. During each stage of the intellectual, political, and religious development of the United States, great orators, standing at the rostrum, on the Stump, and in the pulpit, used words and gestures to influence their audiences. Usually striving for the noble, sometimes achieving the base, they urge their fellow citizens toward a more perfect Union. The books in this series chronicle and explain the accomplishments of representative American leaders as orators.

A series of book-length studies on American persuaders honors the role men and women have played in U.S. history. Previously, if one desired to assess the impact of a speaker or a speech upon history, the path was, at best, not well marked and, at worst, littered with obstacles. To be sure, one might turn to biographies and general histories to learn about an orator, but for the public address scholar these sources often proved unhelpful. Rhetorical topics, such as speech invention, style, delivery, organizational strategies, and persuasive effect, are often treated in passing, if mentioned at all. Authoritative speech texts are often difficult to locate, and the problem of textual accuracy is frequently encountered. This is especially true for those figures who spoke one or two hundred years ago or for those whose persuasive role, though significant, was secondary to other leading lights of the age.

Each book in this series is organized to meet the needs of scholars and students of the history and criticism of American public address. Part I is a critical analysis of the orator and his or her speeches. Within the format of a case study, one may expect considerable latitude. For instance, in a given chapter an author might explicate a single speech or a group of related speeches, or examine orations that comprise a genre of rhetoric such as forensic speaking. But the critic's focus remains on the rhetorical considerations of speaker, speech, occasion, and effect. Part II contains the texts of important addresses that are discussed in the critical analysis that precedes it. To the extent possible, each author has endeavored to collect authoritative speech texts, which have often been found through original research in collections of primary source material. In a few instances, because of the extreme length of a speech, texts have been edited, but the authors have been careful to delete material that is least important to the speech, and these deletions have been held to a minimum.

In each book there is a chronology of major speeches that serves more purposes than may be apparent at first. Pragmatically, it typically lists all of the orator's known speeches and addresses. Places and dates of the speeches are also listed, although this is information that is sometimes difficult to determine precisely. But in a wider sense, the chronology attests to the scope of rhetoric in the United States. Certainly in quantity if not always in quality, Americans are historically talkers and listeners.

Because of the disparate nature of the speakers examined in the series, there is some latitude in the nature of the bibliographical materials that have been included in each book. But in every instance, authors have carefully described original historical materials and collections and gathered critical studies, biographies and autobiographies, and a variety of secondary sources that bear on the speaker and the oratory. By combining in each book bibliographical materials, speech texts, and critical chapters, this series notes that text and research sources are interwoven in the act of rhetorical criticism.

May the books in this series serve to memorialize the nation's greatest orators.

Bernard K. Duffy
Halford R. Ryan

Foreword

Was Margaret Chase Smith a great American orator? If she is judged by standards of the nineteenth century — a stentorian voice and a spread-eagled delivery — then she fails to qualify, for her *actio*, the classical term for platform delivery, was subdued. Perhaps her stature as a U.S. senator, and the first female senator elected in her own right to that hitherto male club, would qualify her for inclusion as a great American orator. Alas, she was not a Senator Daniel Webster or a Henry Clay or a John C. Calhoun of America's Golden Age of Oratory, nor was she a Senator Huey Long, a William Borah, or an Everett Dirksen in the twentieth century. Yet she has left her mark on American politics and oratory.

Perhaps she was a great twentieth-century speaker. On this criterion, Smith certainly qualifies. As an archetype of the female speaker and politician in this century, Smith addressed audiences in two of Aristotle's three genres of political rhetoric. With regard to deliberative oratory, Smith was the first woman to speak as a congresswoman and senator. As for occasional oratory, she also used the rostrum to address epideictic audiences, particularly as a commencement speaker and as the guest of numerable civic and service clubs.

Perhaps she was a great twentieth-century American. Margaret Chase Smith was a solid citizen who exemplified the Greek notion of *arête*. She believed in civic duty and piety in which she strove for, and attained, excellence; she championed democracy; and she attacked Senator Joseph McCarthy while her male colleagues in the U.S. Senate cowered. Her many political campaigns, mounted without being bought and paid for with other people's money (here alone is Smith's lesson for our times), attest to her independence as a moderate Republican from Maine.

But last of all, Margaret Chase Smith was a woman. How she worked out the tensions of a woman's working in a man's world and still remained a female is worth reading in itself. In fact, Smith broke the old stereotype of the cult of true womanhood that was anchored in domesticity—

and submissiveness — for she clearly violated both, but the citizens of Maine evidently did not mind. But neither was Smith an advocate of feminism, as it was conceived in the 1960s and 1970s, for she believed women's and men's roles were interchangeable at least with regard to politics. Indeed, she stood for personhood wherein gender roles were irrelevant, as indeed they should be with regard to justice and citizenship rights.

And Professor Marlene Vallin, the author of this book, is a woman. Like Smith, Vallin pursues her task as a scholar without reference to gender. To be sure, Vallin notes that Smith fell out of favor with feminists, for Smith regarded her brand of domesticity an important role for the home as well as the national government. Would a male writer have caught Vallin's perception? On the other hand, Vallin is sensitive to Smith's "maleness" as an orator: Smith argued, she debated, she used evidence to warrant her claims, and she campaigned against males. In short, as Smith was a rhetor who happened to be a woman, Vallin is a rhetorical critic who happens to be a woman. Those expecting more or less from either Smith or Vallin, solely as a function of gender, will be sorely disappointed.

Indeed, Vallin's work on Smith's papers and archives has already born fruit, for the professor has spoken to many audiences, both lay and academic, about various facets of Smith's oratory. But in this book Vallin ably assembles the whole narrative history of Smith's remarkable oratorical career. In sum, Vallin explicates how and why Margaret Chase Smith's rhetoric gained and maintained her tenure in elected office.

Halford R. Ryan

Preface

The purpose of this book is to demonstrate that Margaret Chase Smith, U.S. senator from Maine, was a great American orator. She was a petite, rather quiet woman of average education and ordinary background who successfully used her rhetorical talent to create a most successful career in the hitherto exclusive male domain of politics. For thirty-two years she convinced her constituents to choose her continually as their representative in the U.S. Congress. In particular, during her four terms in the U.S. Senate, regarded as the most powerful deliberative body in the world, she never hesitated to speak out when necessary. When her Republican colleague Senator Joseph McCarthy of Wisconsin was using the Senate floor to irresponsibly defame the reputations of individuals who did not have an opportunity to defend themselves, she addressed the offensive situation and the collective offenders, boldly censuring all in that hallowed arena for allowing such behavior. Her courage to risk her career for the defense of democratic values was celebrated by many in the media. She was not intimidated by the fact that she was the only female member; she was solely motivated by the need to "do the right thing."

Throughout her career Margaret Chase Smith of Maine was noteworthy for her moral courage. She was answerable only to her constituents, her conscience, and the Constitution of the United States. In her pursuit to be the best American representative she could be, she skillfully used the speaker's platform to contest controlling traditional belief. When the party politicians tried to deter her from winning the primary election for the Senate in 1948 by reviving the traditional claim that the Senate was no place for a woman, Margaret Chase Smith's determination to win only grew stronger. Although her vocal tone tended to be soft and her image slight, her message was powerful. Many of her Senate colleagues soon realized that Margaret Chase Smith was a bold contender, and they, along with the people of Maine and the nation, grew to admire her.

     The study of Margaret Chase Smith's oratory is significant for several
reasons. First, it offers insight into the stormiest times of the twentieth
century. Serving in Congress from 1940 to 1972, Margaret Chase Smith was
involved in political policy regarding World War II, the Korean War, the
Vietnam War, and the Cold War. She participated in the momentous debates
over nuclear power and domestic upheaval. Second, Smith's speeches
demonstrate that a woman can succeed in politics, a world traditionally
regarded as exclusive to men. Third, the study of Smith's oratory presents a
model for political integrity. The senator's refusal to be coerced or bought by
political machines and special interest groups is a worthwhile lesson for
politicians. Finally, the study of Smith's oratory illustrates the enduring
strength of the American character. Like the common man ideal of the
nineteeth century, Margaret Chase Smith's achievements confirm that
opportunities abound in America if one has the will and determination to
make them happen.

     The book is divided into two parts. Part I contains five chapters.
Chapter 1 introduces the study, including the rationale, background information, objectives, and organization. Chapters 2 through 5 are devoted to critical
analysis of selected speeches. Chapter 2, "I Speak as an American," discusses
the rhetorical value of both "Declaration of Conscience" speeches, delivered
in 1950 and 1970. Chapter 3, "I Speak as a United States Senator," investi-
gates three of Senator Smith's strong responses to the foreign policy of the
Kennedy administration: "Nuclear Credibility," 1961 and 1962, and "Nuclear
Test Ban Treaty." Chapter 4, "I Speak as a Woman," studies samples of the
numerous speeches Smith delivered to women's groups: "Women and
Leadership," "Women's Progress," "No Place for a Woman," and "The
Importance of Individual Thinking." Chapter 5, "I Speak as a Republican,"
focuses on two important speeches Smith delivered during her 1948 primary
campaign for the Senate — "Answer to a Smear" and "Election Eve Radio
Speech" and — at the pinnacle of her career, the "Presidential Candidacy
Announcement" speech. The title of each chapter was taken from Smith's first
"Declaration of Conscience."

     Part II of the book is composed of reference materials that relate to
Part I. Texts of the speeches chosen for analysis in Part I are found here. In
addition, there are texts of selected speeches included that are mentioned in
Part I and also serve to illustrate the value of Smith's oratory: "Anti-ABM,"
"The Kennedy Twist," "Response to Professor Fullam's 'Are You Proud?'
Speech," "Celebrating the Fortieth Anniversary," and "I Speak as a Woman."
Also included in this part is a chronology of the speaking events, indicating the
date and place of presentation of each speech studied. The final segment
consists of a bibliography that includes information about the Northwood
University Margaret Chase Smith Library, a congressional research library
located in Senator Smith's hometown of Skowhegan, Maine, and lists of
primary and secondary source material.

I would like to express particular appreciation to the librarians at Penn State Berks, especially Nancy Dewald, for their cooperative responses to my calls for assistance; to faculty secretary Anna Esterly, for her clerical aid; and to the staff, especially Angela Stockwell, of the Margaret Chase Smith Library, for facilitating the research phase of my study. I would also like to formally thank my devoted family— my husband Richard, our son David, his wife Kimberly, and our daughter Allison — for their faithful support and understanding. Above all, I want to thank Margaret Chase Smith for her inspiration.

PART I
CRITICAL ANALYSIS

1
Margaret Chase Smith: A Great American Orator

> My creed is that public service must be more than doing a
> job efficiently and honestly. It must be a complete dedica-
> tion to the people and to the nation with full recognition that
> every human being is entitled to courtesy and consideration,
> that constructive criticism is not only to be expected but
> sought, that smears are not only to be expected but fought,
> that honor is to be earned but not bought.

— Margaret Chase Smith, November 11, 1953[1]

At the 1964 Republican National Convention in San Francisco, Margaret
Chase Smith, senator from Maine, sat in the stands at the Cow Palace along
with her enthusiastic supporters and listened intently while her friend and
colleague Senator George Aiken of Vermont placed her name in nomination
for the president of the United States. Although tradition dictated that
nominees not be present at the time of their nomination, she insisted on
witnessing the event, the pinnacle of her long political career. She had to be
consumed with contentment as Senator Aiken described her as the "best
qualified for the job." In an enumerated list, he described Senator Smith's
presidential qualities: integrity, ability, experience, courage, and common
sense. Referring to her enormous popularity— nationally, internationally, as
well as with the voters of Maine, the prestigious senator from her neighboring
state summarized her appeal: "[S]he 'can walk with Kings nor lose the
common touch.'"[2]

Margaret Chase Smith, the high school graduate from a working-class
family in rural central Maine, became the first woman nominated for the
presidency by a major political party. She knew she had no chance of
winning, for she had no organization, only devoted volunteers, and no
campaign funds. (She refused to accept money from others.) In addition, she

was competing with the most powerful leaders of the Republican Party —
Barry Goldwater of Arizona, Nelson Rockefeller of New York, Richard Nixon
of California, George Romney of Michigan, Henry Cabot Lodge of Massachusetts, and William Scranton of Pennsylvania. Her decision to have her name
placed in nomination was more of a symbolic gesture. Simply, she wanted
to demonstrate that a moderate with the most federal experience of all the
nominees and the encouragement of a good many voters had the right to run.
As she explained in her "Presidential Candidacy Announcement" speech to the
Women's National Press Club on January 27, 1964, she decided to run for the
presidency for the sake of women's progress. The act presented her with "an
opportunity to break the barrier against women being seriously considered" for
the office.

Margaret Chase Smith's life reads like the stuff of American legends.
Like the log cabin presidents, she rose from obscurity to national prominence.
Her early years were similar to those of the nineteenth-century common man,
that democratic ideal credited with fostering America's greatness. Born just
before the dawn of the twentieth century, on December 14, 1897, in the rural
town of Skowhegan, Maine, she was the oldest of six children produced by
George Chase, a descendant of the early Puritan settlers, and Carrie Murray,
of French-Canadian stock. Life was especially challenging for the Chases as
they struggled to keep above the poverty line. Margaret's father, a ne'er-do-
well who eventually became a barber, was remote and unhappy. He was not
proud of the fact that his family had to live in his father-in-law's house. Her
mother, on the other hand, doted on her, helping her to sense her importance.
Skowhegan was a mill town, and the struggle to survive economically was
commonplace. However, the typical Mainers did not bemoan their travail, as
they were determined to persevere. They were imprinted with the legacy of
their Puritan forbears to believe that hard work, frugality, and self-reliance
were virtues. The rugged terrain and the harsh winters, like those experienced
by the American frontiersman, honed rugged individualists. Mainers, true to
the Yankee tradition, were a proud people, independent, and fiercely patriotic.
The culture that influenced the development of Margaret Chase Smith's
character was one committed to the belief in the indomitable quality of the
American spirit.

Except for her membership on the basketball team, Margaret Chase
showed little interest in school. She was more interested in earning money
and, therefore, worked at a number of jobs after school. During her senior
year in 1915, two events proved fateful. On a class trip, she saw Washington,
D.C., for the first time, and as a telephone operator, she met Skowhegan
Selectman Clyde Smith. For the remainder of her senior year, she worked in
his office, completing her schoolwork in the evenings and on weekends.

Her relationship and eventual marriage to the popular politician
Clyde Smith, her membership in the Business and Professional Women's Club,
and her partnership with William C. Lewis were the experiences that pro-

moted her political ambitions. Clyde Smith introduced her to political life —
his death opened the door to Margaret's congressional career. The Business
and Professional Women's Club taught her the requisite skills, such as public
speaking, for leadership. Bill Lewis, as her companion, confidant, and coach,
urged her on to glory during her tenure in Congress.

Margaret Smith's election to the Congress of the United States in
1940 came only twenty years after women gained the right to vote. She
entered the U.S. Senate, the most powerful legislative body in the world, eight
years later. Forty-four years after the passage of the Nineteenth Amendment,
she became the first woman nominated for the presidency of the United
States, the most powerful position in the world. Her life spanned the course
of the twentieth century, and her years in Congress covered the most dramatic
events in American history. Serving in the Congress during the administrations of Presidents Franklin D. Roosevelt, Harry S. Truman, Dwight D.
Eisenhower, John F. Kennedy, Lyndon B. Johnson, and Richard M. Nixon, she
was a front-row participant in the deliberations regarding the U.S. involvement
in World War II, the Cold War, and the Vietnam War. With seniority from
her three terms in the Senate, she held a ranking position on the powerful
Armed Services and Appropriations Committees. In 1967, she was chosen by
her thirty-five male colleagues to preside over the Senate Republican
Conference, a position that included her in bipartisan meetings at the White
House.

RATIONALE FOR THE STUDY

The study of Margaret Chase Smith's rise to political power is
significant. The fact that she gained entry into the U.S. Senate and thrived
there for twelve years, that she was considered for the vice presidency twice,
and that she was nominated by a major political party for the presidency is
nothing less than phenomenal! Tradition, as well as the consensus of
contemporary studies, has demonstrated that the political arena was strictly
a male domain.[3] The contention, confronted by Smith, that the Senate and
the presidency was no place for a woman was based on the long-held
judgment that public speaking and femininity are mutually exclusive. To
persuade others from the platform was to exert power. For women to speak
on an equal basis with men was still considered by many a challenge to male
authority and ability. For women to appeal to traditional values, especially
common in campaign rhetoric, would put their candidacy into question
because the act itself was contradictory to conventional belief. In addition, the
requisite attributes for political leadership — the ability to orate, argue, and
debate — were supposedly alien to the customary perception of women's
spheres. Women's traditional roles dictated that they speak softly and
demurely, and the notion of women in politics was incomprehensible.

The purpose of this study is to explore Margaret Chase Smith's ascent to the highest realms of political power through oratory. The question governing the investigation is a natural one: How did this obviously feminine person with a common background and a history of ordinary accomplishments manage to reach such heights in the quintessential male domain? The book presents analyses of several of her speeches that illuminate the answer. The discourses are organized in chapters labeled according to how she viewed her position as a politician. The identifications are taken from her most famous speech, "Declaration of Conscience," when she boldly faced the all-male assembly in the Senate and prefaced her message with the assertion: "I speak as a Republican. I speak as a woman. I speak as a United States Senator. I speak as an American."

In spite of the obvious value in studying the rhetoric of Margaret Chase Smith, no such studies have been published to date. As a matter of fact, the *Index to Journals in Communication Studies* mentions only two articles, but neither offers a critical analysis of her oratory.[4] Smith's "Declaration of Conscience" is her only speech included in two public address anthologies.[5] All of the three unpublished theses on Smith, two doctoral and one master's, focus on the "Declaration of Conscience" speech; two present rhetorical overviews.[6]

Senator Smith's rhetoric is worthy of study. Her carefully crafted style reveals a great deal of information about her ability to succeed in a man's world. Her messages tended to have a moral theme, generally focused on preserving America's basic democratic values. Her arguments were organized in inductive structure, depending for support on example and commonsense logic. Her language was concise and deliberate, devoid of any ambiguity. Contrary to the common assumptions posed by researchers of feminist rhetoric,[7] the style of her speeches offered no evidence of her gender. Her purposes were passionate, but the speeches were not dependent on emotional appeal. Also, contrary to research studies on women's speech, Senator Smith's discourses demonstrated that she was a master of the deliberative and forensic form, for she argued as aggressively and debated as skillfully as any man. Her introductions tended to be brief, often with an air of urgency and a take-charge tone. Otherwise, the pleasantries in her greetings were spare. To be colloquial, the senator's oratorical style was true to her personal behavior — she cut right to the chase. Metaphors were few, more purposeful than literary. She was a master at creating impact in structure and style of language. For example, in order to instill a surprise effect in "Presidential Candidacy Announcement," she used the inductive organizational structure. She revealed her decision to run after reviewing the powerful arguments against her running. Other devices used to advance her rhetorical strategy were the repetition of parallel phrases in litany fashion, cleverly positioned rhetorical questions, and the use of the climactic conclusion. Her speeches indicated that she was very aware of the power of identification in effecting communication. She usually adopted the stance of the generic American woman, when addressing women's groups, and that of a democratic reformer, moving her listeners to relate to her ethos. The appeals were very persuasive.

BACKGROUND INFORMATION

Margaret Chase Smith was a model public servant. She devoted her life to serving the American people, and especially the people of Maine, to the utmost of her ability. She was proud to call herself a politician, taking great care to explain to the voters her meaning of the label: "I'm your errand girl in Washington."[8] While some of the occupants of Congress tend to be suspected of legislating according to personal ambition, her motives were selfless. Never silent in the face of injustice, complacency, and corruption, she continually risked reputation for the higher purpose of "doing the right thing." Her political philosophy, simple yet strong, was based on the Golden Rule and the principles of government as conceived by our Founding Fathers. Like Abraham Lincoln, whom she often quoted, she believed firmly in "government of the people, by the people, and for the people."

For thirty-two years, from 1940 to 1972, Margaret Chase Smith won election to the Congress of the United States, first in the House of Representatives for four two-year terms (1940-1948), followed by four six-year terms in the Senate (1948-1972). She has the distinction of being the first woman duly elected to both houses of Congress.

The petite, soft-spoken woman from Skowhegan, Maine, rose in stature to international prominence. The quality of her character, especially her relentless determination to defend America's revered democratic values, won her the hearts and minds of the Maine voters. She was the greatest vote-getter in Maine history. She shook up the collective consciences of the national and world communities with her straightforward speeches on political morality. When her reputedly formidable colleagues in the Senate cowered in fear of the threatening tactics of Senator Joseph McCarthy, Margaret Chase Smith, the sole woman in that hallowed chamber, rose to the challenge. In her first major speech as a senator, the "Declaration of Conscience" speech, delivered on June 1, 1950, she soundly censured her Republican colleague and all others in the Senate who watched idly as the very legislators sworn to uphold the Constitution gave tacit consent to the wanton defamation of character exercised by one of its own members. She faced them head-on and scolded: "Those of us who shout the loudest about Americanism . . . are all too frequently those who, by our own words and acts, ignore some of the basic principles of Americanism." As the so-called Quiet Woman, Smith risked personal and political reputation by beginning the move to combat McCarthyism, the ideology that bred fear in the American mind.

Strongly believing that one should speak only if one could say something worthwhile, Margaret Smith rose from her seat again and again during those tumultuous times to speak in the name of democratic morality. Twenty years later, on the same date, June 1, 1970, she found the need to issue a second "Declaration of Conscience." Once more, the urgency was the rise of political extremism, but this time from the Left. The proliferation of angry demonstrations against the Nixon administration's policy on the war in Vietnam moved her to warn Americans that "[e]xtremism bent upon polarization of our people is increasingly forcing upon the American people the narrow choice between anarchy and repression." Once more she called for action on the part of the "great center of our people, those who reject the violence and unreasonableness of both the extreme right and the extreme left [to muster] their moral and physical courage, shed their intimidated silence, and [to declare] their consciences."

Margaret Chase Smith cared little for whose wrath she might incur. She was pledged to safeguard the nation as she saw fit. For example, she fiercely debated President Kennedy's attempts to reach some form of rapprochement with the Soviet Union during the Cold War with his program for nuclear disarmament. In two of her speeches bearing the same title, "Nuclear Credibility," delivered one year apart on the same date, September 21, 1961 and 1962, she promoted the need for nuclear superiority for the nation's best interest while ridiculing the president for weakness when confronting the Communists: "I sense a tendency, strange to the American character in world affairs, to retreat from circumstances rather than to face up to them realistically and master them." Her 1961 speech so angered Soviet leader Nikita Khrushchev that he referred to her as "the devil in a disguise of a woman."[9] Even Mrs. Khrushchev accused her of threatening "to destroy our homes, to kill our husbands, to take the lives of our children."[10]

Like the rose that daily adorned her dress, Margaret Chase Smith appeared gentle, almost fragile, but many who got too close felt the sting of her thorns. Those who dared to impugn her reputation, to question her motives, or to impede her rights soon left smarting with the realization that she could fight like any man. She was not to be dismissed lightly or taken for granted. She consistently demonstrated that she was her own person, impervious to any outside influence. For example, when she announced her decision to run for the Senate, the general response was the conventional remark that "the Senate was no place for a woman." Both friend and foe, male and female, tried to dissuade her, but her mind was made up. Rather than a roadblock, she saw such restrictions on her freedom as a challenge. She welcomed the position of underdog, making it the focus of her rhetorical strategy. For instance, when the male contenders for the Senate seat in the primary campaign of 1948 used bully tactics, such as the distribution of anonymous smear sheets, to try to force her out of the race, she responded with strength. Rather than quit, she waited until the right moment and struck the final blow. The speech "Answer to a Smear," which she called her "most crucial political speech,"[11] rebutted every accusation on the sheets, in a display of moral superiority. Her demonstration of courage and fortitude to face the powerful political machine and to expose its corruptive practices won her the respect of the voters of Maine and a resounding victory. Margaret Chase Smith had broken the "glass ceiling" for women. Aside from Hattie Caraway, Democrat from Arkansas, who fulfilled her deceased husband's term and then won election for one term with the aid of the popular vote-getter Huey Long, Smith was the first woman truly elected to the U.S. Senate in her own right.

Margaret Chase Smith's speeches reveal her role as democratic educator. Her orations to women's groups and to the graduates of women's college were lectures on the value, power, and responsibility of women, particularly toward the preservation of the democracy and the pursuit of world peace. For example, her discourses to significant groups, such as the Women's Christian Temperance Union and the Federation of Business and Professional Women's Clubs, were sermons of gratitude and encouragement. She entreated them to continue their work for women's progress. Employing her ethos as model, she preached her constant message of self-reliance: "You can if you think you can." She reasoned that the right to vote gave women equality with men, proclaiming that "[c]itizenship has no sex."[12] In a speech to the League of Women Voters in Washington, D.C., on June 29, 1949, she articulated the basic premise of her message to women:

> Women are no different from men in their voting and politics. Just as men do, women have the responsibility as citizens to vote and keep our true democracy alive. Women have the same obligation to think, articulate, and act in the defense of our priceless heritage of liberty.

At times, she boldly chastised women for not taking advantage of their voting power, claiming: "Those that make the breaks, get the breaks."[13] She contended that "[f]ailing to vote is indicative of something far more dangerous than non-voting itself. Such failure reveals a state of mind and an attitude that is basically unAmerican."[14] In response to the age-old question regarding a woman's place, she dismissed it bluntly: "Everywhere."[15]

In her commencement speeches, her rhetorical stance was softer, more maternal. Acknowledging the potential of the younger generation, she advised them to realize their responsibility. In "The Importance of Individual Thinking," an example of her stock speech for such occasions, she encouraged the young women to think before they speak, but "once you have made up your mind, don't hesitate to speak your mind." That, she explained, is the way to protect the democracy from demagogues. The senator used her renowned reputation to teach them about the need for moral courage, her signature characteristic.

Margaret Chase Smith, always the independent, often boldly announced her refusal to accept the feminist label. She was a person who happened to be female. She attacked the feminist movement for demanding more than equal status, for it demanded equality with the retention of special privileges. She stubbornly supported her rationale that the Nineteenth Amendment gave women equality, implying that a women's movement was not necessary. As a politician, she eschewed the feminist tag because it would categorize her as a one-issue candidate. She reasoned that such a stance would weaken her appeal to the electorate, and moreover, it would constrict her purpose as a representative of the people.

Nevertheless, Margaret Chase Smith did work for the advancement of women, particularly when she was a member of the Naval Affairs Committee in the House of Representatives. She is credited for playing an active role in the struggle to secure women a permanent place in the armed forces. She also supported the Equal Rights Amendment. Overall, Margaret Smith never ceased advocating her claim that the most important role for women in the democracy is the traditional one, that of homemaker. She reasoned that the home was the fundamental unit of democracy and that homemakers are governors of the home: "Woman moulds the citizens of tomorrow in the rearing that she gives the children."[16] She often concluded her commencement speeches to young women graduates with this advice:

> [W]hether you enter public service or not, there is no finer
> role that you can play in the defense of democracy and our
> American way of life than that of wife, mother, and home-
> maker. Run your homes and raise your children in the very
> best traditions and fundamentals of our American way of
> life.[17]

Margaret Chase Smith's speeches also serve as evidence of her role as democratic reformer. She undertook her pledge to uphold the Constitution with the fervor of a moral crusader. For example, in both "Declaration of Conscience" speeches, she warned the nation about the threat of extremism to the freedoms we hold so dear. In 1950, she displayed moral courage in attacking Joseph McCarthy. She castigated her Senate colleagues for their silence, calling it moral cowardice. In general, her speeches encouraged the citizens of America to speak out against demagoguery. Her sermonic style speech to the Women's Christian Temperance Union in 1949 presents a simple solution to the problems of creating world peace: "the total mobiliza- tion of our moral forces." Her discourses were replete with references to morality. Above all, her public persona was presented as a symbol of democratic morality.

Margaret Chase Smith's character loomed in popularity above her accomplishments. She received many awards and honors in the name of her Americanism. The Reserve Officer's Association granted her their Minuteman Award in 1964. The United Press International voted her one of the ten most influential women in the world in 1967. For her service in Congress, she was named the "Woman of the Year in Politics" by the Associated Press for the years 1948, 1949, 1950, and 1957. In 1973, she was given the U.S. Senate Service Award. In 1989, President George Bush bestowed on her the Presidential Medal of Freedom, her highest tribute. In addition, colleges and universities presented her with ninety-five honorary doctoral degrees.

Margaret Chase Smith's greatest contribution to American life was in the field of politics. She was indeed the first woman to make major advances in the American political arena, but above all, she was a model public servant. Her political integrity was remarkable. She regarded her election to public office as a mandate by the voters to represent them to the best of her ability. She took her oath to uphold the Constitution as a sacred duty. Nothing in her life took precedence over the responsibility to fulfill the obligations of her duties. She paid meticulous attention to even the smallest details, never failing to acknowledge the requests from her constituents as quickly as possible. She *was* "their errand girl in Washington."

Her campaign efforts were herculean by any human measure. She literally drove the length and breadth of the state to share her plans and gain the support of islanders, coast dwellers, and rugged inhabitants of the wild northern territory. She preferred the personal touch rather than the public platform, enjoying the conversational chatter of chastised, country stores, and cozy kitchens. The effort that she exerted in the performance of her duties was legendary. She prided herself on her perfect attendance record in Congress. She held the all-time consecutive roll-call voting record, 2,941, in the history of the U.S. Senate until 1981. She was master of her own mind, never allowing herself to be influenced by others. She disdained party politics, always voting her conscience over the party line. She conducted her campaigns and the business of her office with great frugal restraint, declining to abuse the voters' trust by participating in congressional junkets and by accepting campaign contributions. She paid for her trips and campaign expenses out of her own pocket. She had no political organization to manage her campaigns, depending solely on the support of volunteers. Whether on the floor of the Senate or at the myriad campaign sites, she never attacked her opponents by name, no matter how evil their intentions. She was a professional in the true sense of the word. She conducted her office with the strong moral sense that won her the hearts of Maine voters and the admiration of her colleagues and the nation.

Margaret Chase Smith was more than a stateswoman; she symbolized the essence of American democracy. She deserves a special place in the annals of American history. Future generations need to know of the accomplishments of the indomitable lady from Maine. They need to read of her humble beginnings and meteoric rise to fame. They need to learn of her unique courage and determination. They need to appreciate her model of political integrity. They need to realize that this mere mite of a woman packed the rhetorical clout of a heavyweight. They need to study her portrait displaying her erect posture, clear blue eyes, and firm chin, all fixed on her faith in herself, her country, and her moral code. Above all, they need to remember her as a representative American orator, the embodiment of the American character that made America great.

2
"I Speak as an American"

Margaret Chase Smith did not make many major speeches during her thirty-two-year career in the U.S. Congress, professing only to do so when she had "something worthwhile to say."[1] On June 1, 1950, after spending her first spring in the Senate watching "the greatest deliberative body in the world" sink "to the level of a forum of hate and character assassination,"[2] she felt compelled to speak out. Despite threats of smear campaigns and possible political suicide, the "Quiet Woman,"[3] who was heretofore simply overlooked by her all-male colleagues, responded to her own voice, her interpretation of her position, her political philosophy. Simply stated, she saw herself as a public servant, elected to serve the American people by safeguarding the principles of the Constitution. During her first session in the Senate, she witnessed the forces of political extremism of the Right abuse those principles. Worse, she saw her more experienced, more prestigious colleagues react with apparent indifference to the defamation. To Smith, such behavior was tantamount to sacrilege, as it was downright immoral. She spoke out to the Senate to warn it that the "serious national condition" that threatened "the end of everything that we Americans hold dear" was the result of ineffective leadership in the federal government.[4]

Within fifteen-minutes, Margaret Chase Smith, the lone woman in that celebrated male arena, revealed the strength of her character to all. She, too, had muscle— moral muscle, and she was not afraid to use it. She became front-page news; newspapers and national magazines lauded her courage. Many hailed her as the Joan of Arc of the Senate. One highly reputed statesman, Bernard Baruch, was quoted as saying, "If a man had made the Declaration of Conscience, he would be the next President of the United States."[5] The "Declaration of Conscience" speech of June 1, 1950 can be credited for casting Margaret Smith's destiny in national politics.

On June 1, 1970, twenty years to the day, a more venerable Margaret Chase Smith found it necessary to reassert the principles she championed in her "Declaration of Conscience." Following the form of her signature address almost to the letter, she again alerted the nation to a new threat of political extremism, this time from the Left. To her, unchecked political extremism, whether from the Right or from the Left, was the greatest threat to the basic principles of Americanism. The June 1, 1970, address has the same title and form. True to her notion of public service, Senator Smith repeated the crux of her message:

> The American people are sick and tired of being afraid to speak their minds lest they be politically smeared as "Communists" or "Fascists" by their opponents. Freedom of speech is not what it used to be in America. It has been so abused by some that it is not exercised by others.[6]

Although Senator Smith addressed two specific rhetorical situations and two specific audiences— in 1950, she spoke directly to her fellow senators about the damage being done by their Republican colleague Joseph McCarthy, and in 1970, she spoke directly to the Senate and to the American people about the threat of the anti-establishment riots— her statement of purpose on both occasions expressed her resolute political philosophy that unchecked extremism can only result in a government of repression— the very antithesis of democracy.

This chapter will discuss each speech separately, devoting most of the discussion to "Declaration of Conscience I" because it served as the pattern for the second speech and, of course, because it impacted Margaret Chase Smith's career significantly. The analysis will follow a neo-Aristotelian form for the most part, starting with an in-depth overview of the rhetorical situation. The analysis will focus on the exigence, the conditions in the nation and in the Senate that provoked the exigence, and the impact of Senator Joseph McCarthy on the exigence. A summary of the results of the rhetorical act, followed by an evaluation of its effectiveness, will serve as the conclusion.

"DECLARATION OF CONSCIENCE I"

On June 1, 1950, Margaret Chase Smith of Maine, newly elected to the U.S. Senate and its sole woman member, rose from her seat on the Republican side of the aisle and delivered the speech that propelled her to nation prominence. Although it was her first major address and lasted only fifteen minutes, it was profound — because of its purpose, its style, and the speaker herself. With carefully measured terms, Senator Smith delivered a clarion call to the consciences of her colleagues. A "national condition" had pushed the United States to the brink of "national suicide," and they were responsible. The ineffective leadership of the Democratic administration and the members of the U.S. Senate were permitting "the end of everything that we Americans hold dear." Mrs. Smith's speech was a stern warning. The seemingly demure lady from Maine articulated a verbal thrashing to her so-called omnipotent male colleagues. She indicted them for what she perceived to be moral cowardice. Urging them to recall the democratic principles on which the nation was founded, she called on them "to do some soul-searching . . . on the manner in which we are performing our duty to the people of America." Her speech was aptly titled "Declaration of Conscience."

THE STATE OF THE NATION IN 1950

The "national condition" Senator Smith alluded to on June 1, 1950 was, in her words, "a national feeling of fear and frustration." The nation was disillusioned with the results of World War II. America, with the aid of the Allied forces, had won the war and saved the world from the nefarious Axis forces, yet there was no sense of peace. As soon as the demilitarization of American forces in Europe began — the good news that the boys were coming home — the bad news began. The reality was that World War II may have ended the perceived major hostilities, but its ending resulted not in world peace but in the outbreak of new, and seemingly, more insidious threats. The Communist movement, present in the world since the nineteenth-century writings of Marx and Engels, and made real with the rise of Bolshevism and the revolution in Russia in 1917, gained strength after World War II because of the democratic nations' alliance with the Soviet Union. Josef Stalin, the megalomaniacal leader, was determined to fulfill Marx's dream of world domination. Ironically, the Allied conferences to plan the end of the war, in particular, the Yalta Conference, actually promoted the beginning of what was termed the Cold War. (Yalta, by the way, became part of the political lexicon meaning "betrayal.") The Soviet occupational forces in the eastern sector of Germany and Berlin became permanent, with the installation of a Communist regime. By January 1950, the "Iron Curtain," forewarned by Winston Churchill, seemed to be implacably in place. Soviet expansion engulfed the war-torn nations of Eastern Europe and parts of the Far East. In May 1949, China fell to the Communists, and the Nationalists fled to Formosa. The Communist government of North Korea threatened to invade the Republic of South Korea. Fearful that the Communist threat was everywhere, the American people became anxious.

The national paranoia that pervaded the American psyche was not totally irrational. Reputable sources, particularly in the media, fed the quasi-hysteria. For example, the June 2, 1947, issue of *Newsweek* informed its readership of the growing Communist membership in labor unions, of an increase of Communist publications, and of the effectiveness of the American Labor Party, considered a pro-Communist organization, which was represented by Vito Marcantonio, who happened to be a representative in the U.S. Congress.[7] The following week, on June 9, 1947, *Newsweek* published "How to Fight Communism," an article by J. Edgar Hoover, director of the Federal Bureau of Investigation (FBI). The article emphasized the increase in membership in the Communist Party. Hoover warned of the deceitful methods used by the Party to carry out their power quest. He cited the formation of front organizations with appealing titles, such as American Youth for Democracy. This organization was formerly known as the Young Communist League.[8] Hoover, America's chief crime fighter, urged Americans to fight Communism with truth and justice. Alarming news coverage on Communist territorial expansion dominated the airwaves as well as the print media. Spy stories proliferated within the popular culture. Books, films, and television shows focused on the potential enemy within, often promoting the "Better dead than Red" panacea. People tended to believe what they saw in print or heard on the airwaves. As Margaret Chase Smith surveyed in the "Declaration of Conscience," the country was on the brink of "national suicide."

Few attempts were made to modify the situation. In a speech delivered in May 1948, Justice William O. Douglas warned against undue concern about communism, urging the need to counteract fear based on ignorance and the need for better understanding of the "threat."[9] However, the fear prevailed.

The collective desperation for some rational resolve grew worse when the news was announced that the United States had lost its atomic monopoly. In 1949, scientists discerned that the Soviet Union had exploded a nuclear device. The United States was no longer the invulnerable superpower. The world was again at the brink of disaster, more cataclysmic than ever before.

SENATOR JOSEPH M. McCARTHY

Sitting on the Republican side in the U.S. Senate at the time that this fear was festering was the freshman senator from Wisconsin, Joseph M. McCarthy. He was elected in 1946, when a landslide victory for the Republicans resulted in their gaining the majority in both houses of Congress. For the first time since the Hoover administration, in 1932, the Republicans claimed the majority in both houses. The 80th Congress would make its mark in the history books for a number of reasons.

McCarthy seemed to have been sent to the U.S. Senate not so much for his attributes as a potential statesman, or for his political savvy, but because of his "instinct" for publicity.[10] He managed to convince the media to exploit his stint as a marine in World War II. Photos of "Tail-gunner Joe," commandeering a tank in full combat gear, promoted the working-class "common man" as an American hero. He loved publicity, and the reporters grew to love him. He had a talent for making news, the kind that fascinated the American public. Despite the fact that those who knew him saw him as nothing more than a rude, arrogant, low-class lout, noted for barroom brawls and dirty fighting, Joe McCarthy was useful to them. Prior to his fateful Wheeling speech, on February 9, 1950, Senator McCarthy had proved ineffective. The leadership of the Senate did not find him interesting. As a matter of fact, he was rated by Washington correspondents and political scientists as "the worst Senator in the Senate."[11] Needless to say, McCarthy was desperate to find an issue that would win him popular appeal, at least to assure him reelection in 1952. According to biographer Richard Rovere, "He was on the make with all the devices of ambition, and he was unencumbered by any sort of morality."[12]

On January 7, 1950, at a dinner with Father Edmund A. Walsh, regent of the School of Foreign Service at Georgetown University and author of several books on the threat of world communism, Walsh suggested that McCarthy might consider the issue of communism and its capacity for subversion. McCarthy had struck paydirt, but he did not realize that it was the motherload.

As luck would have it, or so he believed, Joe McCarthy, who gained his Senate seat by portraying himself as the blood and guts type that the American public fictionalized was the stuff of patriots, found the issue that would catapult him to national fame — Communist spies and traitors in the Truman Administration.

Invited to deliver a traditional Lincoln's birthday address to the Ohio County Women's Republican Club of Wheeling, West Virginia, on February 9, McCarthy planned to test his new issue. With the help of Willard Edwards, a member of the Washington bureau of the Chicago *Tribune*, McCarthy got his hands on information regarding State Department loyalty procedures gathered by the House Committee on Appropriations and a letter written by James F. Byrnes, Truman's secretary of state, on July 26, 1946, which discussed changes in personnel at State. According to Rovere: "From this dusty veteran of the file drawers, with its obsolete statistics, compiled for the predecessor of the predecessor for the then Secretary of State, McCarthy elaborated the myth on which his whole subsequent career was based."[13] Rovere attests that McCarthy had said time and again that the Byrnes letter was what he waved before the Wheeling ladies. According to a report by Frank Desmond of the Wheeling *Intelligencer*, that letter and some hasty notes were all that McCarthy had when he initiated his rhetoric of implication:

> While I cannot take the time to name all of the men in the
> State Department who have been named as members of the
> Communist Party and members of a spy ring, I have here in
> my hand a list of two-hundred and five that were known to
> the Secretary of State as being members of the Communist

party and who nevertheless are still working and shaping the
policy of the State Department.[14]

On February 20, 1950, McCarthy read the above excerpt of what he
claimed was the text of his Wheeling speech into the *Congressional Record*.
The text of the speech was never found and, according to Rovere, it is
believed that a member of his staff wrote the excerpt above.[15]

Whether the wording was exact or not did not seem to matter. The
gist of the message offered the American public a reason for their psychological malaise. McCarthy presented *his* view of this perplexing situation —
betrayal — which seemed to be the only reasonable answer. The need to
ferret out the enemy within eclipsed the American mind. McCarthy's
assertion, that Communists, bent on overthrowing our democracy, had
infiltrated the government and American society, crystallized these fears.
They now had a cause to fight for. It was American versus "Un-American,"
"patriot" against "traitor." Joseph McCarthy became their champion. With his
infamous "I have a little list" speech, which he repeated compulsively over and
over again, he "defined" the "betrayers." Interestingly, in each of his sequential
speeches, the number of names on the list changed. The few names that he
finally uttered were exonerated. Nevertheless, the "I have a little list" became
the rallying cry. With the mere gesture of reaching into his pocket and
producing a piece of paper, McCarthy dramatized "the dark imaginings of
many millions of his contemporaries."[16] Like a grisly reprise of seventeenth-
century Salem, the witch-hunts began.

McCarthy began his very public crusade to expose the traitors. He
became the conquering hero, and his name gave a label to the phenomenon:
"McCarthyism."[17] Millions of Americans became convinced that the Senator's
book *McCarthyism: The Fight for America* which detailed his plan, was the
answer to safeguarding America.

Pleasantly surprised by the impact of the Wheeling speech, McCarthy
raced to capitalize on the publicity by giving similar speeches wherever he
could. On every occasion, he performed what was to become his signature
gesture— "I hold in my hand," followed by varying numbers and later specific
names. The senator's words were fodder for front-page readers. Reporters
flocked about him like seagulls to a boatful of fish. The senator was prime
copy. A member of the "greatest deliberative body in the world," the bulwark
of democracy, he broadcasted the dirty secrets of men in high government
places.

Many of his performances were presented on the floor of the Senate.
Senator Smith recalled in her book *Declaration of Conscience*, that McCarthy's
"'I hold in my hand a photostatic copy,' had a most impressive tone and ring
of authenticity."[18] However, when she finally got McCarthy to show her
some of the photostatic copies, she discovered that they did not seem to relate
to his claims.[19] Nevertheless, McCarthy's unproven accusations continued
to fill the historical chamber. McCarthy blatantly abused the privilege of

congressional immunity, and he denied the accused the right of innocence until proven guilty. Reputations and lives were destroyed summarily. Some senators whispered their concern, hiding behind closed doors, but none did anything about it. The Senate's silence was condonement. The sole woman member remembered: "McCarthy had created an atmosphere of such political fear that people were not only afraid to talk but they were afraid of whom they might be seen with."[20]

An example of the inflammatory rhetoric spouted by McCarthy on the Senate floor involved his insidious attack on Professor Owen Lattimore, a faculty member of John Hopkins University. Rumors began to circulate about Lattimore's Communist leanings while he was working for the State Department on a United Nations Technical Assistance Mission in Afghanistan.[21] On March 30, 1950, McCarthy took the Senate floor to accuse Lattimore of what he perceived to be a superior attitude: "I might say that if we study him we cannot help but see that here is a brilliant individual. That is what makes him dangerous."[22]

The *Congressional Record* shows how the senator continued his character assassination:

> We wonder why a man so brilliant as Lattimore would set forth his aims so clearly over a number of years — especially now when he denies these aims so loudly. I suppose, however, if we had the answer to that question, we would also have the answer to why Hitler wrote his *Mein Kamp* and why Stalin wrote his *Principles of Leninism*.

> He is undoubtedly the most brilliant and scholarly of all the Communist propagandists, and also the most subtle of the evangelists who have deceived the American people about the Chinese Communists.

> . . . [N]o one can read his books carefully without realizing that they are replete with pro-Soviet propaganda; twisted with the half-truths about America; misinformation about the Chinese Communists; and historical distortions and omissions designed to trick the American public into support of policies advantageous to Moscow.[23]

Accusations such as this forced a special investigative subcommittee of the Senate Foreign Relations Committee, chaired by Senator Millard E. Tydings (D-Maryland), to call for hearings on Lattimore. Hearings went on for months, with Lattimore last appearing before the committee on May 3. On July 20, 1950, the subcommittee reported in the *Congressional Record*:

[W]ith reference to Lattimore, four members of the committee saw fit to file reports. The majority report and the one
by the Senator from Massachusetts (Henry Cabot Lodge) say
the charges are not proved.[24]

McCarthy was not satisfied. Instead, he attacked the way the
Administration was handling the investigations. In a speech on the Senate
floor, he presented a scathing evaluation of the work of the subcommittee:

This cover-up . . . is a deliberate fraud, originated and
propagandized with one idea in mind: conceal, cover up,
keep the American people from the truth. This, ladies and
gentlemen, makes one sick way down deep inside. I cannot
stomach it. I doubt if any American would. . . . For it is the
sinister effort to avoid honesty. It bears a basic corruption
that permeates the State Department's small closely knit
high command. Instead of shooting square with the American people, we find men in high positions who offer us bits
and pieces of evidence to help them conceal instead of reveal
the truth.[25]

Even after Senator Smith had the courage to demand that her
colleagues behave more responsibly, McCarthy continued his maniacal
harangues. He continued them at the 1952 Republican national convention,
where he was the star. He was reelected to the Senate and resumed his
messianic fervor to ferret out the spectral enemy within until 1954. Ironically,
McCarthy rose to fame as a "media darling" of the print media. It took the
revelation of his madness on the televised Army-McCarthy hearings to
convince the public that he was sick.

THE AUDIENCE: THE U.S. SENATE

The legislators that sat in that avowed august body in 1950 had their
motives for not publicly expressing their reaction to Joe McCarthy's abusive
harangues. Most were downright fearful of incurring McCarthy's wrath. To
do so would have been political suicide. The media-made demagogue made
sure that anyone who dared challenge him rued the day. His smear tactics
were notorious. "[W]hile sensitive to violations of Senate rules and courtesies,
they were quite unwilling to fight fire with fire. Tussling with McCarthy, they
believed, would mean a gutter brawl and an accompanying loss of stature."[26]
Democrats refrained from going to the defense of the administration. By
June, only twelve Democrats had spoken out against him — three Tydings
Committee members and a handful of northern liberals. "The others talked

only in private — a posture that infuriated Truman and no doubt encouraged McCarthy."[27] Besides, the Democratic power bloc happened to be comprised of southern conservatives who joined with the Republican conservatives in their criticism of the Truman administration.

The consensus of the fifteen silent Republican moderates across the aisle was that, as Leverett Saltonstall of Massachusetts, confessed "attacking McCarthy was no easy matter."[28] They considered themselves good Republicans, and attacking McCarthy would be an attack on their party. Also, they did not want to appear to appease the opposition party. They humbly acknowledged that McCarthy had a great deal of popular support — among Irish Catholics, conservatives, midwesterners, and westerners. According to historian David Oshinsky, "[T]hey had straddled the fence. The dilemma of satisfying party, conscience, and the national interest seemed to paralyze them."[29]

Some members, however, like minority leader Robert Taft and the conservative contingent of the Republican Party, remained silent from satisfaction. With McCarthy's repeated accusations associating the Truman administration with Communist infiltration and the perceived threat to the country, they had finally found a way to express their frustrations. Here was a means to destroy the power hold of the Democratic party on the executive branch. Since Franklin Delano Roosevelt had defeated the Republican Herbert Hoover in 1932 and ushered in his liberal New Deal programs, the Republicans had failed to win national leadership. It had been eighteen years of being the minority party. Something had to be done. Joe McCarthy's street-fighting tactics seemed to be the solution. According to David Halberstam in *The Fifties*, McCarthy was a partisan ploy, allowing "worthier men to keep their hands clean. 'Joe, you're a real SOB,' Senator John Bricker of Ohio once said, 'but sometimes it's useful to have SOBs around to do the Dirty work.'"[30]

A closer examination of the Senate in the spring of 1950 reveals greater division among its members than party affiliation. The Senators appeared to be aligned more according to position on the political spectrum than to party. The conservative wings of both parties seemed to be more sympathetic with one another than with the other members of their affiliation. The conflict within the Senate was not simply Democrats versus Republicans; there was division among the conservatives, moderates, and liberals or "New Dealers," as the conservatives called them. Further, there was evidence of an even stronger and definitely more passionate division between the right and the left wing, so to speak. That was the specter of class conflict. For example, the conservatives, composed chiefly of representatives from the Republican rural Midwest and the Democratic rural South, criticized those members of the Democratic administration from the East who happened to be wealthy, well educated, and liberal. On February 20, 1950, McCarthy chose to become their standard-bearer and spelled out this conflict for inclusion in the *Congressional Record*:

> The reason why we find ourselves in a position of impotency
> . . . is the traitorous actions of those who have been treated
> so well by this nation. It is not the less fortunate or mem-
> bers of the minority groups who have been selling this nation
> out but rather those who have had all the benefits the
> wealthiest nation on earth has had to offer — the finest
> homes, the finest college educations, and the finest jobs in
> the government that we can give. This is glaringly true of
> the State Department. There the bright young men who are
> born with silver spoons in their mouth [*sic*] are the ones who
> have been worse [*sic*].[31]

Margaret Chase Smith listened to McCarthy, watched her so-called powerful colleagues, and winced from the conviction that something wrong was being allowed to happen. Perhaps she may have recalled from a lesson long ago the admonition of the influential New England philosopher Ralph Waldo Emerson: "When a whole nation is roaring Patriotism at the top of its voice, I am fain to explore the cleanness of its hands and the purity of its heart."[32]

However, despite the pleading of Democratic liberals, such as columnist Doris Fleeson and broadcaster Ed Hart, who were convinced that she was the one who could confront McCarthy, she hesitated about speaking out because she was a newcomer with little influence.[33] She had been regarded so far with indifference by the Senate leaders, but from her eight years in the lower house of Congress, she had gained a widespread reputation for patience and integrity. According to Oshinsky: "[T]o raise her hacks, someone would have to step far out of line. In 1950, that someone was Joe McCarthy."[34]

After mustering six signers to support her statement — Senators Charles W. Tobey of New Hampshire, George D. Aiken of Vermont, Wayne L. Morse of Oregon, Irving Ives of New York, Edward J. Thye of Minnesota, and Robert C. Hendrickson of New Jersey— she retreated to her home in Skowhegan, Maine, with her trusted assistant Bill Lewis, that Memorial Day weekend, and together they wrote the "Declaration of Conscience."

THE RHETORICAL EVENT

The exigence that Senator Smith responded to with her hallmark speech had to do not so much with the sick climate in the country or with the increasing threat of the Soviet Union or with directly accusing Joseph McCarthy. She targeted the national condition and alluded to the abusive tactics of Joseph McCarthy, which were effects. The root cause of the national crisis was the lack of effective leadership in Washington.

Margaret Smith chose to address the Senate on the first of June in 1950 because she had had enough. She watched as her powerful colleagues on both sides of the aisle sat silently while one of them, Joseph M. McCarthy, the junior Republican from Wisconsin, repeatedly took the floor of that hallowed hall to repeatedly abuse the sacred privilege of congressional immunity. The privilege, granted by the framers of the Constitution for the purpose of protecting the deliberative environment of Congress, is stated specifically in Article I, Section 1:

> Senators and Representatives shall . . . in all Cases, except Treason, Felony, and Breach of the Peace, be privileged from Arrest during their Attendance at the Session of their respective Houses, and in going to and returning from the same; and for any Speech or Debate in either House, they shall not be questioned in any other Place.[35]

Obviously, the assumption by the erudite students of the Enlightenment was that those elected to office by the people would be honorable. Alas, the assumption proved false on numerous occasions. Our elected officials proved to be what they were basically— human, with a range of finite virtues; some more noble than others and some quite ignoble and downright malevolent. Psychology has taught that humans behave according to motives, overt and covert. Politicians tend to be preoccupied with self-seeking and partisan interests.

The occasion for the speech favored the opportunity for its effectiveness. The Senate on June 1, 1950, was conducting debates on the Amerasia Case, which was concerned with security risks, and as Senator Smith reports in her book, the atmosphere was tense.

Just before noon, in the midst of the Amerasia debates,[36] and with her plans kept secret from all except her secretary William Lewis, Margaret Chase Smith obtained the floor. Facing the majority party, the Democrats, to her right, and her Republican colleagues on her side of the aisle, with her nameless target, Senator McCarthy, only two rows behind, the diminutive Mrs. Smith courageously proceeded with her delivery. Her slight physical appearance and soft vocal tones contrasted sharply with the magnitude of her message. The element of surprise had been used masterfully. When the speaker's platform was set on her desk, the press, in particular, was curious. The woman member who had hardly been heard before was going to say something. Earlier, McCarthy himself expressed curiosity. In the *Declaration of Conscience*, Senator Smith recalled that when she boarded the subway train from the Senate Office Building to the Capitol that morning, McCarthy was also on board. He remarked, "Margaret, you look very serious. Are you going to make a speech?" She responded, "Yes, and you will not like it." McCarthy frowned, and, true to form, threatened: "Remember, Margaret, I control Wisconsin's twenty-seven convention votes," alluding to the possibility of her being considered for the vice presidency.[37] To add to the impact of her message, she had instructed Bill Lewis to hand out copies to the press at the moment the Chair recognized her to speak. Margaret Chase Smith had been stereotyped by some as a conservative New Englander from Maine— the progressiveness of her message surprised many.

Barely five-foot-four inches tall and of petite build, obviously feminine from the cut of her clothes to the trademark rose pinned carefully to her lapel, she stood ramrod straight, her feminine dignity most attractive. Of course, she felt some trepidation about the speech; it was very risky. But she had no doubts about the need for her message to be heard. It was the right thing to do — that was reason enough. In agreement with Aristotle's admonition that "[p]olitical society exists for the sake of noble actions, and not for mere companionship,"[38] Margaret Smith never saw her elected position as a personal gain. Ego satisfaction had little to do with the job. She often repeated in her speeches from 1940, when she was elected to the House of Representatives, that she was simply a public servant. She continually encouraged the citizens of Maine to consider her their "errand girl."[39] Simply, *they* chose her to do *their* bidding in their Congress.

In barely audible tones from what some may have heretofore perceived as a mere wisp of a woman, Senator Smith dispensed with a formal introduction to launch into her indictment with urgency. There was a "serious national condition," a "national feeling of fear and frustration that could result in national suicide and the end of everything we hold dear." And with the dead aim of the Maine hunter, she laid the blame on the Senate and the Democratic administration: "The condition" is the result of "lack of effective leadership."

Her message sounded more like that of a New England preacher, but the soft tones of her delivery resembled that of an inner voice:

> I think that it is high time for the United States Senate and
> its members to do some soul-searching — for us to weigh
> our consciences — on the manner in which we are perform-
> ing our duty to the people of America — on the manner in
> which we are using or abusing our individual powers and
> privileges.

Fortified with the firm belief that the democratic principles on which our forebears built the country were immutable and downright sacred, the lady from Maine delivered a refresher lesson in citizenship to her esteemed colleagues:

> Those of us who shout the loudest about Americanism in making character assassinations are all too frequently those who, by our own words and acts, ignore some of the basic principles of Americanism:
>
>> The right to criticize;
>> The right to hold unpopular beliefs;
>> The right to protest;
>> The right of independent thought.
>
> The exercise of these rights should not cost one single American citizen his reputation or his right to livelihood merely because he happens to know someone who holds unpopular beliefs.

Her scolding was evenhanded and from a more universal viewpoint. Identifying herself as "a Republican," "a woman," "a United States Senator," and "an American," she cited the general transgressions of the Republicans as well as the Democratic administration. For example, she blamed the decline of America as world leader because "the Democratic Administration has pitifully failed to provide effective leadership." She indicted the Democratic administration for confusing the American people "by its daily contradictory grave warnings and optimistic assurances— that show the people that our Democratic Administration has no idea of where it is going." She summarized that the American people have lost confidence in the administration because of "its complacency to the threat of communism here at home and the leak of vital secrets to Russia through key officials of the Democratic Administration."[40] Smith concluded that it is time for a change, agreeing with her party that "a Republican victory is necessary to the security of this country." However, she warned the Republicans about "embracing a philosophy that lacks political integrity or intellectual honesty," commenting forcefully: "I don't want to see the Republican Party ride to political victory on the Four Horsemen of Calumny— Fear, Ignorance, Bigotry, and Smear." She concluded: "I don't believe the American people will uphold any political party that puts political exploitation above national interest." "As an American," she chastised both parties for "playing directly into the Communist design of 'confuse, divide, and conquer. . . . I don't want a Democratic Administration 'whitewash' or 'cover-up' any more than I want a Republican smear or witch hunt."

Smith further took her colleagues to task by describing the immoral tactics of one of their own. She never mentioned McCarthy by name, but her criticism, although in the plural, pointed clearly to him:

> I don't like the way the Senate has been made a rendezvous

for vilification, for selfish political gain at the sacrifice of
individual reputations and national unity. I am not proud of
the way we smear outsiders from the Floor of the Senate
and hide behind the cloak of congressional immunity and
still place ourselves beyond criticism on the Floor of the
Senate.

Demonstrating that the preservation of our precious democratic
principles takes precedence over all other loyalties, Margaret Chase Smith
expressed disgust with the current "national condition" directly. There was no
doubt about where she stood: "The American people are sick and tired of
seeing innocent people smeared and guilty people whitewashed."
      The speech concluded with a summary statement of the major points
of the speech signed by "Seven Republican Senators."

THE ANALYSIS

The chief purpose of Senator Smith's speech was to deliver a moral
message. The time had come to shake the Senate out of its apathetic state —
whether collective paralysis or not — to face reality. Her straightforward
description of the national crisis and its causes served as a mirror, to shock
the members into seeing what the Senate had become. As a rhetor, Smith
intended to motivate the members to remember the true purpose of their
position and to reform their ways before all "that we Americans hold most
dear" is lost.   Smith firmly believed that the Senate was "the greatest
deliberative body in the world," that the framers of the Constitution planned
it to be so. However, from her view, in the spring of 1950, debate was dead.
Rather than an arena of active and articulate argumentation for the purpose
of discovering decisions that were right and proper, the Senate, to the
dismayed freshman, was a tomb, its hallowed walls resounding solely with the
whining charges of external threats and character assassination.   Smith
reasoned: McCarthy was not the root cause; the leadership was, for it was
guilty of mismanagement, for allowing the abuse of the entrusted privilege of
congressional immunity. The members were more concerned about their
personal and political needs than about the needs of the nation. Worst yet,
they had abused their primary responsibility as legislators: to serve the
American people by safeguarding the rights granted to them by the Constitution.
      Embedded in the overall moral message was a political purpose.
Midway into the speech, Smith addresses the members of her party,
acknowledging their goal to become the majority party.
      Margaret Chase Smith delivered an epideictic speech to a deliberative
assembly. Her argument left little room for debate, for she clearly aimed to

censure her colleagues in the name of the American people. As soon as she began speaking, she cited the exigency, succinctly stated its cause, and indicted the perpetrators:

> The United States Senate has long enjoyed worldwide respect as the greatest deliberative body in the world. But recently that deliberative character has too often been debased to the level of a forum of hate and character assassination sheltered by the shield of congressional immunity.

Cleverly realizing that her ethos alone was not powerful enough to achieve her purpose and also as a means to reinforce her point that the members of the Senate exist for the benefit of the people, that they were elected to represent the people, Smith defined her perspective and her voice right before she began her indictment: "I speak as a Republican. I speak as a woman. I speak as a United States Senator. I speak as an American."

After stating her thesis calling for the need for the senators to "weigh our consciences" as to how "we are performing our duty to the people of America," she clarified her statement by stating what she believed to be "some of the basic principles of Americanism":

> The right to criticize;
> The right to hold unpopular beliefs;
> The right to protest;
> The right of independent thought.

The body of the speech was introduced and concluded with the perspective of the American people. That is, before and after delineating the views of each of her personas, Smith stated the position of the American people. As a prelude to her specific points, she posited:

> The American people are sick and tired of being afraid to speak their minds lest they be politically smeared as "Communists" or "Fascists" by their opponents. Freedom of speech is not what it used to be in America. It has been so abused by some that it is not exercised by others.

After defining the different points of view on how the Senate is at fault, she concluded the body with the following summary statement:

> As an American, I condemn a Republican "Fascist" just as much as I condemn a Democrat "Communist." I condemn a Democrat "Fascist" just as much as I condemn a Republi-

can "Communist." They are equally dangerous to you and
me and to our country. As an American, I want to see our
nation recapture the strength and unity it once had when we
fought the enemy instead of ourselves.

The first points that Smith states in the body tended to be more
political than the rest of the speech. In an effort to engage the support of her
Republican colleagues, she reminds them that they belong to the party of
Lincoln, the party that united the nation after the Civil War. She compares
that challenge with the present. Then she impugned the Democratic
administration for gross ineptitude by listing its faults:

The Democratic Administration has completely confused the
American people by its daily contradictory grave warnings
and optimistic assurances — that show the people that our
Democratic Administration has no idea of where it is going.

Stating that "this nation will continue to suffer as long as it is governed by the
present ineffective Democratic Administration," Smith summarized her
partisan appeal by stating the ultimate goal of her colleagues: "[I]t is time for
a change and . . . a Republican victory is necessary to the security of this
country."

The praise was short-lived. The political appeal proved to be simply
a statement of possibility. For the second main point in the body, the senator
returned to the chief purpose of her speech: to censure. She warned
Republicans that they must change their errant ways of "embracing a
philosophy that lacks political integrity or intellectual honesty. . . . I don't want
to see the Republican Party ride to political victory on the Four Horsemen of
Calumny— Fear, Ignorance, Bigotry, and Smear."

The other points in the body stated her viewpoints as a woman and
as a U.S. Senator. The last point states the view of her most powerful
persona, that of an American. Her perspective as a woman seemed weak,
more of a token statement. Her comments regarding her view as a senator
were stronger. She repeated her concern for the silent sanction of the abusive
practices of McCarthy: "I don't like the way the Senate has been made a
rendezvous for vilification, for selfish political gain at the sacrifice of individual
reputations and national unity." As an American, she accused both Republicans and Democrats alike for "playing directly into the Communist design of
'confuse, divide, and conquer.'" She concluded: "I don't want a Democratic
Administration 'whitewash' or 'cover-up' any more than I want a Republican
smear or witch hunt."

The excellence of her oratory is found in the use of ethical proof.
Smith attempted to present an infallible argument. She based her reasoning
on the unassailable democratic principles found in the Constitution and,

especially, the Bill of Rights. These documents codify the moral code on which American democracy functions. They serve as the rationale for the government of the United States; they are revered in the company of patriots. Smith further strengthened her argument by presenting her claims from a multipersona view. She empowered her ethos by defining herself as a Republican, a senator, a woman, and an American. The audience members could not readily dismiss her argument as that simply of the newly arrived "mere woman" moderate from the rather remote state of Maine. With the multiple identity, she expressed the point of view of each and every member. She planned that all could identify with her and her message.

Smith's dependence on ethical appeal is evident in her use of value-laden language. In her effort to move the listeners to reflect on the relationship between the deteriorated national condition and their personal characters, she used terms of shame throughout the speech: "irresponsible words of bitterness," "selfish political opportunism," "debased to the level of a forum of hate and character assassination," "abusing our individual powers and privileges," "irresponsible sensationalism," "rendezvous for vilification." Although Smith's style of expression was more forthright than figurative, she did use two powerful images to communicate her intent: She blamed the Senate for the country's confused and suspicious psychological state caused by the "cancerous tentacles of [their] 'know nothing, suspect everything' attitudes." She warns the Republican Party of its "corrupt political philoso-phy" based on "the Four Horsemen of Calumny— Fear, Ignorance, Bigotry, and Smear."

In deprecating terms, she moved her listeners to examine their sense of justice and fairplay:

> It is strange that we can verbally attack anyone else without restraint and with full protection and yet we hold ourselves above the same type of criticism here on the Senate Floor. Surely the United States Senate is big enough to take self-criticism and self-appraisal. Surely, we should be able to take the same kind of character attacks that we "dish out" to outsiders.

For the most part, her call to "do some soul-searching" was more scolding than constructive criticism. She dealt more with blame and shame rather than with praise. Emulating Lincoln's Second Inaugural Address, Smith may have intended to "bind up the country's wounds" by appealing to the audience's "better angels of their nature," but her address lacked the conciliatory tone of Lincoln's. The lady from Maine's tone was more one of righteous indignation, reminiscent of the type echoed in the austere steepled clapboard churches and menial schoolhouses of her youth.

Above all, the speech was excellent because of the ethos of the speaker. Smith, person of exemplary character, demonstrated her courage to admonish the most powerful legislators of the land about their lack of character. Only a person of impeccable moral courage could dare to lecture the Senate about its moral cowardice. The fact that she was the only female in the historically all-male assembly also contributed to the strength of her ethos. Like the biblical David, Margaret Chase Smith emerged from the crowd to confront the Goliath Joe McCarthy with a slingshot load of moral might. Her no-nonsense style, austere tone, and honest argument communicated the anger of a true patriot, which was in stark contrast to the bombastic, emotion-laden rhetoric of her nemesis. McCarthy had a penchant for naming names; Margaret Smith chose to do the opposite. McCarthy warned vindictively; she advised instructively. His belabored dependence on the term *patriotism* revealed a mock chauvinism; her message defined the true meaning of Americanism. Justice to him meant ferreting out traitors; justice to her meant tolerance. The "rugged individualist" confronted the conformist.

Smith's logical proof served to reinforce the ethical appeal of her argument. Rather than using specific evidence, she depended on the deductive reasoning structure of the enthymeme. In other words, to pursue her probe into the belief system of her auditors, she based her reasoning on generally accepted principles rather than on concrete data. To illustrate, the major premise of the argument in these speeches is that evil conditions prevail in a nation where there is lack of leadership and irresponsible criticism. Smith then used general examples to demonstrate the minor premise of a lack of leadership and irresponsible criticism in America today. Her implied conclusion was that evil conditions exist in America. Another example of the enthymemic construct in Senator Smith's argument is as follows: Basing her logic on the premise that American tradition allows us to hold unpopular beliefs, she presented examples to show that attacking dissenters endangers their reputations and livelihood. The implied conclusion is that to attack dissenters for speaking freely is against American tradition. Another example of such deductive reasoning calls to mind the moral outrage of smear tactics. Basing her logic on the belief that accusations that smear innocent people are wrong, the senator demonstrated the validity of that belief with examples showing that innocent people were being smeared.

Smith's rhetorical strategy is evident not only in the structure of her argument but also in her style of expression. The "Quiet Woman" with the soft voice cleverly empowered her rather weak delivery with her decisive language. She apprised her colleagues of their corrupt way with candor. When she demanded that it was "high time" for senators to do "some soul-searching" about how they perform their jobs, she spoke with the fervor of her revolutionary forebears.

To emphasize particular parts of her message, Smith relied on parallelism. Concerned with defining her ethos as the speaker, she clearly uses both stylistic devices: "I speak as a Republican. I speak as a woman.

I speak as a United States Senator. I speak as an American." Smith also uses the parallel construct to pronounce "the basic principles of Americanism": "the right to criticize; the to hold unpopular beliefs; the right to protest; the right of independent thought." To underscore the urgency of the matter, she repeated the need to speak "briefly and simply" at the beginning of the speech. She also repeated "I think that it is high time" in an attempt to shake her listeners out of their lethargy and into reality.

Senator Smith's strategy seems carefully planned, especially for the beginning of the speech. Recognizing the importance of gaining the attention of the audience, particularly in her case, she accomplished this with several devices. As she kept the fact that she was going to speak and the subject of her address secret until the time came, she purposely dispensed with the traditional introduction because her message was urgent, and she repeated the need to speak "briefly and simply."

As soon as she established the fact that she would address an emergency situation, she defined the exigency that the nation is in a crisis state. To motivate the audience to comprehend the magnitude of the crisis, Senator Smith created word clusters with the term *national*. She pairs the term *national* with increasingly alarming terms: "national condition," "national feeling of fear and frustration," "national suicide." The repetition of the term *national* reinforced Smith's conviction that the nation, above all, should be the most important concern. She implied to the Senate that it existed for the greater good, beyond itself and above party needs.

Smith's delivery also reflected her rhetorical strategy. The senator was not renowned for her oratorical skill, as her mode of declaiming was far from grand. To the contrary, her delivery was understated. Her voice was hardly audible, her gestures and bodily movement were almost nonexistent, and her platform presence was very unimposing. Indeed, she was certainly not a speaker familiar to the Senate. But perhaps her individual mode of presentation worked for her rather than against her. Because she was a woman among males and rarely spoke, her asking to be recognized to speak not only attracted the attention of the audience; it also emphasized the urgency of the situation. Her colleagues must, in fact, have wondered what was so important to move Margaret to speak. In fact, the *New Republic* comprehended the impact of her understated presentation: "In the hushed all-male audience, Mrs. Smith's hardly audible tones had visible effect. It was like another still, small voice saying something to listeners which, in their hearts, they already knew."[41]

Unfortunately, for all her honest intentions, the aftermath of the speech indicates that Senator Smith did not achieve closure with her audience. The senators in attendance, except for the very few that immediately wished her words of congratulations, seemed oblivious to her call. Rather than search their souls to do the right thing, they became even greater supporters of McCarthy and his tactics.

The moderates soon drifted apart. Margaret Chase Smith saw the signers of the "Declaration of Conscience" desert her cause to champion that of McCarthy. For example, Senator Irving Ives publicly applauded Joe's attacks, offering him his cooperation. Senator Charles Tobey wrote a constituent that "I have not disavowed Senator McCarthy. Many senators feel that his objectives are good, and I share that feeling."[42]   Only Senator Wayne Morse remained at her side.

THE AFTERMATH

Although Senator Smith's speech seemed successful at the national level, it had little effect on her senatorial audience. "Politically speaking," wrote David Oshinsky, "the Declaration had no real impact. . . . Its sponsors were essentially a leaderless band. . . . Strangely isolated from one another, the moderates could not easily combat the advances of McCarthy's powerful allies."[43] "In what remained of the Truman years," Richard Rovere comments in his biography of McCarthy, "McCarthy was nothing but an engine of denunciation. He denounced and accused and blamed and insulted and vilified and demeaned."[44]   Rovere explains that McCarthy was used by colleagues, that he would bring in documents against "anyone who was giving them trouble."[45]

Instead of his critics increasing as the result of Smith's address, the opposite occurred. McCarthy's popularity grew. He became the chief celebrity at the 1952 Republican National Convention where he was introduced to the wild demonstration as "Wisconsin's Fighting Marine," a man much maligned for his courage in "exposing the traitors in our government."[46]

The chief reason why Margaret Chase Smith's "Declaration of Conscience" speech was not successful with the senators was simply that it was a speech of principle to an audience more motivated by political power than principles. As the representative of the small group of moderates, she entreated those on the opposing ends of the political spectrum to listen to their conscience, whereas they were more concerned with party loyalty. Hers was, indeed, a noble posture, but few seemed to pay heed. To the powerful assembly, hers was a minor voice of little import. However, she took her charge as a representative of the American people very seriously. Perhaps she believed that her colleagues did too. Perhaps she believed that underneath their collective veil of expediency there lay a noble soul and that if reminded firmly, the better quality of their character would emerge.

Margaret Smith's speech proved weak because she failed to see that in actuality she was addressing a conflict common to the American character — that of morality versus expediency.[47] According to James R. Andrews in "Reflections of the National Character in American Rhetoric":

A measure of ambivalence toward goals and values is inherent in the American character. A rhetoric that seeks to establish the *ultimate* truth, a rhetoric that defines its task as defending *absolute* morality, is a rhetoric that can only succeed in engendering intense hostility and may be more likely to provoke civil war than to promote civil progress.[48]

Andrews concludes: "Only a rhetoric that takes into account the need to understand and to balance conflicting pressures will finally contribute to the realization of our noblest aspirations."[49]

When Senator Margaret Chase Smith concluded her speech, she was complimented by a few of her colleagues. She waited at her seat for McCarthy, who sat through the whole speech, to respond, but he simply left the chamber.

However, the "Declaration of Conscience" attracted national attention. Favorable press reports from across the nation lauded the sanity of the speech and the moral strength of the speaker. The *New York Times* ran as front-page headline "Mrs. Smith Warns of Repression," along with her photograph.[50] On June 3, the *Times* included the following editorial comment under the title "Plain Talk in the Senate": "It was high time that some responsible Republicans in the Senate spoke up . . . against the tacit encouragement which certain members of their party have given to the smear tactics of Senator McCarthy."[51] The *Anniston, Alabama Star*, under the laudatory headline "Speech That May Make History," observed:

> It was the sort of speech that long has been needed, one that, we hope, will make history. For not only members of Congress, many of those in the other departments, and other Democrats and Republicans alike in high places have so lost their balance and sense of values in recent months that the whole American people is about to become psychopathic in fear of the Russian menace.[52]

Newsweek put her photograph on the cover of its weekly issue with the caption "Senator Smith: A Woman Vice-President?" The accompanying article stated: "What many a bewildered citizen had waited to hear for a long time was said by a woman last week. After months of shocking charges on one side and evasive alibiing on the other, her precise, restrained phrases worked as neatly as a broom sweeping out a mess."[53]

In spite of the fact that the speech had relatively no impact on the immediate audience, the national audience, for the most part, raved about it. The American public cheered the sole female member of the most illustrious legislative assembly because she showed that she had the courage of her conviction, a most revered American ideal. Her speech was a demonstration of the very principles that she accused her colleagues of lacking— freedom of speech, especially the right to criticize. The news of the speech prompted the heaviest mail she had ever received, running eight-to-one in favor.

As predicted, Joseph McCarthy, true to his vengeful reputation, retaliated. He was bent on making Margaret Smith pay for attacking him. At first, his tactics were rather mild: He attempted to belittle Senator Smith and her Republican colleagues who cosigned the Declaration by sarcastically labeling them "Snow White and the Seven Dwarfs."[54] When he saw that she would not succumb to such intimidation, he attempted to attack her reputation and career. He demonstrated his political clout and got her kicked off the Investigations Subcommittee in 1951. On August 20, 1951, McCarthy took the Senate floor, and for two hours he defended himself, then took a swipe at her and signer Senator Henrickson by citing the "Declaration of Conscience" as evidence of their prejudice against him: "One of the most vigorous attacks . . . upon my exposure of Communists was made by the Senator from Maine . . . in which the Senator from New Jersey joined."[55] Senator Smith stood strong. When he was finished, she responded by placing her "Declaration of Conscience" into the *Record* for the third time, with the comment: "Opposition to Communism is surely not the exclusive possession of Senator McCarthy. Nor does differing with him on tactics automatically make one a Communist."[56]

In early 1952, McCarthy made his most serious attack on Senator Smith. A book entitled *U.S.A. Confidential*, written by Jack Lait and Lee Mortimer, contended that she was pro-Communist. The book criticized her as "a stunted visionary" who was given to "boneheaded speeches."[57] The authors alluded to a Senate doorman's complaints that she was "a lesson why women should not be in politics" and that she "reacted to all situations as a woman scorned, not as a representative of the people."[58] Senator Smith sued both the authors and the publishers for libel. After four and a half years of publicized lies and misrepresentations, on October 17, 1956, Lee Mortimer finally acknowledged that the statements about her were false.[59] She fought McCarthy's style of political smear tenaciously. Indeed, she battled every other attempt to defame her for daring to criticize him publicly strongly and soundly and won. Her victories led to his defeat. McCarthy once remarked in frustration: "There's too damn many women in the Senate!"[60]

In 1954, McCarthy plotted to stop her reelection to the Senate by running his own candidate, Robert L. Jones, against her. Margaret Smith beat McCarthy's candidate in the primaries by a record number of votes, a five to one margin. The story goes that McCarthy, at a press conference in Portland, Maine, asked if there was anyone more popular than Senator Smith in Maine. A reporter responded, "Yes." "Who?" questioned McCarthy hopefully. The reporter responded, "Almighty God."[61] In defeating Senator McCarthy's candidate by such a great margin, the lady from Maine also destroyed his power in the U.S. Senate.[62]

After his failed attempt to get Margaret defeated in the Maine primaries in 1954, McCarthy and Smith often found themselves riding on the same little subway train that transports senators from the Senate Office Building to the Senate wing of the Capitol Building. McCarthy remarked, "Margaret, we seem to be following each other and riding together." "Yes, Joe," she smiled. "If you don't watch out, people will say we are fellow travelers."[63]

As Smith's career ascended, McCarthy's declined. On December 2, 1954, he was finally censured by the Senate for making insulting remarks about his colleagues. Unfortunately, he was not censured for abusing the privilege of congressional immunity by slandering the reputations of American citizens. As former ambassador to the Soviet Union George Kennan lamented with great disillusionment in his memoirs: The practice of McCarthyism "was never decisively rejected by the political establishment of the country."[64] According to Oshinsky, "If his fellow Senators had been ready to challenge each mendacity, or if either of the two Presidents of his day had been willing and able to denounce him regularly, it would have worked. But that was not to be."[65]

Three years after being censured, at the age of forty-eight, Joseph McCarthy died of cirrhosis of the liver. David Halberstam comments in epic work: "If nothing else, he had illuminated the timidity of his fellow man."[66] Margaret Chase Smith, on the other hand, went on to be reelected to the Senate continuously until 1972. The "Declaration of Conscience" speech proved to be effective in the long run. She proved to be the better representative of the people.

"DECLARATION OF CONSCIENCE II"

On June 1, 1970, Senator Margaret Chase Smith found it necessary to repeat the message she delivered twenty years earlier. The exigence was the same, but the situation was more complex. Again, she spoke that "a national feeling of fear and frustration" threatened "the end of everything we Americans hold dear." In 1950, the offenders came from the political Right; in 1970, the perpetrators were from the political Left. Both extremists justified their actions in the name of Americanism, and in pursuing their objectives, both factions abused those very democratic principles on which Americanism is based. The situation seemed simpler in 1950: McCarthyism was the threatening ideology, and the chief culprits were Smith's conservative colleagues in the U.S. Senate. In 1970, the instigators came from various segments of society. In 1970, television played an active role in replaying the mayhem created by the clash of extremist forces on the streets and campuses for the American public. Exercising the right to dissent and the right to assemble often resulted in chaos. Mob violence provoked repressive police action. In her speech, Smith attacked the leftists and their disruptive practices for endangering American democracy.   She warned that the anarchy perpetrated by these forces against what was referred to as "the establishment" was an even greater threat to the notion of Americanism because it tended to result in repressive measures advocated by those of the extreme Right: "Extremism bent upon polarization of our people is increasingly forcing upon the American people the narrow choice between anarchy and repression."[67]

Intimidated by the sights of increasing upheaval, mainstream America remained mute. The voice of moderation and sanity, in the person of the now-venerable Senator Margaret Chase Smith, had to speak out. Once more, the senator was driven by her moral compunction to repeat the message that confronted McCarthy and his cronies in 1950. The speech delivered to the U.S. Senate in 1970 confirms the infallible strength of the senator's character. Hers was the recognized voice of reason, the conscience of the Senate. Despite the passage of twenty years, at age seventy-three she demonstrated the constancy of her convictions about the function of government and of the citizenry in a democracy.

RHETORICAL SITUATION

Civil unrest on American streets and college campuses was provoked by two major militant forces that grew and festered in the countercultural movement of the 1960s — the antiwar movement and the civil rights movement. Both groups demanded greater recognition and involvement in matters of policy and procedure, especially in the government and the university. Zealots from the political Left seized the opportunity to spread their nihilistic philosophy. The notion of law and order was anathema to their cause, as anarchy was their aim. All forms of authority were challenged; law enforcement agents, such as the police, were called "pigs." Groups such as the Black Panthers and the Yippies focused on disruption of life as it was. College students organized as Students for a Democratic Society boldly demanded changes from college administrators, reinforcing their willfulness with the illegal occupation of offices and buildings. Government was attacked, forcing the government, in some instances, to fight back.   The violence intensified beyond the democratic principles of civil disobedience and passive resistance. Violence often became an end in itself. Reason had fled, often leaving anarchy in its wake.

The cause of the anger that pervaded the land was the perception that the government was increasingly disregarding the voice of the people. Promises of change were unfulfilled. The civil rights movement that had worked so hard in the early 1960s to gain greater equality for African-Americans felt thwarted. Martin Luther King's Dream seemed impossible. The attention of government was drawn away from domestic issues by the increasing demand for involvement in the Vietnam War. Presidents Johnson and Nixon promised peace in their election campaigns, only to carry on covert plans to escalate America's involvement. Consequently, a great credibility gap emerged between the American people and their leaders.

At the same time that young Americans, brimming with idealistic visions of peace and brotherhood, were calling for changes in the old order, the government was surreptitiously making deals with the Diem regime of South Vietnam. The first agreement began during Eisenhower's administration. He "took Americans fully across the Asian Rubicon by pledging to support President Diem."[68] President John Kennedy continued the policy by sending advisers to help train South Vietnamese troops in their war against the invading Communist North. Kennedy secretly ordered 500 of the elite fighting force called the Green Beret to South Vietnam. In 1962, these "advisers" were "firing back" in self-defense. By October 1963, there were 16,000 American troops on active duty in Vietnam. Under President Johnson, the number of "advisers" kept increasing, and so did the clandestine military operations. In 1964, the Congress almost unanimously passed the Tonkin Gulf Resolution, which officially authorized American military action in Vietnam. American involvement increased dramatically. By 1969, there were about 550,000 American troops in Vietnam. Although Richard Nixon campaigned on the promise to end the war, he made covert plans with his secretary of state, Henry Kissinger, to expand the war into Cambodia and Laos. Plans to bomb the North Vietnamese cities of Hanoi and Haiphong were among their secret plans. Nixon spoke of seeking "peace with honor."

By June 1970, the country was sickened by the seemingly endlessness of the war. The Communists were relentless in their determination for total revolution. American involvement was escalating. News of the war dominated the media. All the American public saw was the senseless waste of money and lives. Many citizens questioned the legality and the morality of the government's actions. Peace protests and draft resistance movements conducted antiwar demonstrations at the Capitol and on campuses across the country. The members of the Senate were labeled "hawks" or "doves," in accordance with their view of foreign policy. The majority of Americans, law-abiding citizens, remained stunned and silent and fearful.

Supporters of the civil rights movement also made demands. The decade that began with the promise of greater equality and peace grew ugly as it aged. Both antiwar and civil rights advocates joined in protest marches on Washington. Discontent spread like brushfire. On August 15, 1965, race riots in the Watts section of Los Angeles turned the area into a war zone. On August 1, 1967, black power advocates such as H. Rapp Brown and Stokely Carmichael called for revolution. In the summer of 1967, race riots severely damaged sections of New York, Newark, and Detroit. In the summer of 1968, the violence between the police and thousands of radicals who converged on Chicago for the Democratic National Convention was televised for all to see.

On November 15, 1969, more than a quarter million protesters marched on Washington, D.C., demanding the end to the Vietnam War. Inside the Justice Department and the Pentagon, hundreds of paratroopers stood at alert with rifles loaded. In November 1969, news of the My Lai massacre, in which American soldiers led by Lt. William Calley slew 567 unarmed peasants on March 16, 1968, alarmed America's moral sense and further intensified the war protest movement of the Left and the disillusionment of the majority. In December 1969, the Chicago police conducted a predawn raid on the headquarters of the Black Panthers, killing two and resulting in weeks of bloody confrontations between the police and the city's black community. On April 30, 1970, President Nixon's order for the arbitrary invasion of neutral Cambodia, contrary to U.S. international law, precipitated the most violent protests in American history. On May 9, 1970, there was another rally in Washington, D.C., asking the United States to pull out of Cambodia.

Violence became part of campus life at colleges and universities across the nation. On May 4, 1970, at Kent State University, the ROTC building was burned down, and national guard troops, brought in to quell the disturbance, fired into a student antiwar rally and killed four and wounded nine. On May 15, 1970, police opened fire on a women's dormitory at Jackson State University in Mississippi, killing two students and wounding twelve and resulting in a black boycott of white businesses.

The day after Kent State, a group of students from Colby College in Maine released to the press a telegram the group reported it was sending to Margaret Chase Smith. The message was a demand that she return home to explain her position on the war and the ensuing domestic violence.[69]

The telegram was never delivered, but the conscientious Smith did travel to Colby to meet the students and to endure what turned out to be "the most unpleasant" experience of her career.[70] On Saturday, May 9, the senator confronted a crowd of approximately 2,000 students from several campuses, answering their questions and enduring their taunts and obscenities. Although Smith denied that the experience had anything to do with her decision to make a second "Declaration of Conscience" speech, she admitted that it did influence her choice of language, claiming that the event "brought home to me, as nothing else had, the threateningly high intensity of the polarization."[71]

In her book *Declaration of Conscience*, Smith defined the national sickness that had weakened the country in the years preceding 1970 as the growing ethic of "unlimited and crass pragmatism — the creed that the end justifies the means."[72] She acknowledged that although there was much of this element in McCarthyism, it was more pervasive in 1970: "[I]t had a sanction and credibility that McCarthyism never even remotely approached."[73] She faulted many national leaders — from academia, theater, sports, the military, and government — for embracing the ethic. From her perspective, traditional values were being disregarded and openly derided.

Terms that reflected such formerly revered human values as fairness and honesty became sources of satire. Society was being instructed by those in the avant-garde — those who were "cool" — that it was not "hip" to be square.[74]

Smith was deeply troubled by what she viewed as the moral decay of America, in particular, the impact on the young people. Most disturbing was evidence of moral decline in her own field. She cited leaders in the executive and legislative branches who were putting the achievement of personal power above their duty to the people: "Being a Senator to them was not a dedicated career but only the pragmatic means to an end— outside the Senate."[75] With characteristic candor, the senator expressed her estimation of the total situation:

> The seeds for disillusionment, disrespect, disgust, resentment, and ultimately revolution were not only planted by leaders in the various fields, but they were cultivated and nurtured, consciously and unconsciously by them. It is no wonder what followed. Vietnam did not cause it. Vietnam was only a convenient rally point and a useful excuse for the extremism of the revolt that exploded into murder, arson, assault, and violent trespass.[76]

Although she supported the policies of fellow Republicans Nixon and Agnew, she did not approve of the manner in which they handled the antigovernment sentiment. She felt that it would have been better not to speak at all, rather than to risk the further polarization of the people. When Nixon referred to the troublesome students as "bums," it was interpreted that he meant all students. Smith writes that the comment "contributed to the growing split."[77]

In the *Declaration of Conscience*, the senator cited the Kent State happening of May 4, 1970, as the impetus to deliver another "Declaration of Conscience." With the aid of her assistant Bill Lewis and inspiration from an editorial written by ABC-TV commentator Howard K. Smith in the *Wall Street Journal*, she wrote the second "Declaration." This time she announced to the Senate that she would speak, but, as in 1950, she did not disclose the subject matter. Unlike the first "Declaration," she did not need the support of cosigners. In 1970, she had earned the title of stateswoman; her credibility was above reproach. Her reputation to speak only when she had something important to say garnered the interest of all her colleagues on that June 1.

ANALYSIS

On June 1, 1970, Senator Margaret Chase Smith rose from the same desk she occupied twenty years earlier and delivered almost the same speech she presented on June 1, 1950. Her purpose for repeating the message that established her reputation as a courageous servant of the people and defender of democracy was the same. In 1950, the threat to our democracy could be focused on one man, Senator Joseph McCarthy, and his conservative supporters. The audience was a direct one — the U.S. Senate — and the purpose of the message was clear — to censure her colleagues for allowing one of their own to blatantly abuse the privilege of congressional immunity. In 1970, the threat was also from the forces of political extremism, but this time from the Left. However, the threat was compounded: Those from the Left were the perpetrators of violent acts that were resulting in the greater threat to democracy— repression from the Right. As Senator Smith instructs clearly toward the end of her speech:

> The excessiveness of overreaction on both sides is a clear
> and present danger to American democracy. That danger is
> ultimately from the political right even though it is initially
> spawned by the antidemocratic arrogance and nihilism from
> the political extreme left.

The speech in 1970 was more complicated than that of 1950 because their was no specific leader of the Left. Adherents to the doctrine of nihilism — the belief that all social, political, and economic institutions must be completely destroyed to make way for new institutions— were numerous and from divergent segments of society. However, they were all countercultural revolutionaries, producers and products of the permissivism that permeated American culture in the 1960s. The extremists such as the Yippies, the Weathermen, and the Black Panthers were anarchists, but their philosophy had many sympathizers and supporters who believed strongly that change, particularly social change, was necessary. Liberal voices tended to sympathize with the anarchists when they spoke out for greater social and economic equality. Many of them were respected intellectuals and artists who expressed their views in their work. They supported the radicals' right to express their revolutionary ideas verbally. They marched along with them on Washington several times, in peaceful protest to the escalating involvement of America in the seemingly endless Vietnam War. These well-informed citizens were professors and playwrights, musicians and media moguls. Along with them went the altruistic youth — the bright college student bent on making the world a better place. They reflected the positive side of the countercultural revolution. The extremists of the Left whom Smith indicts in her second "Declaration of Conscience" speech are those who promoted the negative — those who abandoned reason for reaction. Their actions had no purpose except to destroy. "Burn, baby, burn" was their rallying cry. Their notion of revolution involved blood and destruction.

The audience that Smith targeted in 1970 was not simply the

members of the U.S. Senate. She expands her message to "the people themselves." She accuses them, along with the Senate — as she also did in 1950, of having "'know nothing, suspect everything' attitudes." She specifically indicts the "militant intellectuals of 'hear nothing' attitudes" — the ignorant conviction that their point of view is the only valid one. Margaret Chase Smith is particularly concerned about the students. College campuses in the 1960s were common sites for protest — in the form of literature, speech, and action. The Kent State tragedy demonstrated her contention that extremist behavior from the Left will result in repression from the Right. She believed that although freedomloving the American people would opt for law and order over unbridled expression. In this address, the senator speaks to both sides — the Left and the Right. She illustrates her perspective with a quote from a letter sent to her by a Colby college student: "I am striking with my heart against the fighting in Cambodia but I am intimidated by those who scream protests and clench their fist and cannot listen to people who oppose their views."

In the final two paragraphs of the speech, Smith addresses the "great center of our people," those moderates who have remained mute in this time of national crisis. These are her people, and she has been their stalwart spokesperson in Congress these past thirty years. She calls them to search their consciences, muster up their courage, and speak out:

> It is time that with dignity, firmness and friendliness, they
> reason with, rather than capitulate to, the extremists on both
> sides — at all levels — and caution that their patience ends
> at the border of violence and anarchy that threatens our
> American democracy.

The purpose of the second "Declaration" is the same as that of the first: to warn the nation about the threat of political extremism to American democracy. Therefore, her rhetorical strategy is to model the second speech on the first "Declaration." She almost repeats the message verbatim. For example, as with the first "Declaration," Smith eschews a formal introduction to signify the seriousness of her speech. She reminds the audience of her message twenty years ago and proceeds to recall portions of the first speech as they apply to the exigence in 1970. She follows a repetitive structure of "I said then," followed by how that comment applies to today. Often she adds more specific information about the present situation. For example, when she refers to the harm done twenty years ago by the "irresponsible words and the selfish political opportunism," she expands that harm to include "the irresponsible words [that] have exploded into trespass, violence, arson, and killings." When she accuses her audience of ignoring "some of the basic principles of Americanism," she adds "the right to dissent against the dissenters." In other words, in using the first "Declaration" as model, Smith plans to awaken the American people to the grave danger America is in once more. By conjuring up images of the dark days of McCarthyism, and adding how the national situation in 1970 is even worse, she hopes to shame those on the Left and the Right who are abusing the very rights they are shouting about and to shake middle America out of its malaise. Again, like the patriot Paul Revere, she articulates a warning that repression was on its way.

The second "Declaration" appears to be more a lesson in citizenship rather than the censure of the first speech. Unlike the first "Declaration" that offered different viewpoints and, at times, sounded political, the speaker was the voice of the spirit of America in the highly respected persona of Senator Margaret Chase Smith. Imbued with the fervor of her forefathers, the Senator was more the venerable New England schoolteacher. In her life or death lecture, with calm but stern tones, she aims to enlighten her listeners about the fragile nature of democracy. She reasons that freedom of speech includes the right to dissent, but it also includes the right to dissent against the dissenters. It does not allow for lawlessness. According to Smith, an effective democracy demands a responsible, enlightened, respectful citizenry.

The speech has a more solemn tone, rather than the angry, impatient voice of the first "Declaration." Perhaps the senator was concerned that this speech would be her last opportunity to address the subject that was dearest to her heart. She was seventy-three years old, and she was coming up for reelection in two years. The world had changed since she delivered her first "Declaration" twenty years ago. True, the times in 1970 had been terrible. The war was a disaster, and all faith in government seemed to have waned. But, as she warned the militant intellectuals, there is no "just cause" for jeopardizing the basic tenets of American democracy. Times change, and people change, but the principles that founded and fortified American democracy for almost 200 years proved constant. Extremists will always try to threaten these fundamental rights; therefore, she consistently professed, it is the duty of the American people to be ever vigilant.

RESULTS

The speech received overwhelming approval in newspapers, magazines, television, and radio. The mail was heavier and more favorable than it had been for the first "Declaration." Reaction in the Senate had been positive from both sides. President Nixon wrote her a note of gratitude. She received a similar message from moderate Democrat Hubert Humphrey and glowing responses from liberal Democrats such as Edward Kennedy of Massachusetts.

Most of the criticism came from Smith's raising the prospect of the Right reacting with repression to the anarchy of the Left. A number of the comments cited were delivered by FBI director J. Edgar Hoover a few days after Senator Smith's speech; he took issue with Smith's reasoning that the choice is between anarchy and repression, implying that she was in sympathy with the "revolutionary violence."[78] A few letters from the Left accused her of threatening them with repression.

EFFECT

The senator received notes from some that her speech had opened up opportunities for parents to communicate with their children. A high official lecturing at the National War College on the student revolutionary movement indicated that there was a noticeable cooling-off change as result of the speech.[79] She also received letters from students who wanted to know how she intended to put her words into action, offering to do what they could to help her. On August 18, 1970, she accepted the offer to chair the Freedom House, an organization formed to fight political extremism. In 1971 she joined with the Student National Education Association in its efforts to fight polarization.

At best, the speech raised some of her listeners to talking — to understanding the seriousness of the situation and to looking for solutions. However, as would be expected, it had little impact on the causes of the exigence. The war raged on, and so did civil strife. Despite the Senate's repeal of the Gulf of Tonkin Resolution on June 24, 1970, President Nixon said the resolution did not guide his policies. On June 29, 1970, the last of the 18,000 American soldiers, after two months of what President Nixon called his Cambodian incursion, retreated to South Vietnam. Nixon announced the pullout of 40,000 more Vietnam troops by Christmas. In October 1970, there were prison riots in New York City prisons and the bombing of police stations. In November, six members of the Weathermen were arrested as the bomb plotters. On November 21, U.S. planes conducted widespread bombing raids on North Vietnam. On February 8, 1971, South Vietnam invaded Laos with U.S. air support. On March 7, a thousand U.S. planes bombed Cambodia and Laos. On April 24, 1971, 700 Vietnam War veterans tossed their war medals away in protest at the Capitol. The antiwar demonstrations in Washington continued. On March 1, a bomb exploded in the Senate wing of the Capitol in protest of the U.S. military action in Laos. On April 21, 1971, eleven mayors warned of collapse of U.S. cities. On May 3, 10,000 antiwar protesters battled with police in an effort to shut down Washington. On December 26, 1971, a band of Vietnam veterans seized the Statue of Liberty in protest of the indiscriminate bombing of Indochina. On May 13, 1972, Americans heavily bomb Hanoi and Haiphong. Finally, on December 3, 1972, President Nixon ordered an end to the bombing. On January 27, 1973, the United States agreed to stop fighting in Vietnam. On March 29, 1973, American troops were withdrawn from Vietnam.

The war has had a devastating impact on all involved. The waste of lives and resources alone was shocking. The conflict took some 55,000 American lives and an additional 350,000 casualties; the financial cost was over $160 billion. More than two million Vietnamese were killed. Laos and Cambodia were devastated. The cease-fire agreement was broken as soon as the Americans left. The war waged on until April 30, 1975, when the victorious North Vietnamese captured the South's capital city of Saigon.

3
"I Speak as a United States Senator"

During the twenty-four years that Margaret Chase Smith served in the U.S. Senate, the Chamber was consumed with issues of foreign policy. From her first term, in 1948, to her forced retirement, after losing reelection in 1972, the subject that dominated debate had to do with Soviet aggression and the spread of communism. From the administrations of Presidents Truman to Nixon, the position of the United States vis-à-vis the USSR in world affairs, the predicament called the Cold War, was the source of much controversy. The idealistic domestic programs, such as the New Frontier and the Great Society — promised by Presidents Kennedy and Johnson, respectively — were forced to take a secondary position to the persistent disruptive demands provoked by Soviet saber rattling.

These were times of great fear and frustration for the American people and their leadership. Supposedly, World War II was fought to end Fascist aggression and to restore peace. However, there was no peace because a new form of aggression threatened the world — Communist aggression. Although united in the common cause to defeat the Nazis, the end of the war revealed the conflicting ideologies between the USSR and the other Allies. In retrospect, the Soviet leader's plans for Communist expansion were in operation at the Allied forces conference in Yalta in February 1945. Decisions on how to handle the end of the war gave the Soviet Union a strong foothold in Eastern Europe and in Germany in particular. Soviet plans were furthered when, at the end of the war, President Harry Truman acquiesced to the demands of the war-weary American people and demobilized American forces in Europe too rapidly. The vacuum created by the removal of the dominant American presence in the area was advantageous to the Soviets. As the United States demilitarized, the USSR increased its military strength. Josef Stalin, the Soviet leader, saw the defeat of Germany as the go-ahead for Communist expansionism, the beginning of the fulfillment of the ultimate goal of communism: world domination. Americans grew disillusioned: the notion of achieving peace in the world seemed remote.

The ideological contest between the Soviet Union and the United States became even more complicated with the introduction of nuclear weapons. The United States introduced the world to the ferocity of such weaponry when it dropped an atomic bomb on the Japanese cities of Hiroshima and Nagasaki in August 1945, in an effort to end the war in Asia. By October 1949, the world learned that America's atomic secret was out, for the Soviet Union had exploded a nuclear device. The arms race between the two opposing political systems intensified, leading to the building of nuclear stockpiles. Missiles with nuclear warheads were focused on major American and Soviet cities. Americans spent the 1950s taking precautions for the eventual Soviet nuclear attack. Air raid drills were mandatory once more, and the building of bomb shelters grew in popularity. The grim specter of total obliteration of human existence on the planet loomed like a dark cloud over the future. Nuclear bombs became more and more powerful, each having the power to level several major cities.

The threat of war moved into the stratosphere. The control of space became a shocking reality when, in October 1957, the Soviets surprised the world with the launch of the first man-made satellite, Sputnik. The United States was particularly surprised at the advanced Russian technology. The nation rushed to catch up by charging its educational sources to improve training in science and technology. Americans were beginning to feel that their country was losing its prime position in the world.

By 1950, the world was divided between the West and the East, the Free World and the Communist world. Nations organized for purposes of defense: The Western allies formed the North Atlantic Treaty Organization [NATO] to protect Europe; the Communists countered with the Warsaw Pact. Communism had spread, as Winston Churchill had predicted in 1946 in his famous "Iron Curtain" speech, from the Baltic to the Balkans to the Mediterranean and the Dardanelles. By 1949, the Marxist Mao Tse-tung and his Communist forces had overtaken the Republic of China and established the People's Republic of China. The humiliated Kuomintang Nationalists under Chiang Kai-shek were forced to flee to the island of Taiwan (Formosa). The "domino theory" was proving itself in Asia. As soon as China fell to the Communists, Manchuria, Korea, and Indochina witnessed the incursion of insurgent forces. These "wars of liberation," according to Soviet propaganda, were promoted to free people of the yoke of colonial imperialism. In 1956, Communism came within ninety miles of the United States when Fidel Castro and his rebels successfully invaded Cuba and defeated dictator Fulgencio Batista. Like the other Communist leaders, he allied Cuba with the USSR and vowed to spread communism to the surrounding countries.

The Soviets appeared to have little fear of attack from the United States. They surmised that although American military might was more powerful than theirs, the United States would be reluctant to use nuclear warfare for fear of risking the devastating consequences of a possible third world war. The policy of the United States was that of world leadership with the implication that the American military would be used to defend and maintain world peace when necessary.

The tension between the opposing forces exploded twice during Senator Smith's tenure in the Senate. First, the United States and other countries supported United Nations action to defend South Korea against invasion by the Communist North. The Korean War raged on from 1950 until 1953, when both countries signed a cease-fire agreement. At the onset of the next decade, the United States became embroiled in the war between South Vietnam and the Communists in the North, which lasted for more than a decade. American involvement escalated from Eisenhower's administration through Kennedy's, Johnson's, and Nixon's, ending in 1973, with an ignominious cease-fire agreement and victory for the Communist insurgents.

Senator Margaret Chase Smith had a strong interest in military affairs. Before she became an elected representative, as the wife of Representative Clyde Smith, she revealed her belief in military preparedness in a speech delivered on the occasion of Navy Day, October 27, 1938, to the Kennebec County Women's Republican Club. In the House of Representatives, she sat on the powerful Naval Affairs Committee, where she fought valiantly for women in the military. On July 14, 1950, she was commissioned as a lieutenant colonel in the U.S. Air Force Reserve in gratitude for her support of the need for a new Department of the Air Force, which she championed when she was in the House. In the Senate, she was chairperson of key subcommittees of the Senate Armed Services Committee, in particular, the Preparedness Investigating Subcommittee. As chairperson of this committee, the Senator was privy to secret information concerning the arms race. Further, Senator Smith gained firsthand foreign policy experience from her world tour in 1954-1955. Sponsored by Edward R. Murrow's See It Now program on CBS-TV, she met with many world leaders, such as the British Winston Churchill, the French Charles De Gaulle, the West German Konrad Adenauer, and the Russian V. M. Molotov, as well as with common folk.[1] Hers was the first trip of its kind for American leaders, and she was the first U.S. Senator to be welcomed in Moscow since the 1930s.[2] Such experience most likely gave her the confidence to speak as an expert on foreign affairs.

Undoubtedly, Margaret Smith's view of national and international affairs had to be colored by her enduring support of the military. Maine's economy, with its air bases and shipyards, was dependent on the defense industry. An even greater influence on her perception was her association with William C. Lewis, Jr., her steadfast assistant and confidant throughout most of her congressional career. Bill Lewis was a military man from a military family. His father, William C. Lewis, Sr., was an Army Air Corps Reserve colonel. He served as general counsel of the Old House Naval Affairs Committee and, later, was offered and accepted the rank of major

general in the Army Air Corps Reserve. Both he and Senator Smith were
strong supporters of the military. In her book *Declaration of Conscience*,
Senator Smith revealed that a memorandum from Air Force Brigadier
General Jerry D. Page supplied the basic ideas for both "Nuclear Credibility"
speeches.[3]

This chapter will analyze three speeches dealing with foreign policy
that the senator delivered on the floor of the Senate in 1961, 1962, and 1963.
She delivered "Nuclear Credibility" on September 21, 1961. A year later to the
day, on September 21, 1962, she presented the second "Nuclear Credibility."
The third speech to be discussed here is "Nuclear Test Ban Treaty," given on
September 9, 1963.

All three speeches addressed the same collective audience— members
of the U.S. Senate, the American people and in particular, the president of the
United States, John F. Kennedy. The "Nuclear Test Ban Treaty" spoke to the
Senate specifically, on the occasion of the ratification vote. Each speech
disputed the administration's foreign policy as it related to the Soviet Union.
The arguments in each address were prefaced on Senator Smith's adamant
conviction that national security could only be assured by the maintenance of
a strong military defense system, including nuclear tactical weapons. Further,
she contended that such assurance was dependent on the degree that
America's leaders asserted their will and determination to use such military
power when necessary. According to her perspective, the only guarantee for
the effective deterrence of Communist aggression was a superior military
counterforce.

Margaret Chase Smith's adversary in these three speeches was the
young president, Democrat John F. Kennedy. The only similarity between
these two was that they were both New Englanders who knew each other from
their common experiences in the House and the Senate. However, their
visions of the world and the position of the United States in it were diametri-
cal. Smith, the rugged individualist whose character was honed by the rigors
of the working class in small-town Maine, seemed to have little respect for the
manor-born, Harvard-educated Kennedy. Besides their partisan differences,
she was critical of his demeanor. She never forgot when he participated in a
major campaign to unseat her in the Senate. During the 1954 campaign, then
Senator John Kennedy came to Maine expressly to support her opponent,
claiming that the Democrat, Colby Professor Paul Fuller, would be a better
representative for the entire New England area.[4] She also was suspicious of
his brother Robert's association with McCarthy during the Army-McCarthy
hearings in 1954. Senator Smith connected John Kennedy with McCarthy as
the only two senators who traveled to Maine to campaign for her defeat.[5]

Margaret Chase Smith's political philosophy was clearly evident in all
her speeches. She believed strongly in the moral superiority of the United
States. Motivated by the philosophy of the Founding Fathers and the vision
of the early settlers, such as the signers of the Mayflower Compact, she was

devoted to the notion that the founding of America was God ordained. It was her commitment to ensure that philosophy endured. She had no tolerance for counterphilosophies, such as fascism and communism; the notion of mutual coexistence was fallacious. In other words, political systems that oppose American democracy were the enemy. The American political system was superior to all others. In a speech on foreign policy that she delivered to the Overseas Press Club, on April 19, 1955, she summed up her view of America's position in the world, concluded from her recent twenty-three-country tour, with an affirmation of her political beliefs:

> *The time has come* when our leadership in world affairs *must* increase in boldness and firmness if *we are* to cope success-fully with the threat to the freedom of the world. . . . We *must* start charting our course in the confident realism that *we are* the greatest nation in the world — and the world's *greatest* hope for peace — that *we* are through with letting Russia scare us — that we *must* strive for positive construc-tion instead of *fear-minded*, negative defensiveness that stresses *countermove* instead of maintaining the *initiative*.[6]

According to Smith, America was a nation built on moral principles; it represented right, and she firmly believed that "right makes might." Demanding firmness and resolve from herself and all Americans, she had no tolerance for weakness and conciliation. Think first, she professed; then speak with absolute conviction. She believed that having the moral strength to defend one's convictions, especially in the face of adversity, was an American virtue that should be evident in all forms of leadership. Smith's view of reality was supported with references to proof from the past. She was convinced that truth is made evident with what she called "hardheaded facts."

John F. Kennedy had a more pluralistic and futuristic view of the world. While Margaret Chase Smith, moralist and realist, was committed to the preservation of national security, he was most concerned with achieving world peace. He is quoted as stating: "I am almost a 'peace at any price' President."[7] He maintained the traditional policy of containment, but he regarded the Eisenhower-Dulles defense policy of massive retaliation as risking the possibility of nuclear war. Kennedy was not a fan of war; he rejected the contention by some Americans that "we should enter every military conflict as a moral crusade requiring the unconditional surrender of the enemy."[8] Kennedy believed in negotiating with the Soviets, stating that "[i]t is far better that we meet at the summit than at the brink." Mutual coexistence seemed to be the more realistic course. He believed that both the United States and the USSR were led by rational human beings who naturally feared the consequences of nuclear war; therefore, each would be open to agreement on how to reduce that threat.

Margaret Smith spoke from a national perspective; she reasoned from fact. John Kennedy's view was more global; he concentrated on probability. He saw the world in the throes of great political change — from imperialism to nationalism; and he felt positive about the transformation. In a speech he delivered in October 1961, he commented:

> [T]he United States is neither omnipotent nor omniscient —
> that we are only six percent of the world's population — that
> we cannot right every wrong or reverse each adversity — and
> that therefore there cannot be an American solution to every
> world problem.[9]

In a speech on March 23, 1962, at the University of California at Berkeley, President Kennedy looked ahead to what he called "a world of diversity . . . where, within a framework of international cooperation, every country can solve its own problems according to its own traditions and ideals."[10]

In his American University speech of June 10, 1963, the president defined the type of peace he believed would work:

> Not a *Pax Americana* enforced on the world by American
> weapons of war . . . a genuine peace, the kind of peace that
> makes life on earth worth living . . . not merely peace for
> Americans, but peace for all men and women; not merely
> peace in our time, but peace for all time.[11]

In what is considered by many to be his best speech, the president hinted to a proposal for a nuclear test ban treaty, explaining that "nuclear powers must avert those confrontations which bring an adversary to a choice of either a humiliating retreat or a nuclear war."[12] He believed, in contrast to Senator Smith's view, that "we can seek a relaxation of tensions without relaxing our guard."[13]

"NUCLEAR CREDIBILITY" (1961)

On September 21, 1961, Senator Smith delivered her first "Nuclear Credibility" speech. As in 1950, a Democratic president was in office, and the threat to our national security from communism was even greater. President Kennedy refused to continue the hard-line posture of his predecessor Dwight D. Eisenhower, a stance that Senator Smith celebrated because it had "produced the greatest and longest period of peace for the United States since the days of pre-World War II.[14] In contrast, Kennedy believed that the policy of massive retaliation to enforce deterrence promoted by Eisenhower's secretary of state, John Foster Dulles, actually threatened war. Acknowledging that no sane person would want nuclear war, the young president sought to achieve detente with the Soviets through communication and mutual agreement.   On March 23, 1961, Senator Smith commented that "John Kennedy was impressive to me,"[15] when he eloquently delivered an ultimatum to Khrushchev to remove the Communist forces from Laos. However, she was disillusioned when, instead, Khrushchev defied the demand and pushed farther into Laos. Khrushchev further spurned Kennedy's strong words by precipitating a crisis in Berlin for the purpose of making a separate peace with East Germany and to sealing Berlin off from the Free World. To Margaret Smith, the president's credibility was suspect. He seemed to be talking like Churchill but acting like Chamberlain: His words were bold, but his action was weak.

The occasion that prompted Margaret Chase Smith's extremely powerful speech was the fact that President Kennedy was planning to deliver his first speech to the United Nations in a few days. As Smith expressed in "Nuclear Credibility," the United Nations was an organization "threatened with collapse for lack of will and determination." Her speech, which distinctly addressed members of the Senate and the American people, targeted President Kennedy in particular, accusing him of lacking will and determination.   One may surmise that she chose this particular occasion and this particular message to warn the president to represent America by speaking with greater will and determination.

Senator Smith's attack on the president was severe. She accused him outrightly of misrepresenting American leadership style, specifically, of lacking the courage to stand up to Nikita Khrushchev of the Soviet Union: "I sense a tendency, strange to the American character in world affairs, to retreat from circumstances rather than to face up to them realistically and master them."

With carefully chosen words and a clearly delineated argument, Senator Smith demonstrated that she was a master of the deliberative style of oratory. Characteristic of her businesslike manner, she got right to the point by stating the exigence of the situation succinctly:

> Everywhere the Communists press forward stronger. Khru-
> shchev, vowing to take over the world for communism, and
> acting with all the confidence of a winner, threatens to put
> an end to civilized survival for the world if we do not let him
> have his way.

The purpose of her speech was clear; she intended to reveal that Khrushchev was an immoral leader with malevolent intentions and that President Kennedy's reluctance to fortify his tough words with action encouraged the Soviets to be successful. Her implication was that Kennedy was guilty of moral cowardice. Using the president's own words from his celebrated inaugural address, she demonstrated that he spoke strongly but acted weakly. Smith portrayed Kennedy as a "paper tiger." He was risking the loss of national security for the sake of Secretary of Defense Robert McNamara's theory that "we can do *more* in deterring the Soviets by preparing to do *less* against them if they should provoke armed hostilities." The theory postulated that "increasing conventional forces is the best way to create more effective deterrence."

Senator Smith's speech is a counterargument aimed at exposing the fallacy and the danger of such thinking. After reviewing the deteriorating state of foreign affairs and indicting the permissive policy of the administration, the senator warned:

> [If] we *fail* to meet the Soviets at the ultimate levels of *will and purpose*, the danger will be greatly widened that we will have no choice later on but to meet them at the ultimate levels of *force and violence*; either that or submit to their will.

In other words, Smith believed that the strong articulation of our military readiness to the Soviet Union would avoid war.

Senator Smith defined her case as an effort to present a realistic perspective. The people needed to see the present national crisis more coherently. She executed her purpose by reviewing past events in which the Soviet Union succeeded in effecting its ends much to the dismay of the United States. Intent on moving her listeners to identify with her logic she posed her thesis in probing form: "*What has happened that permits Khrushchev to act as he does?*" She drove the quandary into the hearts and minds of her listeners by repeating the problem: "[W]hy does he feel free to do as he does?" "Why does Khrushchev so often have the initiative and we are satisfied only to react?"

Structuring her purpose statement in question form provided the basis for her rhetorical strategy. It helped her to achieve her objective of letting the people decide after a process of carefully planned inductive reasoning. The question style permitted the speaker to get inside the minds of her listeners, to move them to think along with her. In other words, the interrogatory style advanced rhetorical efficiency by effecting identification with the audience; both speaker and listeners are on common ground.

With clear, calculated language, the senator delineated her argument effectively. Basing her logic on truths supported with recent and historical fact, she moved her auditors toward closure with her. After listening to her speech, they would be convinced that America was losing the struggle with the Soviets not because it was weaker militarily but because the president was an ineffective leader. They would realize that Khrushchev was duping the president because he had been told by Kennedy that America would never initiate a nuclear strike. Khrushchev behaved like a naughty child because he knew he would not be punished. The president facilitated his immoral behavior even more by bargaining for peace with America's military strength. The speaker intended that the audience would realize that Kennedy's hope for mutual coexistence was simply "wishful thinking," that there were no facts to support the theory. The president seemed oblivious to the hard-core reality that the Soviets were pledged to pose a clear and present danger. Smith, as efficient rhetor, moved her audience to agree that the only effective deterrent to the onslaught of communism lay in the American character. The will and determination that won the country and kept it a winner needed to be demonstrated with greater forcefulness. Smith led the audience to conclude that there was no real reason for Americans to be intimidated by the Soviets. America had the military advantage; now its leader needed to take the moral advantage.

The thesis question also established the cornerstone on which her argument was mounted. The pivotal points of the speech were also in the form of questions: "Why does he feel free to do as he does?" "Is Khrushchev free to act as he does because the Soviets have suddenly gained the over-all military advantage?" "What is the origin of this fear of risks?" *"Is it conceivable that Khrushchev could assess that the will of the American people has collapsed?* . . . That Americans, as the saying goes, would rather be RED than dead?" "How much longer can we afford to lose?" "If we fail to stand firm in Berlin . . . there with the best we have, where in the world will we draw the line?"

With cause-and-effect style, Smith led her listeners to respond to each question by demonstrating her reasoning with facts, example, and testimony. She summarized each point of argument with emphatic statements of truth. By organizing those truths in logical order, the rhetor motivated her listeners to come to the intended resolution of the dilemma:

> The primary determinant for over-all military advantage today is the capacity for total nuclear war.
> The over-all military advantage is on our side.
> The greatness of this country was not won by people who were afraid of risks.
> We can defeat the USSR at any intensity of armed conflict unless we have degraded our fighting capacity greatly by self-imposed restrictions, such as restrictions on the use of tactical nuclear weapons.
> To say that we can count on achieving and maintaining a balance or stability in these conditions — even if we had the Soviet's cooperation, much less their opposition — is nothing short of wishful thinking . . . a form of "nuclear escapism" to dodge the hard, cold facts.

[W]e have the nuclear capability — but not the nuclear
credibility.

Smith's mastery of logical appeal was also evident in her use of
language. She reinforced her argument and influenced her listeners' logic in
three particular ways. First, she juxtaposed contrasting terms in key
statements. In the beginning of the speech, she initiated her purpose by
putting "the need to *command*" in direct relationship to *deter*. The following
illustrate similar structures: fail/free, peace/war, fear/freedom, life/death,
weak/strong, winning/losing, resolution/retreat, firmness/passivity, strength/
submission, will and determination/force and violence. The either/or
construct served to free her listeners from indecisiveness and also intensified
the "do or die" demand of the situation.

Another effective stylistic device used by the senator was the
technique of intensifying key thoughts by proceeding each with statements in
the negative. For example, to arouse her auditors' attention to her thesis,
which she characterized as a "vital question," Smith first stated what the
question was not in repetitive structure: "Not a question that I have
composed. . . . Not a question of selfish or parochial origin. But one far more
important. A question of national interest."

Smith used the rhetorical device of repetition throughout her speech.
For example, to further prompt her listeners to realize that her thesis posed
a "vital question," she revealed its relevance with the repetition of the personal
pronoun *we* and the objective pronoun *it*: "We must do this now. If we fail
to do it now, we may not be free to do it later. . . . [W]hat we learn from our
experience, what we do about it." Also: "It is a question. . . . It is a
challenge." The senator created a dramatic introduction to her thesis, one
that extended for two pages.

Finally, Smith demonstrated the power of language by using the
president's words to reinforce her argument. Focusing on the term *inexhaustible,* which he had used in the phrase "our restraint is not inexhaustible" in a
recent speech, Smith used that term to describe the sentiments of the
American people: "Our deterrent capacity is not inexhaustible. The confidence the American people is not inexhaustible." She summarized: "How
much longer can we afford to lose?"

Margaret Chase Smith further displayed rhetorical mastery when she
used her adversary's own words to debate his viewpoint. For example, she
quoted the bold expressions from his famed inaugural address to demonstrate
that his was an empty promise: "We dare not tempt them with weakness. For
only when our arms are sufficient beyond doubt can we be certain beyond
doubt that they will never be employed." In reality, Smith argued, citing the
aggression of Castro in Cuba and Khrushchev in Berlin, the president's policy
promoted the weakening of American military might. The senator borrowed
the president's famous phrase about fear and negotiation to make her
argument final: "While I agree with him that we should not negotiate from

fear or fear to negotiate — I say we should not fear to refuse to negotiate on any matter that is not negotiable."

Another outstanding feature of this speech was the use of ethical appeal. Margaret Chase Smith demonstrated the strength of her ethos by confronting the President aggressively. The implication seemed to be that she was the better leader for America.[16] For example, she articulated the fact that she was better informed about the military, intimating that the president lacked the necessary courage to defy the Soviets:

> We have the military basis for clearly demonstrating our will and purpose . . . for making deterrence work. But we will never deter the Soviets by backing away, or by offering to fight *on their terms* because we are fearful of provoking them by indicating beyond all doubt that we will fight, if fight we must, on *our terms*.

Assuming the president's place, she audaciously declared that she would be "the first to urge great caution . . . also . . . great firmness . . . and the last to cease opposing the submission of the unlimited interests of 180 million Americans to the stupidity of limited deterrence."

Throughout the speech, Margaret Smith presented herself as the defender of American morality. Her argument focused on revealing the fact that the president thought and acted in opposition to American beliefs. She made reference to American values in her attack on his perspective. She demonstrated that he may have contributed to the loss of freedom, the most revered value. She criticized his moral character as weak in contrast to his predecessors and, in particular, those pioneers who fought for America. She indicted his position on world affairs as "strange to the American character." She even hinted that he lacked devotion to the American people because he had devalued the importance of national security and national pride. She faulted him for not having faith in the destiny of America. She also accused him of sympathizing with the enemy, of selling out our political system and all that we hold most dear in exchange for a flimsy notion of world peace.

The senator invoked the patriotic sense of her listeners with passionate references to Americans and freedom. For example, she stipulated that her message was directed to "every American . . . to every free man and woman . . . to every person who yearns to know what freedom is, or to gain a freedom wrested from him by force, or lost to him by inaction or bad advice." She stirred up ire among her listeners by describing Khrushchev's aggression in Berlin as "a frontal attack on Freedom." She incited strong feelings of nationalism by reminding them of their heritage:

> *The greatness of this country was not won by people who were afraid to take risks.* It was won for us by men and women

with little physical power at their command who nevertheless
were willing to submit to risks. Could it not be lost for us
by people with great physical power at their command but
nevertheless willing to risk submitting? I believe it could.

She fired the flames of patriotism with her attempt to heighten the seriousness
of the situation with this description:

[It is] the most crucial the American people faced since the
Declaration of Independence launched us as the United
States into the world of nations . . . not the strongest, not the
largest; but nevertheless confident, firm, and fearing no one.

She blamed the president for Khrushchev's sense of confidence,
claiming: "We have in effect played into his hands — for the kind of warfare
in which he knows he can beat us. We have restricted ourselves on the
freedom of choice to use the nuclear tactical weapons which he knows would
defeat him if he started war. *In short, we have the nuclear capability— but not
the nuclear credibility.*

Finally, Margaret Smith appealed to the emotions of her listeners.
She was intent on alarming them to the paramount danger the president's
policy portended. The seriousness of her message was intoned with the first
sentence when she defined her audience as all-inclusive: "What I am about
to say is addressed not only to the members of the United States Senate but
to all Americans — and most specifically to the President of the United
States." The importance of her thesis was dramatized with a climactic
introduction that increased in urgency for two pages. For example, she
appealed to her listeners' feelings about their country and the present danger
by characterizing the thesis question as the "most crucial the American people
have faced since the Declaration of Independence." The drama was further
enhanced with the repetition of the personal pronoun *it,* referring to the
"question of national interest" that comprised the thesis, interplayed with the
personal pronoun *we,* referring to the audience. This stylistic device caused
the audience to feel directly responsible for the message that was about to be
told. Smith intensified their sense of responsibility with the repetition of the
deeply probing term *why.* For example: "Why does he [Khrushchev] feel free
to do as he does?" She urged her listeners to "go straight to the reasons *why*
the conflict so often runs against us and burdens us so heavily."

The speaker's desire to stimulate her listeners emotionally as well as
cognitively is reflected clearly in her argument. She simply presented them
with an either/or, do-or-die choice. She wanted them to feel that there was
no time for discussion; realistic decisions must be made. Smith also
influenced the thoughts and feelings of her audience with the use of emotion-
laden words: *against us, burdens us.* Other such terms are found in the

following statements, underlined for illustrative purposes: "Khrushchev . . . *threatens* to put an *end to civilized survival for the world*." "He has dared to make a *frontal attack on Freedom*." "[T]his is a time of *corroding fears and tensions*." "We have wandered into the never-never land of *high hope and deep despair*." "I see *no hope* of deterring them." The speaker further demonstrated her stylistic talent with several metaphors that served to stir up intended feelings of foreboding: "It is a *grim spectacle* as we have never seen." "[Khrushchev] has *stained* the sky and *polluted* the air with nuclear bursts." She also spoke of "*foul* clouds of his nuclear *blackmail* blasts."

To sum, the rhetor wanted her auditors to be worried. She wanted them to see and feel the futility of the present foreign policy. She wanted to move for immediate change before it was too late. Recalling the president's strong yet meaningless words against Soviet aggression in Laos and Cuba, Senator Smith exhorted: "God forbid that the pattern of brave words on Laos and Cuba followed by no brave action be repeated on Berlin."

The feisty Margaret Smith, admired by many for having the courage of her convictions, concluded her life-threatening revelation on a positive note. Assuming the leadership position, she used her powerful ethos to empower her listeners to have faith in her argument: "I am confident that we can do better." After restating the most probing questions of her message, the senator, as in a prayer, invoked their sacred American heritage: "In the name of the courage, determination, and sacrifices of our forebears, *let us not be afraid to be right* at this critical time." She then offered President Kennedy some final words of advice. Margaret Smith maintained her steely stance to the end by adapting the President's famous phrase from his inaugural address to fortify her view: "While I agree with him that we should not negotiate from fear or fear to negotiate — I say we should not fear to refuse to negotiate on any matter that is not negotiable." To Senator Smith, America's traditions were inviolable.

Apparently, Senator Smith's speech was effective. President Kennedy did address the United Nations General Assembly with greater will and determination, as she had warned him to do. He let the world audience know that the United States would not hesitate to use its nuclear capacity. Historian Michael Beschloss noted in *The Crisis Years* that the president felt that the American people were "ready to go to the brink of war" on Berlin.[17] Beschloss also states that the president was concerned by Senator Smith and others who accused him of lacking the will to use nuclear weapons.[18]

Senator Smith's speech achieved international attention, particularly in the Soviet Union. On September 23, 1961, commentators on Russian radio accused her of having "another attack of cannibal instinct" and referred to her as "that bloodthirsty little woman."[19] Soviet leader Nikita Khrushchev called for American Communists, through the *Daily Worker*, to conduct a letter-writing campaign against her.[20] He denounced her as "the devil in a disguise of a woman" in a letter to the British Labor Party members of

Parliament.[21] Mrs. Khrushchev, in a letter to the organization Women for Peace, called Margaret Chase Smith a warmonger: "Threats are made to destroy our homes, to kill our husbands, to take the lives of our children . . . just one American name — Margaret Smith."[22]

"NUCLEAR CREDIBILITY" (1962)

Exactly one year after she delivered the first "Nuclear Credibility" speech, Margaret Chase Smith found it necessary to deliver a second. Although President Kennedy seemed to have acknowledged her warning in the 1961 address, the senator felt that his words remained meaningless— that they still were not supported with any action. She felt that his policy "continued to undermine the nuclear credibility of the United States to the detriment of our Nation, and to the advantage and the increasing boldness of Khrushchev."[23] In particular, she was concerned about the reports of missile bases in Cuba, which, by the way, the White House angrily denied.[24] After consulting several friends and advisers, and after much thought and deliberation, the senator decided to once more warn the members of the Senate, the American people, and the president of the United States of the dire consequences that might result from relating to the Communists with weakness rather than strength.

She began her 1962 speech by getting right to the problem: The questions she had the year before that had served to probe the efficacy of the foreign policy of the Kennedy dministration needed repeating. The Senator reiterated four central questions— the last one being the prime focus: "When will we start winning?" According to her view, the exigence that prompted the 1961 address had worsened:

> The Communists, far from exploring new frontiers of friendship and cooperation, have continued the pressures of their attacks against liberty. . . . Indeed, they have *increased* their efforts. And there is little in their attitude toward any problem anywhere to indicate that they intend to change for the better.

In her 1961 speech, Senator Smith argued the claim that the Kennedy plan was detrimental to America's superior position in world affairs. She reasoned that the United States was losing to the USSR because the plan was based on the unrealistically optimistic notion that peace could best be obtained if the United States downplayed its nuclear might, reducing such weapons to parity with the Soviets. The Kennedy policy advocated the use of conventional forces over nuclear weapons, debated Smith, in a misguided effort to "level the playing field." Rather than continuing Eisenhower's policy of containment through the threat of "massive retaliation," a posture that reinforced America's superior status in the world, Smith concluded that Kennedy's fallacious notions on how to achieve world peace reduced the United States to the level of a "second rate" nation. The Kennedy policy, she reasoned, promoted reactive decision making, allowing the Soviets to take the initiative.

In the 1962 address, Smith further criticized the rhetoric of the administration, accusing Kennedy and McNamara of "[w]ords and more words" and no action: "It is inconceivable that any amount of polished phrases — no matter how expertly put together and how adroitly presented — could longer conceal the hard facts from the American people." She commanded her audience to "face the truth": "No amount of contrived double-talk can longer divert the impacts of reality." She quoted the essence of the not-to-worry replies that had been articulated by Administration spokespersons in response to the exigence: "We are far behind. But we will catch up. And meanwhile, there's no great military significance in the Soviets' feat. And Cuba really presents no threat."

The Senator added to the claim made in 1961 by presenting what she considered the only logical solution to the problem, the traditional stance of maintaining an overall military advantage. Addressing the president directly, Smith asserted that "there is a route back" to "the position of eminence, influence, and well-being that our country enjoyed in better days." She clarified that "the starting point" must be to build up our military advantage to the level of a "realistic over-all military advantage reposing in a capability to win our objectives at any level of conflict, from the lowest to the highest." The claim that Smith posited is that Communist aggression could be deterred through strengthening military defense: "We must counter the *military capabilities* that constitute a threat to us. We must protect ourselves against that which we know the Communists are *capable of doing*." In other words, according to the senator, the only way that the United States could regain its superior position in the world was to rely on "a counterforce": "Our 'second-strike' must be stronger than the force remaining to the enemy after his initial strike."

Senator Smith clearly summarized the grounds for her claim by citing specific data that attested to her perception that the United States was losing the Cold War to the Communists. First, she announced that the Communists had not changed as the administration's policy had hoped: "The Communists, far from exploring new frontiers of friendship and cooperation, have continued the pressures of their attacks against liberty." She supported her observation by listing abrupt negative statements in parallel form. The mere mention of the location was sufficient to kindle common images among her listeners: "Not in the U.N. — Not in Berlin — Not at Geneva — Not in Cuba — Not in Southeast Asia — Not anywhere."

The senator framed her second supporting point in a pivotal question: "And why should they change . . . as long as they are making progress toward their goals?" First, she mentioned the growing weakness of the West in Europe: "The NATO Alliance, protecting an area of the non-Communist world that was of great and immediate importance to the United States, was plagued by troubles, doubt, criticisms, and uncertainties." To the reality that the confidence of NATO must be strengthened, she dismissed the idea, given the Administration's foreign policy. She queried: "Could we possibly hope to build this confidence by demanding acceptance of U.S. policies that are not palatable to them? Would not this course be more likely to destroy their confidence than to build it?" She warned that Khrushchev, aware of the weak situation in NATO, may cast "an acquisitive eye toward the Western doorstep of the Soviet Empire." He may assess "that the Free World's will is so low as to negate its power." She supported her logic with testimony from "a good friend of President Kennedy" who "reported that Khrushchev had stated that he believes that the United States will not fight to protect itself."

Her third point in support of her claim also relates to the administration's wish for positive change in the menacing situation. She disputes the notion by reviewing realistic events, asserting that the only change has been in increased Communist aggression:

> In Laos our objective of a truly neutral and independent country is stalled by the refusal of the pro-Communist elements to comply with the peace agreement that was signed only a short time ago at Geneva. . . .
>
> In Cuba, the Bloc countries and Castro blatantly defy the principles of the Monroe Doctrine and proceed with the Communization of that island— and in recent weeks an acceleration of transforming Cuba into a Communist arsenal.
> . . .
>
> In Vietnam we are committing ourselves, bit by bit, to a more involved war, as the result of fashioning our responses to the patterns chosen by the enemy.
>
> And in the realm of space the Soviets' new achievements cast the shadow of a tremendous new military potential across the whole Free World.

In other words, what had changed, she asserted, was the fact that the position of the United States in world affairs had deteriorated to "a disturbingly low level."

After demonstrating that the Kennedy administration's policy of strength through weakness had only served to imperil national security, Senator Smith further supported her claim that a counterforce was necessary in order to win by addressing and rebutting counterclaims to her notion.

First, she dealt with the contention that by building up the military the United States was promoting an arms race. She quickly dismissed such an idea as "fiction":

> If this *were* our intention, would we not be stupid indeed to burden ourselves with the expense of an *aerospace defense system*, our ballistic missile *early warning* facilities, the Strategic Air Command *alert*, and other precautions of that sort? If we *intended* to strike *first*, could we not *forego* these things and put *all* of our effort and resources into *offensive* means?

The second counterpoint Smith rebutted dealt with administration's concern with "subject of risks": "We have been cautioned on more than one occasion that we cannot do thus-and-so because it would risk provoking the Communists." Fear of that risk, she reasoned, was responsible for the weakening of our military defense, especially in regard to the policy of increasing conventional force and decreasing nuclear force. With the agility of a master fencer, the senator thrust the point of her rebuttal at the very foundation of the counterargument:

> I have heard comparatively little about the risks of adopting wishful thinking as a substitute for hardheaded realism in overcoming the Communists' drive for power and keeping the balance on our side.

She pressed her criticism of the administration's seemingly vacuous logic as illustrated in the following statements: "Can we risk the survival of our country on anyone's 'opinions' as to what the Communists' *intentions* are?" She characterized such reasoning about the Communist risk as "gambling on a guess that the Communists *do not intend* to use every part of the military capabilities" and as "gambling on the dangerous assumption that *their intentions will be good*." In other words, the senator boldly portrayed the rationale for the Administration's policy as simple conjecture, hardly the evidence on which to decide the fate of the world. With the final blow, she declared sternly: "We must protect ourselves against that which we *know the Communists are capable of doing*."

Margaret Smith concluded the rebuttal with a revealing commentary on the absurd reasoning of the counterforce opponents. Her model is the "anti-counterforce" advertisement in the *New York Times* of August 21, 1962, signed by 175 highly respected academics. She claimed that the critics inferred that the United States "is to blame for the Soviets' continued intransigence." They argued that building a counterforce gave "the Soviets reason to fear that we are preparing to attack them." Our military might caused the Soviets "to be driven to excessive secrecy and distrust by the apprehension of our strength." Scornfully, she summed up the ludicrous argument of the noteworthy anticounterforce proponents: "In substance, these critics contend that the Soviets are bad because *we* make them bad. Hence, if we reduce *our* military strength, their attitude will improve, and they well become more tractable." With almost mocking tones, the forthright lady from Maine impugned the judgment of some of America's leading intellectuals:

> Do these good and sincere people who are so critical really believe that we would be better off *without* a margin of military advantage across the board? Are they really willing to risk the survival of our country on their opinion of the Soviets' intentions?

The intrepid Senator Smith then challenged those "who seem to think that deterrence is . . . old-fashioned . . . has no future." Mustering up her moral muscle, she rebutted such a notion with the historical rationale: "We have had effective deterrence for the majority of time over the last fifteen years. We have effective deterrence now. And I believe we can continue to have effective deterrence in the future." She summarized her point firmly: "And in the future, as in the past, there is no doubt that effective deterrence will stem fundamentally from our counterforce capability."

The senator concluded her argument by addressing the fundamental fear of counterforce: the risk of precipitating the most destructive war of all, a nuclear war. To those who say that "in nuclear war there could be no winner," she asserted defiantly: "We *can* win." She defended her declaration by acknowledging that such a win would be costly but that it did "not *have* to be a Pyrrhic victory." She moved her listeners to regard the concept of winning and losing on moral grounds: "We *could lose by eroded resolve* and ultimate capitulation without suffering any physical damage at all from the enemy who defeated us." The senator reaffirmed her claim with the following emphatic conviction:

> [I]f we are attacked, I hold with the concept that our "second-strike" force must be stronger than the force remaining to the enemy after his initial strike. If we retained this advantage we would be in a winning position.

The second "Nuclear Credibility" speech is clear proof of Margaret Chase Smith's oratorical mastery. The discussion on the structure of her argument demonstrated her debating skill. It showed how she, with insightful logic, pitted her win-lose resolution to the foreign policy dilemma provoked by Communists against the weak lose-lose rationale resolution of her opponents. Senator Smith's rhetorical competence was also evident in her style of expression. Similar to her 1961 address, she chiefly depended on poignant questions to probe the psyche of her listeners in order to compel conscientious thinking. The stylistic device was used most effectively in the conclusion of her speech. In an effort to move all her listeners toward closure, she prompted their senses accordingly:

> Don't we want to do everything within reason to avoid needless destruction? . . . Of course we do. Don't we want to provide the enemy with every possible incentive *not to attack our cities?* . . . Of course we do. Do we want to subscribe to or be limited to a policy of indiscriminate devastation, which would provide an enemy with a strong incentive to attack our own cities? . . . Of course we do not.

Her powerful peroration rallied all Americans, in addition to her audience, to better comprehend the crisis more clearly and to embrace her resolution. Using the devices of repetition and contrasting negative with positive phrases that helped to make her 1961 argument so effective, the senator summarized her perspective:

> I do not intend to imply that counterforce is the answer to *everything. It is not.* But even in the very worst context that can be contrived without going to impossible extremes, we are still vastly better off *with* it than we could possibly be *without* it.

The audience was left with Margaret Smith's final, resolute appeal ringing in their minds:

> *No one* claims that it is a panacea. *No one* could say for certain that because we have a counterforce capability the future will be *easier.* But *there* is every reason to believe that if we *resolutely maintain* a counterforce capability the future will be *less difficult* than it might be otherwise. and that is a goal which, although not spectacular, we must not ignore.

The immediate response from her Senate colleagues was one of praise. Senator Stuart Symington, who, as President Kennedy's spokesperson, criticized the first "Nuclear Credibility" speech, was extremely impressed with the second one. He referred to it as "one of the most thought-provoking addresses on our military posture it has been my privilege to listen to in the Senate."[25] Republican Senator Kenneth Keating hailed the speech as a "remarkable analysis," stating that the venerable Smith had "devastated" the anticounterforce argument.[26]

One month later, the validity of Margaret Chase Smith's argument was proven. President Kennedy faced the greatest threat to the United States and the world – the possibility of a nuclear war. As warned by Senator Smith, the Soviets could not be trusted. With blatant disregard for American supremacy, the Soviets moved missiles with nuclear warheads aimed at the United States into western Cuba. When confronted with the fact, Khrushchev denied everything.[27]   Finally, Kennedy saw Chairman Khrushchev for what he really was: "an immoral gangster."[28]   Later, his brother Robert admitted that the Kennedy Administration had been fooled by Khrushchev lies: "We had been deceived by Khrushchev, but we had also fooled ourselves."[29]

The Cuban Missile Crisis, in October 1962, had the potential to become the most feared crisis in the world. In a speech on October 20, President Kennedy informed the American people of the crisis and the fact that he was implementing a quarantine on military shipments to Cuba.[30] Invoking the Monroe Doctrine, he warned Khrushchev that any missile attacks anywhere in the hemisphere would incur "a full retaliatory response upon the Soviet Union."[31]   Addressing the Soviet leader directly, Kennedy appealed to him to consider world peace instead of world domination as his primary objective.[32] The president concluded the momentous address by invoking the same moral justification that Margaret Chase Smith had always advocated: "Our goal is not the victory of might, but the vindication of right."[33]

Khrushchev backed down; the missiles were dismantled. The world was brought to the brink of total devastation and, at the eleventh hour, saved. At last, reason triumphed; the Cold War in Cuba cooled by a small but significant amount.

To sum, Margaret Chase Smith's argument for counterforce capability as the effective deterrent to Communist aggression proved superior. Her interpretation of reality, for which she spoke so passionately, and that was so strongly criticized by many leading intellectuals, saved the day and the world. She lamented that Kennedy "had done it so late as to have the world on the brink of World War III."[34]   Nevertheless, she was proud of the President's new-found determination, in particular, his demand for on-site inspections to ensure that the missiles were removed.[35]

"NUCLEAR TEST BAN TREATY"

On September 24, 1963, the Senate of the United States convened to vote on the ratification of the long-awaited nuclear test ban treaty. As the individual senators rose to present their opinions on the agreement, it became apparent that most were supportive. The senator from Maine chose to speak last, perhaps to reinforce the fact that she labored long and hard on her decision or simply to have the last word. Margaret Chase Smith began her discourse by stating that the vote is "one of the most difficult votes that I have ever cast as a United States Senator — or even in my twenty-three years in Congress."

Such a statement from one respected for her independence, integrity, diligence, and decisiveness must have attracted the attention of her audience. Her colleagues knew that she had studied the treaty with her usual precision. The credibility of her opinion was fortified by the fact that she sat on the Preparedness Investigating Subcommittee where she was privy to a great deal of information on American-Soviet relations. In addition, during the debate that preceded the vote, on September 9, 1963, they heard her remind them of the need to also "examine and evaluate" the "consequent disadvantages which might accrue to the United States." These, she reasoned, must be weighed against the advantages to determine the level of risk to the nation. They listened as she attempted to paint a realistic portrait of the kind of people America plans to share its fate with. The descriptive words Smith used served to communicate her belief that the Soviets were immoral, that they could not be trusted: *shameful, stealthy, surreptitiously, shattered*:

> [This is] the same country which, in recent years, . . . ruthlessly repressed the Hungarian uprising, erection of a shameful wall of tyranny around Berlin, surreptitiously deployed ballistic missiles in Cuba and, after months of stealthy preparations, shattered a moratorium on nuclear testing which had been in effect for thirty-four months. It has also seen fit to abrogate virtually all the agreements and treaties it has ever entered into with other nations whenever it served its purpose to do so.

Her associates heard the distinguished Senator Smith delineate sixteen questions that she felt called attention to the "serious risks" inherent in the document, questions that presented a "cold, hard, impassioned appraisal of the treaty and all its consequences."[36] They were generated from her criticism of the "poor draftsmanship" of the treaty as well as from the sudden attitude change of the Soviets:

> I considerate it more than passing-strange that suddenly the Soviet Union found this limited agreement to be so vital to her national interests that it was negotiated, initialed, and signed with remarkable expediency and haste.

The senator recalled for her listeners the Soviets' "adamant intransigence" to the suggestion for such a treaty the year before in Geneva. She motivated the senators to question why the Soviet Union suddenly found this limited agreement "so vital" to its national interests. They heard Smith insinuate that the Soviet's sudden interest had to do with the ambiguous language of the agreement, which allowed for "varied interpretations." She further probed their thinking by reminding them of the present disparity in knowledge gained from recent nuclear testing. The Soviets' last series of tests was "massive, sophisticated, and impressive; America's was not."

After her speech, Senator Smith forwarded the questions to Defense Secretary McNamara and Secretary of State Dean Rusk. She received an answer from Senator John Sparkman, second senior Majority member of the Senate Foreign Relations Committee, to the effect that there were no single factual answers available to her questions because they were hypothetical, requiring data that could only be collected after a full-scale nuclear war between the U.S. and the USSR. Other answers could not be given because they involved classified data.

Unsatisfied, Margaret Smith had a second set of questions read into the *Congressional Record*. She heard from Secretary of State Dean Rusk and Secretary of Defense McNamara but felt that their "answers were too speculative and without the definitiveness and assurance I had sought."[37] She was also perturbed with the classification of so much relevant data as secret, causing the argument for the treaty to be one-sided.[38]

Since 1956, John F. Kennedy, then the Democratic senator from Massachusetts, had endorsed a nuclear test ban treaty with the Soviet Union. During his presidential campaign in 1960, he emphasized the urgent need to control the spread of the Bomb to other countries. Despite the fact that the United States, Britain, and the Soviet Union had agreed to a voluntary moratorium on nuclear testing from 1958, Kennedy was concerned about the need for a more binding agreement.[39]

When he became president, he advised congressmen that a test ban agreement might lead to the resolution of such conflicting issues as Berlin and Laos. He encouraged his advisers to seek such an agreement when they met with the Soviets in Geneva. Otherwise, he warned that international relations would be an endless arms race if nuclear weapons spread to countries like Israel and China. Above all, he was most concerned about denying the Bomb to China, that austere Communist country with whom the United States had no relations. China with nuclear power would indeed be a real threat to the world.[40]

The Geneva talks, which resumed on March 21, 1961, were not successful; the Soviets maintained their hard-line policy. However, in private conversations with his diplomats and visiting American envoys, as well as in his correspondence with Kennedy, Khrushchev tended to indicate that he was also interested in a nuclear test ban treaty. The point of contention had to deal with on-site inspections.

Believing that the time was right, Kennedy chose peace as the topic for his commencement address at the American University on June 10, 1963. In the acclaimed speech, he defined his notion of "genuine peace": "The kind that enables men and nations to grow and to hope and to build a better life for their children. . . . Not merely peace in our time, but peace for all time."[41] In an effort to communicate his message of detente to Khrushchev, the president addressed the graduates:

> Let us reexamine our attitude toward the Soviet Union. . . .
> As Americans, we can find communism profoundly repug-
> nant. . . . But we can still hail the Russian people for their
> many achievements— in science and space, in economic and
> industrial growth, in culture and acts of courage.

The attitude change the president called for involved his suggestion for a test ban treaty. He implored that such an agreement would "increase our security. It would decrease the prospects of war."[42]

According to historian Michael Beschloss, in actuality the speech was motivated by a political purpose. Kennedy's primary purpose was to gain support for the test ban treaty.[43]

On July 25, 1963, Averill Harriman, Lord Hailsham, and Andrei Gromyko, representatives from the United States, Great Britain, and the Soviet Union, respectively, initialed what they considered the "most important arms-control accord since the start of the Cold War."[44] "The editors of the *Bulletin of the Atomic Scientists* moved the hands of their Doomsday Clock back to twelve minutes before midnight."[45] Pleasing to President Kennedy was the now-publicized divorce between the Chinese and the Soviets.

On July 26, 1963, in a televised speech, President Kennedy informed the American people of the agreement, describing the event as "a shaft of light cut into the darkness."[46] Kennedy hailed the accord as "an important first step, a step towards peace, a step towards reason, a step away from war."[47]

Any act that may result in the thawing of the Cold War was regarded favorably by most Americans. Many must have agreed with former President Truman's exclamation when he was so informed: "I'm in complete agreement with what — what it provides. . . . My goodness life, maybe we can save total war with it."[48] However, the meticulous Senator Smith was not among the majority. As a matter of fact, her attitude toward the treaty was counter to that of her constituency. Her out-of-state mail was "overwhelmingly against the treaty," but "Maine writers were substantially for the treaty."[49] Consider-ing Margaret Smith's extraordinary devotion to the people back home, one can readily begin to understand why she felt that her decision to vote against the treaty was so difficult.

In the *Declaration of Conscience*, she addresses what she refers to as the dilemma that has "plagued" the Senate "ever since its establishment." She refers to the basis for decision making: Should the Senator vote according to the best interests of her state, of the nation, or should she vote according to her "own conviction and conscience"?[50] The senator reasoned that a legislator may vote according to her own personal convictions if she had more information on the issue than her constituents. That was her case. As a member of the Senate Prepared Investigating Subcommittee she was present at both open and closed hearings. Her decision to cast a negative vote was influenced by the classified "devastating" testimony of such opponents of the treaty as scientist Dr. Edward Teller, who worked on the atomic bomb, and Dr. John S. Foster, Jr., the "Number Three" person in the Pentagon.[51]

On the day of the vote, Margaret Chase Smith declared her decision to vote against ratification of the treaty with absolute clarity. She based her conclusion on the grounds that the issue was "dominated by speculation . . . and by emotions." She was convinced that the terms and the language of the treaty as well as the ensuing debate results lacked the kind of clear, hardheaded facts that such decision making should be based on. As she presented in her speech during the debate, the terms and language of the treaty were so ambiguous that they allowed for "varied interpretations." Also, during the debate, she was disappointed to see what she regarded as vital questions go unanswered by the administration because answers would be speculative or involved secret data. She reasoned that the whole notion of signing such a treaty with the Soviets was based on speculation.

Senator Smith asserted to her colleagues that she perceived voting for approval of the treaty as the need to make the choice between what was probable and what was real, between what was an image and what was the real issue. That is, she felt that the debate was between those who saw the treaty as the "first step to peace" and those who argued that it was "a threat to national security." To Margaret Chase Smith, the treaty question was solely one regarding national security. Peace was an ambiguous reference, not a concrete one. She firmly believed that the maintenance of national security was the principal charge of the leadership in America— the previous speeches in this chapter demonstrate her perspective in cogent, powerful arguments. Therefore, she concluded the "Nuclear Test Ban" speech by admitting that although she could not challenge the argument for either choice with "complete certainty in [her] mind . . . the jeopardy that the treaty [imposed] on our national security [was] a more compelling argument against the treaty than the political and psychological disadvantages that would stem from rejection of the treaty."[52]

Senator Smith justified her decision by methodically rebutting the quality of evidence presented by those who believed the treaty should be ratified. First, she asserted that the decision-making process was emotional rather than logical. Citing the smear tactics of the political extremists, she questioned the sanity of those on the extreme Right who charged that those who supported the treaty were "pro-Communists" and of those on the extreme Left who referred to those who opposed the treaty as "murderers" who were "deliberately poisoning the milk for children with lethal doses of Strontium Ninety." In an effort to emphasize the absurdity of such logic, to fortify her relationship with both factions, and to promote her ethos, Margaret Smith informed her colleagues that she was "a target of the extremists of the Right" and that they called her "'pro-Communist' and a 'fellow-traveler' because of my Declaration of Conscience."

She reminded her audience that such negative behavior could be detrimental to the nation. She warned the audience of the damage inflicted by McCarthy-inspired extremists in the 1950s:

> What it did to our scientists and the way that it shackled our
> free scientific effort was revealed in the later fifties when
> Russia's Sputnik revealed how tragically we were lagging
> behind Russia in science and technology.

Second, Senator Smith rebutted the reliability of the sources used to determine that voting for the treaty was the will of the people. She questioned the pronouncement that both the Gallup and Harris Polls reported that "an overwhelming majority of the American people want the treaty to be ratified." She charged that polls were poor indicators of public opinion and contended that the mail, that is, "individual mail in personal handwriting," was much more valid. The level of a person's concern and passion for a subject was more readily observed in a letter than in a survey. Smith also faulted the validity of the Maine mail she received in the summer. Some of the sentiments have been those of summer residents rather than Maine citizens. However, she lauded the mail that she received from outside Maine advocating a negative vote because it was more passionate. That mail was a more reliable indicator of the will of the people. However, Smith submitted that all the above indicators were "too contradictory for me to let the mail have any significant influence on my decision." She voted her conscience.

"In trying to arrive at a conscientious decision," the moderate Mrs. Smith considered the alternative: "[W]hat would happen if the Senate did reject the treaty." She admitted that "we would lose significant ground in the psychological war" from Khrushchev's "false propaganda." However, she pointed out that rejection of the treaty would not cause the United States to resume open air nuclear testing because "President Kennedy has taken the position that the United States would refrain from open air testing as long as Russia refrained from open air testing." Therefore, the truth was that passing or rejecting the treaty would have no impact on the subject of open air testing.

The senator restated what she proclaimed during the debate: the real reason why Khrushchev wanted the treaty:

> [I]t is to the military advantage of Russia to keep us from
> resuming open air tests in the belief that Russia is signifi-
> cantly ahead of us in the high yield weapons and will stay
> ahead as long as we do not make the open air tests that are

necessary if we are to close the high yield weapons gap that
so heavily favors Russia.

In other words, Smith argued that Khrushchev really did not need this treaty
to achieve his objectives. All he needed to do was to refrain from open air
testing. Therefore, she concluded, "it would be most unlikely that Khrushchev
would order resumption of open air testing if the Senate were to reject this
treaty."

Since her argument was based on a hypothetical situation, the senator
admitted that it might be considered "speculative." However, she affirmed the
superiority of her argument by claiming that "it is no more speculative than
the answers given to the question that I have raised in this debate — answers
that even those providing the answers have admitted were 'speculative.'"

Contending that "the national security disadvantages stemming from
ratification of the treaty have not been as fully presented out in the open to
the public" as were the "political and psychological disadvantages stemming
from the rejection of the treaty," and admitting to having "very grave
misgivings about the harmful effect of rejection of the treaty," Margaret Chase
Smith concluded that she would cast "a very troubled vote against the treaty"
because "the jeopardy that the treaty imposes on our national security is a
more compelling argument."

As expected, the Nuclear Test Ban Treaty was ratified by an
overwhelming vote — eighty to nineteen. In addition to moderate Margaret
Chase Smith from Maine, the others who voted against the treaty tended to
be from the conservative wings of both parties. Eleven were Democrats: ten
southerners, including Richard Russell, chairman of the Armed Services
Committee, and John Stennis, chairman of the Preparedness Investigating
Subcommittee, and Ohio conservative Frank Lausche. Seven Republicans also
voted with Senator Smith, all westerners, including Barry Goldwater of
Arizona. Senator Smith's colleagues on the Armed Services Committee voted
for the treaty; those on the Preparedness Investigating Subcommittee voted
four to three against it.

As Bill Lewis comments in *Declaration of Conscience*, Margaret
Chase Smith was subjected to a degree of public ridicule. Columnist Drew
Pearson, in particular, accused her of deciding her vote on political reasons
rather than according to her conscience. He claimed she voted with
Goldwater because she wanted to be his running mate in the presidential
election of 1964.[53] Lewis rebutted Pearson's criticism and defended the
Senator's integrity in a letter to Pearson. In particular, he cited the number
of times Margaret Smith voted against Senator Goldwater's proposals. He
accused the newspaperman of the "guilt by association and trial by accusation
tactics that Senator Smith denounced in her 'Declaration of Conscience'
speech on June 1, 1950."[54]

Her vote against the treaty was used against her by her opponent in the 1966 election, but she was once again returned to the Senate by her constituents. However, the questions she raised in the debate "were a powerful force leading to the establishment and appointment of a Subcommittee on Safeguards on the Test Ban Treaty,"[55] formed for the purpose of keeping a close watch on the Soviets. Senator Smith was appointed a member of this subcommittee.

It was reported that the results gave President Kennedy his most satisfying day in the White House.[56] He was determined to maintain the momentum of the test ban treaty for the 1964 campaign. However, the treaty did not fulfill its promise for leaders Kennedy and Khrushchev. It was weak from the beginning because it was a limited, rather than a comprehensive, test ban treaty. Three years later the nuclear arms race was fiercer than ever.[57]

Sadly, President John F. Kennedy did not live to carry out his plans. On November 22, 1963, on a trip to Dallas, Texas, he was assassinated. On the day after, Margaret Chase Smith placed a red rose on the Senate desk John Kennedy had formerly occupied.

4
"I Speak as a Woman"

When Margaret Chase Smith rose to face the all-male assembly for her first major speech, she immediately defined her persona: "I speak as a Republican. I speak as a woman. I speak as a United States Senator. I speak as an American." With the echoes of her adversaries' pervasive criticism that "the Senate is no place for a woman" fresh in her memory, the sole female member of the Senate proudly proclaimed her gender as equal to the other identities. In doing so, she asserted a woman's right to sit in the most powerful political arena in the world, and she demonstrated that there is no such thing as "the weaker sex." Her forceful message taught her colleagues and the nation not to put too much stock in image. Just because she appeared like the traditional lady — petite, demure, and stylish — did not mean that she was delicate. On the contrary, the "Declaration of Conscience I" speech revealed Margaret Chase Smith to be a powerful force. She demonstrated that despite the conventional conviction, women can succeed in politics if they accept the challenge.

From her first campaign for the congressional seat vacated by the death of her husband in 1940, Margaret Chase Smith was aware of the gender issue. Although women had been elected to the House of Representatives,[1] she could hear both men and women complain that Congress was no place for a woman. As her husband's administrative assistant, she was ready and able to handle the job, but first she had to deal with the idea of woman's place. Throughout her highly successful career, while she was the greatest vote-getter in Maine history, Margaret Smith had to contend with the gender issue. When her name was put into nomination for the presidency on the Republican ticket, again she heard the comment: "The Presidency is no place for a woman."

Margaret Chase Smith was not one to suffer constraints in the pursuit of her goals. After all, freedom of opportunity and freedom of expression were the basic tenets of the American democracy that she so revered. Instead of complaining or accepting defeat, she resolved to handle the gender issue in her own characteristic way: She accepted the challenge and charged on to overcome it. From her fun days in high school basketball, she demonstrated her love for challenges, for she found them stimulating. When the going got tough, she got tougher. Her attitude was more masculine than feminine, for she intended to expose the gender issue for the sham that it was. Smith refused to be labeled a feminist. She contended that such a label would present her as a single-issue candidate. In addition, she felt that the movement was divisive, separating men from women. Smith saw herself as a person. She thought it necessary for men and women to work together for the good of the American system of government. She sought to demonstrate that conviction throughout her political career. As an individual, she refused feminine privileges, but demanded respect. She eschewed the conventional path for her career in Congress. Instead, she preferred to make her mark in military affairs, ordinarily the bailiwick of men. Smith dared to go where her female predecessors did not, and she was successful. In the House of Representatives she sat on the powerful Naval Affairs Committee, where she fought for permanent status for women in the armed forces.[2] In the Senate she became the ranking Republican on the Armed Services Committee. Always fashionably attired with the emblems of traditional femininity, white gloves and high heels, she toured the wartime Pacific and postwar Europe, surveying the damage and meeting heads of state. When most women her age were anticipating grandmotherhood, Margaret Chase Smith sought more battles to fight.

As would be imagined, Margaret Chase Smith was a popular speaker to women's groups. She was the ultimate symbol of women's progress. She proved that a woman can function well in a man's world. Her career success demonstrated that the notion of a woman's proper place is fraudulent. Women wanted to hear of her experiences, and she welcomed the opportunity to voice her philosophy.

The four speeches selected for analysis are representative of the numerous discourses Margaret Chase Smith delivered to women's groups across the nation. They are particularly important to understanding Smith's success because they reveal her views on being female, which remained unchanged throughout her life.[3] Three address women's organizations: the National Federation of Business and Professional Women's Clubs (BPW), Cleveland, Ohio, July 8, 1946; the Woman's Christian Temperance Union (WCTU), Philadelphia, Pennsylvania, August 20, 1949; the Women's Bar Association of the District of Columbia, January 20, 1948. The fourth, "The Importance of Individual Thinking," Hood College, Frederick, Maryland, April 21, 1951, is representative of the many commencement speeches she presented to the graduates of women's colleges. Each details her conviction that women can be the resolution to the world's problems. With characteristic candor, she detailed what a woman is and what a woman could do for herself, for her country, and for the world. Senator Smith had a great admiration for women's organizations, for they proved to be the agents of women's progress. She also had a great deal of admiration for young women college graduates, as they had the greatest opportunity to make the positive changes Smith advocated.

Margaret Chase Smith personified her message. Her struggle was women's struggle; her success was women's success. Her ethos, therefore, was the most persuasive appeal. The basic structure of the content of her speeches consisted of character examination and character development. Like the Greek philosopher Heraclitus, Smith believed that character shaped destiny. That conviction was the underlying theme of the speeches.

The speeches in this chapter, like most of Smith's important discourses, addressed the negative impact of the aftermath of World War II. The positive mood that encouraged American victory at the beginning of the war began to decline dramatically as the war dragged on. Americans naively believed that the end of the war would bring a return to life as it was before the war. They expected that the wartime effort would then be focused on restoring peace. They found the irony of reality difficult to comprehend. How could it be that the United States entered the war to help its Allies defeat the malicious totalitarian regimes of Germany and Japan only to result in the rise of an even greater menace — Communist Russia? Their moral code as well as their purpose was questioned. They had sacrificed much for the lifestyle that was so summarily disrupted by the Japanese attack on Pearl Harbor. The United States entered the war to destroy evil. Americans supported that decision because they believed that it was the right thing to do. However, World War II led not to peace but to the Cold War. The almost wildfirelike spread of Communism through Eastern Europe, stemming from the division of Germany, caused the federal government to increase, rather than decrease, its military forces. Economic and military aid needed to be supplied to other countries ravaged by the war so they would not fall to Communist domination. A rogue political ideology had once more threatened democratic governments. The Allies were once again embroiled in a struggle for the survival of their system of government. The formerly positive American electorate became cynical, fearful, frustrated, and eventually demoralized.

All of the speeches in this chapter reflect the style of consciousness-raising rhetoric associated with the Cold War rhetorical vision.[4] Smith strove to move her listeners to action, to convince them that they were mediators of change and, as such, needed to realize that they had the power to influence the course of events. Her message was predicated on her unwavering belief that a direct correlation existed between women's progress and world peace.

"WOMEN AND LEADERSHIP"

The first speech to be analyzed is Margaret Chase Smith's address to the convention of the National Federation of Business and Professional Women's Clubs in Cleveland, Ohio, on July 8, 1946. The speech is important because it detailed the basic tenets of Smith's philosophy. She incorporates these principles, in various versions, in her other speeches.

As the representative from the Second District in Maine, reelected by wide margins for the fourth time, Margaret Smith appeared confident. She was comfortable with the audience, for she credited the BPW for preparing her for her success.

The Business and Professional Women's Clubs is the world's oldest and largest organization of working women. Since its founding in 1919, the BPW has been an advocate for women's rights. Its specific objectives are to elevate the standards of women in business and professions and to extend opportunities to business and professional women through education. The BPW/USA is represented in every congressional district. In addition, BPW/USA networks abroad through the International Federation of BPW. The organization also maintains official representation at both the UN and the Hague.[5]

Margaret Chase became interested in the BPW as a young working woman. The organization offered her a sense of belonging and purpose and the opportunity to unite with other women of similar interests for the purposes of self-improvement and career advancement. A charter member of the Skowhegan chapter, Margaret was elected president in 1923 and again in 1924. At the age of twenty-eight she won election to the state presidency. Her experiences with the BPW sharpened her leadership skills, developed her character, and defined her public persona. As an officer in the association, Margaret traveled to big cities and met many sophisticated and influential women. The experience heightened her awareness of the importance of image and manners. She won many supporters with her ladylike charm and her scrupulous devotion to duty and the welfare of others. Above all, the ideals fostered by the BPW honed her view of the world and her view of herself in that world. According to a biographer: "For Margaret, the federation's expressions of idealism released longings to become involved with something larger than herself, the organization itself ultimately becoming the means by which she could achieve such an end."[6] Her metamorphosis was in process: The working class girl from the small town and rural state was evolving into the astute, sophisticated politician.

Representative Smith's speech was strong and forthright, thus demonstrating the take-charge attitude she wanted women to assume. Her first words, aimed at complimenting the audience, also served to introduce the crux of her message, the notion of women's place: "This convention is an example of democracy at work. It is more particularly a most impressive example of the acceptance by women of their responsibility as citizens — to think constructively and to make their thinking articulate."

The exigence Smith addressed was the general reluctance of women to assume their rightful position in public affairs. Acknowledging the power of the Business and Professional Women's Association— "Much, if not most, of the past leadership of women in this country has come through civic organizations and through organizations such as your own— "Smith revealed the purpose of her speech: to enlist the aid the Business and Professional Women's Association to continue and extend their "beneficial influence as widely as possible."

The call to action followed Smith's explanation of her rationale. With the premise that "[c]itizenship is without sex," she stated the claim on which she based her position: "Since the granting of suffrage to women, the only differential between men and women as citizens has been the availability and acceptance of leadership." She soundly blamed women themselves for failing to follow through after they won the hard-fought battle for suffrage. Smith abruptly dismissed the charge that leadership opportunities for women are limited by boldly asserting the prized New England ethic of self-reliance: "I have no sympathy with this view because it is only those who 'make the breaks' that 'get the breaks.'" She concluded sternly: "If we are to claim and win our rightful place in the sun on an equal basis with men, then we must not insist upon those privileges and prerogatives identified in the past as exclusively feminine."

Margaret Chase Smith's argument followed the logical organizational pattern. Professing that women can exert leadership, she offered the example of the outstanding performance of women during the war. "Now," she appealed, "the challenge to women is to match their amazing wartime record with the battles for peace and the orderly reconversion to normal living." She intensified the appeal with the claim that women "are far better equipped for the task of winning the peace because they possess certain abilities and understanding of matters basic to peace that men do not possess." Smith used that statement as a transition to the next step in her argument.

Smith states the claim that women as public citizens could exert leadership everywhere: in the home, organizations, industry and business, public offices, politics. She backed up her assertion with evidence in the form of examples and logic. For instance, she supported the authority of women in the home by recalling how Eleanor Roosevelt's influence as a wife led to the increase in the number of women appointments in the Roosevelt administration. In addition, she illustrated the power of the woman in the home with a humorous quotation from General Jimmy Doolittle: "A man who underestimates the power of women is either a bachelor or a fool." She then charged her audience to act upon Doolittle's maxim: "You can quote this to your husbands and observe that they have but one alternative." She

She believed that organizations like the BPW could be the model for effecting mutual understanding that would lead to world peace. Addressing her audience directly, she alerted them to the need to help women gain leadership positions in labor where so many women need representation.

Finally, she referred to the relationship between the home and the government, criticizing that "women have permitted the balance to swing too heavily to the Government's influence over the Home rather than having the Home exercise its proper influence over the Government." This imbalance could be remedied, she advised,

> [b]y taking a greater interest in our greatest investment, our biggest business — our Government — in seeking and accepting public office. In this way, women can bring the wholesome viewpoint and influence of the Home more directly into the formulation and administration of Government policy.

Smith concluded her point by reminding women that they are to blame for not taking "proper advantage of their voting privilege." She reinforced her message with simple logic. Since women make up half the population, then it follows that "women could easily become the most powerful single group in the electorate." She reiterated her purpose by declaring that "women should become more politically minded." She urged women to organize into political groups, to work for political parties, to stimulate women to vote and be active, and to seek public office. In other words, women "must give greater meaning to their role of public citizens."

Smith concluded the speech with a global view of the effect of women's influence on public affairs. First, she illustrated the positive effect American women have had on motivating women of other nations to participate in their governments with reference to the accomplishments of Madame Chiang Kai-shek and Japanese women as examples: "It is a shining example of how women can make the most effective contribution to the enforcement of a lasting peace by becoming leaders in their own nation and then graduating to the roles of leaders of the world." Finally, she emphasized the crux of the issue: Women should help to create the conditions necessary to achieve the ultimate goal of world peace:

> We can't become leaders of the world until we have become leaders within our own Nation. Our influence upon others must come from within ourselves individually. In as great a measure, our influence, as a nation upon the rest of the world in creating and maintaining permanent peace, must first flow from within this country.

When Margaret Chase Smith talked to women's groups about the power of women, she shared her experience, her philosophy, her dream. She knew firsthand about the might of women's organizations, such as the BPW. On another occasion, in honor of the fortieth anniversary of the Maine Federation of Business and Professional Women's Clubs, October 24, 1959, she commends the group's effectiveness:

> Not only did the BPW help get suffrage a year after its formation, but by the time of its thirtieth anniversary in 1949, it had put a woman — and more specifically one of its own members — in the United States Senate. No one should make the slightest mistake about this — for I say to you that I could never have been elected to the United States Senate without the tremendous drive that the Maine BPW did for me.[7]

Specifically, she cited the BPW's successful efforts at getting delegates to vote for her as vice president at the 1952 Republican National Convention.[8] Smith regarded their efforts not as a "tribute to me" but as "dramatic proof of the ability of the BPW to get results once the members of the BPW set their minds on a specific goal." She viewed their accomplishments as "an advance for women generally as I was only a symbol of that advance." Smith predicted that some day the BPW will be successful in getting a woman nominated and elected to vice president and president.

She concluded the speech by thanking the BPW for teaching her the necessary skills for success:

> The BPW taught me how to work with people and how to perform the details on getting things done for the people. So that if I have achieved any efficiency on getting things done for the people of Maine in my job in the Senate, it is greatly because of what the BPW instilled in me.[9]

"WOMEN'S PROGRESS"

On August 20, 1949, Margaret Chase Smith, fortified with the satisfaction of winning a seat over seemingly unsurmountable odds, in what was regarded as the quintessential all-male arena, addressed her audience of the venerable Woman's Christian Temperance Union at its Diamond Jubilee Convention. She greeted the assembly with an accolade expressing her admiration, pleasure, and inclusion: "I know of no higher honor than to have the approval of the Woman's Christian Temperance Union. . . . It is the highest tribute to one's character." With that opening remark, the Senator established common ground between herself and her listeners.

The Woman's Christian Temperance Union has been a moral force in the social development of the United States from the 1870s. Begun by a group of women in Hillsboro, Ohio, who conducted a praying crusade against the saloon in town, the organization was formed officially in 1874 at a convention consisting of delegates from eighteen states. The WCTU quickly became a force in public affairs. Based on the high ideals of good morals and clean living, the WCTU advanced the causes of moderation, prison reform, moral education, woman suffrage, armament reduction, international arbitration, and world peace. In addition, it has combatted child labor, juvenile delinquency, prostitution, and legalized vice. Through Emma Willard's efforts, the World Woman's Christian Temperance Union was founded in 1883.[10]

The exigency that the junior senator from Maine chose to respond to was a concern of many, for she addressed the moral decline of America. The cause stemmed from the sense of national insecurity that pervaded the postwar society. Americans were disillusioned with the results of World War II. Indications of the moral decay appeared everywhere: divorces increased, crime increased, and juvenile delinquency was on the rise. Senator Smith called these moral problems a "wise-guy attitude of immoral cynicism."

Obviously, the intent of the speech was one of great interest to this audience. Smith mounted her strategy to get the members of the WCTU to identify with the situation by clearly stating her belief that the cause of the apathetic mood in the country was indeed the insecurity brought about by Russian Communist aggression. In the clarification step of her introduction she described the conditions that contributed toward military, economic, and moral insecurity. Communist Russia was a godless society that waged "a relentless war against religion and against the principles and leaders of the church." Smith then stated the purpose of her speech, which was to enlist the members of the WCTU to join the fight to save America from the moral erosion that it was experiencing. She explains her choice of the group because they "have two assets that no other organization possesses — (1) you are the champions of temperance and (2) you are women." Thus, her thesis was that the solution to the problem was women's progress because "the progress of women is the progress of temperance and the progress of peace."

Smith constructed her argument with precision. Her first main point supported her claim that women's progress was the solution, listing two major facts that demonstrated that women had proved strong "in the face of formidable opposition." First, she cited the effectiveness of the force of women in the United Nations: The preamble to the Charter included and affirmed "the equal rights of men and women." Second, she listed facts showing the advances made by American women in the job market: "80 years ago women held only 15 per cent of all jobs in America. Today they hold twice that amount — 30 per cent." She summarized the point by stating that "[w]omen have come a long way in the past century."

To further persuade her audience that women had made formidable progress, Smith gave several examples that compared the status of women in 1848 with their status in 1948. In 1848, women could not vote, take part in lawmaking or jury duty, hold public office, or be responsible for their actions. "Today they constitute more than 50 percent of America's total vote," "do jury duty in 35 of the 48 states," and "are eligible to all major elective and appointive positions." Smith summarized this point by repeating that women have "come a long way," but, she warns, "we still have quite a way to go." With this pivotal statement, Smith clarified her position on the notion of women's progress, which she believed would continue to occur if women "remain ever alert and vigilant to our civic responsibility from the standpoint of equality — not perpetuated feminine privileges." She followed the statement with an explanation of her reasons for having "studiously avoided being a feminist." She held that getting equality while keeping feminine privileges was in "direct conflict with the rights sought."

Now that Smith had established that women's progress could make a positive difference in society, she intensified her argument in the next main point. Claiming that since wars seem man-made, "[m]aybe peace should be partially women-made." She fortified her assertion with an overgeneralization:

> The historical belligerency of most nations will be found to be in inverse ratio to the degree of freedom and recognition that the particular nation grants to women. In other words, wherever you find the woman's voice granted even an approach to parity with that of the man's, you will find a more peaceful nation.

Smith warranted the claim that the achievement of world peace can be realized through the advancement of women by reciting her consistent message about women's ability to govern based on the "overlooked . . . fact that women actually do more governing of our daily lives and of shaping our future people [in comparison to men]." She justifies the fact by reasoning that "women are actually the governors of the home." They perform the same responsibilities found in government — legislating, executing, and enforcing rules. She reinforces the connection between homemakers and peacemakers by defining the home as "the most fundamental form of government." With this claim, Smith invited her favorable audience to follow her commonsense reasoning to the conclusion, that since community governments are "no more than a federation of individual home governments," then so follow state governments and the federal government. She concluded simply: "That is the unbroken chain right from your home and my home to the White House."

Smith's solution to the world's problems seemed so simplistic. However, in the midst of this idealistic exercise, the senator admitted that one of the real causes for the dearth of women leaders in the United States, as well as in the world, could be blamed on women themselves, on their "lack of will for public roles." She reminded her listeners: "They cannot become leaders of the world until they have become leaders within their own nation and community." Reflecting on her own values, as was her custom, she emphasized the ethic of individualism and the need for self-reliance: "Our influence upon others must come from within ourselves individually as men and women." Smith summarized the argument on an optimistic note by using an enthymeme to lead her audience to her conclusion: "America, the peace leader of the world, also leads the other nations of the world on opportunity granted to women. There is a definite correlation."

After noting that the audience was firmly in agreement with her argument, Margaret Chase Smith moved the motivated sequence structure to a climactic conclusion. Like a military leader preparing her troops for a major battle, Senator Smith intensified her appeal to the audience by raising her proposed solution to a higher level, to the level of the abstract: "The greatest need of America today — and of the World today — is the total mobilization of our moral forces." She explained wisely:

> We have been stressing physical force to the exclusion of moral force in our zeal for peace. Yet history shows that in the long run physical force never satisfactorily settled differences — and certainly that it never prevented wars and brought peace, but to the contrary bred wars.

Smith used the rhetorical question "What is moral force?" to delineate her final message. At first, she offered a simple definition:

> [n]othing more than the application of reason, common sense, and the Golden Rule. It is the will to see the other fellow's viewpoint. It is the will to give specific and concrete examples of unselfish purpose, good will and sincerity.

Then, with greater eloquence, she enforced the magnitude of the meaning of the term with an extensive definition. For the purpose of creating a cadence with which to rally her forces and also to communicate the impact of the meaning of the term, Smith encoded key elements of her definition with parallel introductory clauses: "It is the will to see the other fellow's viewpoint. . . . It is the cure for frustration and fear. . . . It is placing the guidance of God above nationalism. It is the conscience of men and women." Then, speaking directly to the audience, she specifically defined their involvement: "And you, the members of the WCTU, are our most formal soldiers in our army of moral force."

Smith reminded her audience that "[the] moral and psychological basis for world peace does not yet exist even here at home." What was necessary, she recommended, was "a profound change in human attitudes." Specifically, she cited "hatred, prejudice and contempt for other human beings." She warned: "If the preparation of the necessary moral and psychological basis for world peace seems impossible, then world peace itself is impossible."

Returning to parallelism to continue building the climax and encouraging participation, the senator emphasized that without a firm basis of brotherhood and tolerance, "[i]t is plain that there will be no lasting peace in this world." She intensified her point by repeating: "It is plain that the leaders and the people of all nations must turn their minds to discovering what common interests may exist among them." She concluded the point by mirroring the style of the previous statements and further emphasizing the message with antithesis.

> And it is equally plain that the mental climate for making
> that discovery is not the climate of prejudice and hatred, but
> the willingness of all the people to look and see; the desire
> to know, and to understand; the tolerant acceptance, on
> every side, of live and let live.

For her final appeal, Margaret Chase Smith reiterated the prerequisites for world peace by structuring her sentences with the ultimate intensity. She issued a clarion call for action. Beginning with "What we need, and what the world needs, is the simple old-fashioned neighborly goodwill to get along," she introduced each of the following thoughts with the rallying cry: "[W]e need . . . neighborly goodwill. . . . We need . . . to lay aside our comfortable old prejudices. We need the tolerance. . . . We need to stop living by fear." And with crescendo-like effect, the senator repeated the last statement.

She phrased the final statement of her well-constructed speech in metaphorical terms. The tone was inspirational and called for moral courage:

> We need to take our eyes off the vague shapes and shifting
> shadows in the fateful Valley of Decision, so that we can
> begin to turn the light of trained intelligence upon the real
> objects casting those fearful shadows.

She identified with her audience on moral grounds, implying that both she and they shared the same belief system and the same vision of the world. She asserted that both she and they could function as models to encourage women to summon the will to make a better world through public work. The senator appealed to women in general, honoring their accomplishments as homemakers and promoting their roles as peacemakers. She identified with all women by projecting her persona as that of the representative American woman.

Margaret Chase Smith also spoke as an American moralist. Her address was replete with mention of democratic virtues, such as common sense, equality, freedom, brotherhood, and tolerance, as well as the invocation of God and the Golden Rule. She affirmed that Americans are "peace-minded," the moral leaders of the world.

"NO PLACE FOR A WOMAN"

On January 20, 1948, Congresswoman Margaret Chase Smith, locked in the most momentous battle of her career, opened her address to the Women's Bar Association of the District of Columbia by announcing that the topic of her talk was not a political issue but a more fundamental problem, common to both speaker and audience. She would address the issue of gender: "The most frequent objection that has been raised to my candidacy is that 'the Senate in no place for a woman.'"

The Women's Bar Association was an adjunct of the once all-male American Bar Association, an organization of lawyers admitted to any state bar. The ABA was established in 1878 for the purpose of promoting the standards and practice of the legal profession as well as the uniformity of U.S. laws.

Smith began the speech by acknowledging the contribution the Women's Bar Association had made to the advancement of women. She implied a kinship with her listeners by commending them on their success "in a profession too long regarded as the exclusive bailiwick of men." She commended their efforts: "[T]hose of us in politics are indebted to you because women lawyers have done more to lead the way for greater participation by women in politics than any other group." After establishing common ground with the audience, Smith addressed the common problem that women faced historically, and one that she was presently plagued with in her campaign for the U.S. Senate — the age-old notion of "women's proper place": "The most frequent objection that has been raised to my candidacy is that 'the Senate is no place for a woman.'" Noting that she had often been asked "Where is the proper place of a woman?" Smith stated her purpose simply: "[W]oman's proper place is everywhere . . . [wherever] the particular woman is happiest and best fitted." Acknowledging that her response may seem over-simplified, she explained that "it is a conclusion of mine that has been repeatedly reassured by my experiences in meeting people all over the world."

Smith established her argument on two assumptions that her listeners would likely consider valid. Both were based on the conviction that the American way of life is superior. Her first assumption was that the principle of government by the people leads one to reason that the responsibility for war and the possibility of peace come from the people themselves, not from their leaders. Her second was the contention that the United States is "the most peace-loving nation in the world." On these hypotheses she rested her claim that since "America, the peace leader of the world, has granted the greatest opportunity to the woman — and America's peace leadership stems directly from the influence and participation of American women in shaping the decisions of this country."

Smith supported her conclusion with the claim: "The traditional belligerency of most nations is in inverse ratio to the degree of freedom and recognition that the particular nations grant to women. In other words, wherever you find the woman's voice granted even an approach to parity with that of the man's you will find a more peaceful nation."

She related well to the audience of women lawyers by structuring her rhetoric in forensic form. Smith aimed to correct the injustice perpetrated on women by designating women a proper place and defining that specifically as the home. She reminded her audience of the commonplace — that men are not equally restricted: "You never hear the comment that 'Men are all right in their place.'" She refuted the contention of women's proper place by citing further inconsistencies: If women's roles are to be restricted to those occupations assigned to the home, why are men not barred from the roles performed by women in the home? She cited examples of male chefs, tailors, and interior decorators.

Smith concluded this first phase of her argument by stating that the fact that women, like men, are citizens, and that should be their "one proper role . . . that of alert and responsible citizens in the fullest sense of the word." She elaborated: "Citizenship is without sex. It makes no distinction between the rights and responsibilities of men and women — in America." She then tersely concluded: "Since the granting of suffrage to women, the only differential between men and women as citizens has been the availability and acceptance of leadership."

With the fact established that leadership is available to women, Smith discoursed on the progress women had made and were making by suggesting possibilities, noting the influence of attitude, and exploring the problem of job discrimination in certain fields. But, first, in an effort to keep her listeners on her lines of communication and to assert her firm belief in self-reliance, she preempted those who would complain that such opportunities have been "unfairly limited": "I have no sympathy with this view because it is only those who 'make the breaks' that 'get the breaks.'" Of course, that is how Margaret Chase Smith understood her success — hard work, perseverance, and courage, all attributes of character. She knew that her most persuasive appeal was her public persona, for she was perceived as the prototype of the successful woman. Her rhetorical stance was that if I can do it, so can you.

In response to the possible question as to where women could serve, Smith's response was a simple "everywhere." As always, she asserted her traditional side by underscoring the importance of the home: "Perhaps the most lasting and basic influence of women is in the home — for behind all men, great or small, are women. . . . The fight for decent conditions in communities . . . must be led by the women of the Home — the wives and the mothers." Another area in which women had demonstrated leadership was in civic organizations, particularly those aimed at the advancement of women. She cited the progress of women in industry and business but noted the dearth of women leaders in labor: "Labor unions need the balanced judgment of more women labor leaders."

The major problem area for women in a leadership position, Smith believed, was in "those fields dominated by men to the almost complete exclusion of women — particularly the field of Government and politics." In probing the problem, she mentioned the fact that "women's suffrage is comparatively most recent" but countered that "[w]omen have come a long way in a very short time to increasing equality with men in the business and professional worlds." In probing further, she concluded that the "answer lies greatly with the women themselves." In comparison to the success achieved by women in business and the professions, women considering politics, according to Smith, did not seem to have the requisite determination. She explained that a "controlling factor has been the attitude of the men toward women in their respective fields." Male executives and female secretaries work hand in hand in business, rewarding women with expanding executive responsibilities. In politics, in contrast, the "old prejudice of men against women is given full warning for resistance." As soon as a woman announced her candidacy, "the male cry is that 'public office' is no place a woman." The excuse was weak and dismissive: "[S]he can't hold her own with the men." In refutation Smith offered the excellent performances of her female colleagues in Congress, and she also noted "plenty of examples of women public officials who have successfully maintained their homes and reared their children. A man legislator's division of his professional time as a lawyer oddly enough is never challenged." She summarized this point by blaming both men and women for women's poor success in politics.

Smith concluded her talk by noting the ironic situation regarding the lack of women in politics, citing the fact that women have majority voting power in the country. The solution is that "women need to realize that they hold the power." Since women are keepers of the home and the home is "the most fundamental form of government," women are natural political leaders. She added, "[T]here has been too little of the HOME in the government and too much GOVERNMENT in the home. The most obvious and natural way to reverse this trend is to put more of the HOME GOVERNORS in the government, — and that means WOMEN." She challenged women to act:

> That is why there is a definite and inescapable future in
> politics for women. It is only a question of time — only a
> matter of how long the men oppose women holding public

office and, more important, how long the women themselves are guilty of such political inertia as not to overcome the opposition of the men.

Smith ended with an eloquent and memorable charge to her audience:

The dearth of women in public service can be attributed to women themselves for lack of interest and aggressiveness — and the will to public careers — in this and other countries. Women cannot become leaders of the world until they have become leaders within their own Nation. Our influence upon others must come from within ourselves individually. In as great a measure, our influence, as a Nation upon the rest of the world in creating and maintaining permanent peace, must first flow from within this country.

"THE IMPORTANCE OF INDIVIDUAL THINKING"

"The Importance of Individual Thinking," delivered as a convocation address at Hood College, in Frederick, Maryland, on April 21, 1951, served as a model for the many commencement addresses Senator Margaret Chase Smith gave to graduates of women's colleges.[11] Following traditional epideictic form, the senator began her discourse by acknowledging the audience and the significance of the occasion:

You young women are on the threshold of the finest years of your life. Make the best of those years — not only for yourselves, but for your families, your friends and your country as well. Make better use of those years than has the generation preceding you.

As usual, hers was a moral message. Senator Smith assumed the stance of teacher-preacher wherein the older generation shared its wisdom with the younger generation. She urged the young women to hoist the standard of American right and to rid the world of the threat of moral decay. Regarding them as the hope of the future, she assigned them a moral mission:

Give the young women who follow you a heritage of peace instead of the world of suspicion, aggression, treason, character assassination and moral delinquency that has been thrust upon you by the older generation that has preceded you.

Senator Smith obviously responded to the pervasive exigency that dominated issues throughout her political career, the demoralizing effect of national insecurity. Personally, she referred to the negative repercussions that resulted from her famous "Declaration of Conscience" speech. Although three years had passed, Margaret Chase Smith still fended the fierceness of McCarthy's vengeance. Without mentioning the situation specifically, she championed her deed by motivating her enthusiastic listeners to model her experience — to speak out when the fundamental values of our democracy were threatened: "The right way is not always the popular and easy way. Standing for right when it is unpopular is a true test of moral character." The opportunity to review the McCarthy situation must have had therapeutic value for Smith. By rekindling the memory of her famous speech in the minds of her listeners, she defended her motives and attacked her adversaries. The references also had important rhetorical value, for they heightened her ethos and strengthened her thesis.

The distinguished stateswoman, standing strong in front of her bright, young listeners, opened her presentation in the form of an invocation. She was the paradigm for her message. Using the imperative sentence structure, she entreated the women to assume their civic responsibility as leaders of the next generation. In climactic order, she petitioned them to: "Show them the way to think. . . . Lead them away from bitter cynicism and hatred of those with whom they differ in opinion." And finally:

> Help them to realize that this wonderful country of ours is greater than any individual woman or man — and that its fate, destiny and security should not be made a political football to be kicked around by clashing personalities greedy and envious of political power.

The appeal ended with a powerful call to leadership. She appealed to their ethos, for they had the power and the talent to protect the American way of life. Senator Smith implied that the destiny of the nation was in their hands:

> Your generation can do this. It is your destiny — the greatest challenge. . . . [Y]ou can fulfill your destiny — regardless of what individual role you play in the years to come, whether in the home, in the church, in business or in public office.

This statement was the thesis of the message. It also served as a transition to the lecture portion of the oration. Senator Smith began her argument by stating the basic commandment for moral courage: The need to "Stop, Look, Listen, and THINK" before one speaks but never to be afraid to

speak one's mind: "As long as you speak your minds, dictators and demagogues will never take control of this country."

The purpose of her lesson was "to review the fundamentals that are
so basic and obvious that too often too many of us take them for granted."
In order to teach our democratic values well and to emphasize their
significance, Smith used a traditional teaching technique that actively involves
the audience in the communication process. Her strategy was to intensify the
transaction of meaning with what Kenneth Burke called *consubstantiation*.[12]
She explained: "Instead of making a speech to you today . . . I would rather
just 'think out loud' with you. . . . I would rather say fewer words more slowly
so that they can sink in mentally than to try to crowd in the maximum number
of words in any lengthy speech."

Smith's major point equated thinking with freedom: "The importance
of individual thinking to the preservation of our Democracy and our freedom
cannot be overemphasized." She clarified the meaning of the principle by
instructing that "[t]o 'think' is to . . . put our common sense into action." She
cited two dramatic examples, fresh in the minds of the listeners, to illustrate
the point: When the German and Russian people "defaulted their thinking"
to their dictatorial leaders, they consequently lost their freedom. To drive
home the fact that the "articulate majority . . . rules a Democracy," the senator
warned that Americans were close to losing their freedom:

> Too few people in this country realize that too many people
> in this country are defaulting their thinking to demagogues
> and that we are closer to surrendering our freedom than
> most of us are willing to recognize and admit. When we
> accept the statements and proposals of demagogues because
> we are too lazy to think and test their statements and
> proposals, we can blame no one but ourselves for subsequent
> events.

Her intent was to warn the audience about McCarthyism, a controversial yet
powerful ideology that continued to consume much of public opinion in 1953.
The enthymemic reasoning led the listeners to infer that Nazi Germany and
Communist Russia could happen in America through the vehicle of McCarthyism.

Moving from the abstract to the concrete, Smith adapted her lesson
on democracy to the immediate audience of young, educated women about to
enter the world on their own: "In the more narrow sense of the concept —
the concept that makes a distinction on the basis of sex— the most important
role of the woman in defense of Democracy is her traditional role as
homemaker." Her position on women is clear: "Women, just like men, have
the role of voting, of thinking, of articulation — of taking a stand and
expressing their beliefs."

With the introduction of women's role in a democracy, Smith gently alluded to the feminist movement. She obviously did not wish to alienate her young, well-informed audience: "There is a tendency to set women off separate from men when we think about these aspects. . . . I don't like it simply because women are citizens just like men and have the same responsibilities of citizenship as men do." Smith supported her claim with reasons:

> The articulate action of a citizen, whether man or woman,
> must be constructive — must seek to improve — to build
> instead of tear down and destroy — must be preceded by
> serious and responsible thinking. Criticism unaccompanied
> by positive proposals of substitutes for that criticized
> indicates lack of informed thinking on the part of the critic.

Senator Smith identified with women by heralding their traditional role of homemaker "as being far more important than the role in public office." She explained the direct relationship between the home and our democracy. If the structure of the home is "firm and sound," so will be our democracy. Therefore, she reasoned that woman as "keeper of the home . . . of the home is the key individual of our Democracy on the 'grass roots' level." Therefore, it followed logically that "woman is the primary and basic governor of our Democracy for our governing starts right in the home." The enthymeme invited the young women to question the need for a feminist movement that demands equality while retaining special privileges. The inference is that such an ideology is divisive and hence destructive to our democracy.

She moved the audience toward the conclusion of the speech with encouragement:

> [T]here is no finer role that you can play in the defense of
> Democracy and our American way of life than that of wife,
> mother and homemaker. Run your homes and raise your
> children in the very best traditions and fundamentals of our
> American way of life.

The senator underscored their civic responsibility, warning that "your indifference to your Government and to your full citizenship will be reflected in your children who grow up imitating you." Her final words of advice related their success in preserving the American way of life with the notion of self-reliance: "You don't have to ask anybody but yourself how to do it." Senator Smith's closing thoughts connected individual responsibility with freedom: "Our freedoms today are not so much in danger because people are consciously trying to take them away from us as they are in danger because we forget to use them." With characteristic clarity, she pronounced the ultimate truth of the lecture: "Freedom may be an intangible, but like most everything else it can die because of lack of use. Freedom unexercised may become freedom forfeited. The preservation of freedom is in the hands of the people themselves now— not the Government."

Margaret Chase Smith repeated her democratic lessons and calls to civic responsibility in all the commencement speeches she delivered. Although she never went to college, the senator was well equipped to lecture on the American belief system. Her young audiences respected her authority, and she endeavored to praise their youth and intelligence by appealing to their importance, for the future of America was in their hands. Smith, the national figure, and the young adult women shared their common experiences on the playing field of American values and moral courage.

The gender issue haunted Margaret Chase Smith's career. Political rivals, especially when she decided to run for the Senate in 1948, worked maliciously to convince the voters of Maine that "the Senate was no place for a woman." They distributed anonymous smear sheets and spread vicious gossip attacking her political position as well as her morals. She mounted a feisty counterattack, repudiated the charges, and defeated her opponents at the polls. As she professed in her speeches to women's groups, she was proof that a woman's place was wherever she wished. However, whether the cause was the gender issue or the reluctance of women to undertake their civic responsibility, few women followed in her footsteps. Margaret Chase Smith remained the lone woman in the U.S. Senate for most of her four terms. (Maurine Neuberger, a Democrat from Oregon, joined her for one term in 1960.)

Margaret Chase Smith continued to preach her doctrine regarding a woman's place throughout her long and active life. She was a pioneer for women's progress. Through her achievements, speeches, and her remarkable persona, she taught that gender refers to one facet of a person; it is the strength of the human spirit that counts.

5
"I Speak as a Republican"

Margaret Chase Smith's decision to be a Republican was a natural one; during her early years, most Mainers were. The Republican Party dominated Maine politics from 1910 until 1954, when Democrat Edward Muskie, on his first venture into politics, unseated the Republican governor,[1] thus ushering in the two-party system.

However, party affiliation was not as strong an influence over her decision making as it was with other politicians. She preferred to listen to the dictates of her conscience and her constituents more than to the Republican Party. She was proud of her reputation as an independent voter. Speaking one's own mind was a characteristic much admired at the grassroots level of politics in Maine. That was Smith's preferred milieu; she related best to rural folks, those with whom she had common life experiences. In the rank and file, or the "little people," as she affectionately called them, she saw the idealized democrat — the common man. She was one of them, and fortunately for her, they also represented the majority of Maine voters. Thus, her posture as an independent politician won her the acclaim of the citizens of her state, but at the same time, it incurred the disdain of the Republican Party leadership.

During her eight years in the House as the representative from Maine's Second Congressional District, Margaret Smith had no compunction about voting with the opposition when her conscience dictated. For example, as a freshman congresswoman witnessing the ravages of war in Europe, she boldly supported the defense legislation requested by the Democratic administration in spite of the opposition of the isolationists in the Republican Party. In general, she supported the Democrat's position on appropriations for public spending and on labor legislation, except for the Taft-Hartley bill. While her fellow Republicans voted as a bloc, she willfully broke rank, despite the fact that she was incurring the ire of the Republican organization. She antagonized the conservative wing especially by voting to control rather than increase the power of the House Un-American Activities Committee. Such action caused many Republicans to question her party loyalty; some outrightly labeled her a traitor to the party. Ideologically, Smith classified herself as a moderate Republican, but the conservative Republican power brokers saw her as a "New Dealer," the label used for their enemy — the despised liberal Democratic majority.

Although Margaret Chase Smith naturally identified herself as a Republican, she could not so easily become a Republican politician. As described in Chapter 4, she was a woman, and according to the conventional wisdom of the time, politics was a man's game. However, with her rock-solid will and the support of influential women's groups, she succeeded in destroying the myth of a woman's proper place by becoming the first woman elected to both houses of Congress and the first woman to be nominated for the presidency by a major political party.

To some degree, her fate must have been written in the stars. That is, the story of Margaret Chase's rise from the young working-class woman of rural Skowhegan, Maine, to the political celebrity featured on the front pages of international newspapers and magazines is illustrative of the myth of the American dream. Timing and connections helped along the way. The most prominent example of the influence of these elements was Margaret's meeting and later marrying Skowhegan's popular politician Clyde Smith. Twenty years older than she, the divorced Smith's fascination for the vivacious Margaret caused him to include her as his partner in the business of politics. He saw to it that she became active in the local Republican Party organization. She campaigned with him throughout his constituency, sharing the experience and studying the process. When Clyde won the Second District congressional seat in Congress, Margaret naturally accompanied him. However, she refused to stay home and play the traditional role of a congressman's wife. Instead, she convinced him to appoint her as his secretary. As such, Margaret Chase Smith had the opportunity to study the workings of Congress firsthand, and she was intrigued.

As fate would have it, Clyde suffered a massive heart attack, causing him to relinquish his congressional duties. In a press release issued on April 7, 1940, he paved the way for Margaret: "All that I can ask of my friends and supporters is that in the coming primary and general election, if unable to enter the campaign, they support the candidacy of my wife and partner in public life."[2] The next day Clyde Smith died, and Margaret Chase Smith was officially born as a politician.

Almost immediately, she was thrown into preparing to win the special election that was to be held in May. After the voters of the Second Congressional District agreed that Clyde's widow should fulfill her popular husband's term, the ambitious Mrs. Smith planned for the primary in June and the general election in September. She launched her amazing political career after a vigorous campaign. Margaret Chase Smith served four terms in the House of Representative, from 1940 to 1948. She was now ready for the Senate.

This chapter will discuss the three most significant political speeches in Margaret Chase Smith's career. "Answer to a Smear" and "Election Eve Radio Address" were delivered in her successful battle to achieve her right to run for the U.S. Senate in 1948. "Presidential Candidacy Announcement" was delivered to demonstrate her right to be nominated for the presidency at the 1964 Republican National Convention. In these speeches, Margaret Chase Smith countered the conventional belief that women do not belong in the most powerful political enclaves of the nation. She championed the basic American ethic that right makes might. She proved the moral supremacy of the individual over the political machine. These speeches not only serve as models of the persuasive power of the rhetor's ethos; they also display her mastery of rhetorical skill. Finally, the speeches clearly exhibit the relationship between the rhetorical act and its effectiveness.

"ANSWER TO A SMEAR"

As she wrote in the *Declaration of Conscience,* the "most crucial political speech" she had ever given was "Answer to a Smear," delivered to the Somerset County Republican Women's Club in her hometown of Skowhegan, Maine, on May 21, 1948.[3] Smith termed the decision to move from the House of Representatives to the Senate the "turning point of my career."[4] She was convinced that she was ready to do the job, but she faced the gender issue. No women representatives were in the Senate. The only woman who had managed to get elected to the Senate for a full term was Mrs. Hattie Caraway of Arkansas, who, after fulfilling her deceased husband's term, ran for election on her own with the help of the renown vote-getter Senator Huey Long of Louisiana.[5] Margaret Chase Smith's ambition was to be the first woman duly elected to both houses of Congress.

The idea seemed preposterous to many men and, curiously, to a large number of women as well. Even good friends like correspondent May Craig dismissed her plan when Margaret revealed it to her in 1946: "Margaret, you have reached your peak — you can go no further — so you must adjust yourself to going downhill from now on."[6] "The Senate was no place for a lady" was a common comment, echoed among so-called colleagues and friends in the halls of the Maine State House and the Congress of the United States. The proposition was debated in various newspaper editorials.

However, Margaret Chase Smith was not just another insignificant woman. Her mind was made up, and she would not change it. The greater the challenge, the more fired up she became, for she loved a good fight, and her aim was to prove that she was just as powerful as any man.

The opportunity to run for the Senate from the state of Maine was presented by the resignation of Senate Majority Leader Wallace White. Smith's opponents in the Republican primary were the governor of Maine, Horace Hildreth; the former governor, Sumner Sewall, and the Reverend Albion Beverage. Smith knew that challenge would be a tough one: "Hildreth and Sewall were undefeated top vote-getters."[7] Together, both had the support of the Republican organization. Beverage's claim for support was remote.

The smear campaign became evident when Margaret Chase Smith received an anonymous printed sheet alleging an analysis of her voting record with the obvious intent to paint her as a traitor to her party. The paper attested that of the 242 measures cast by Smith during her tenure in the House of Representatives, 29.3 percent were against her own party, and 44.2 per cent were with Vito Marcantonio, the American Labor Party representative from New York who was reputed to be a radical liberal and Communist sympathizer.[8] The paper accused Smith of being "pro-Communist, a traitor to the Republican party, a tool of the CIO, and a political companion of Representative Vito Marcantonio."[9] The forces responsible for the sheet were never identified, but newspaper reports claimed that Governor Hildreth made critical comments about her being a questionable Republican, called her a New Dealer, and linked her to Marcantonio.[10]

Clearly, Margaret Chase Smith was very disturbed by these assaults on her professional reputation and wished to respond immediately. However, her friend and newly appointed campaign manager, Bill Lewis, conceived a plan that would work to her greater advantage. He advised her to wait:

> Hold back and let them misinterpret your silence as confirmation that you can't, and dare not, try to answer the charges. Then let them get bolder, way out on the limb. Then saw it off at a time of your choosing and place and manner.[11]

As expected, Maine became saturated with the smear sheets, but Mainers heard no word of explanation from Representative Smith. Her silence seemed to validate the accusations, and some concluded that she did not have the courage to reply. Smith commented on such assumptions in her book: "It was such feelings that make them sure that first, I would never announce for the Senate, or second, that I would withdraw from the race before the filing deadline. They should have known better."[12]

Calculating that the full impact of the smear sheets would be reached by May 21, Margaret Chase Smith chose that day, one month before the primary election, to respond. "Answer to a Smear" was to be "the first wholly political speech of her campaign."[13] The audience she chose was the trusted Somerset County Women's Republican Club, "the only women's group in the state that worked for me in addition to the Maine Federation of Business and Professional Women."[14]

Her speech consisted of a methodical refutation of all charges. Margaret feared that its length might cause her to lose her audience, but Lewis argued in support of it: "[I]t would discredit the smears one hundred percent and leave no possible reply."[15] He reasoned that the blow-by-blow style of the speech would show what they needed for her to be considered as a bonafide contender— that, according to Smith, she was "a fighter who could hold my own with the men— and indicate my ability to do the same thing in the Senate — and to fight cleanly and fairly."[16] Sensing the spoils of battle, she concluded: "After all, it contains exactly what the listeners will enjoy. A home county audience will love to hear their daughter defend herself and rip into the smearers."[17]

Aware of the proven philosophy that the best defense is a good offense, Smith came out of her corner with fists fixed. The seemingly bantam-weight amateur demonstrated that she had the rhetorical clout of a champion. She methodically rolled up her sleeves and took on her phantom defamer. Emphasizing the seriousness of her mission, Representative Smith forwent the platitudes that usually initiate a campaign speech. Instead, she got right to the business of proving that she was the better candidate, with a potent double punch of asserting her credibility while debunking his:

> I was in business before I entered Congress. And as a business woman, I respected the principle that real success cannot be gained by running down your competition. I have respected this principle in politics — and particularly in this campaign — and I have not made one word of criticism of my opponents. I had hoped my opponents would respect this principle.

She further discredited her detractor by impugning the corrupt nature of his character by claiming that his resorting to the distribution of "anonymous printed lie sheets" only served to reveal his desperation. Appealing to common ground with her audience, Smith implied the absurdity of the act: "As anyone knows, an anonymous letter is not worth the paper that it is written on. The writer of such a letter, who does not have the courage to identify himself to those charges which he cannot prove, is nothing less than contemptible."

After stating the exigency that prompted her to speak out, Smith defined her credibility as superior to her accusers'. Using parallel introductory phrases, she recited her attributes in litany fashion:

> I refuse to stoop to the smear tactics that my opposition has chosen. I have refused to pursue and participate in the

> charges of State Administration mismanagement. . . . I have
> refused to attack either Governor Hildreth or Governor
> Sewall or Mr. Beverage because I am campaigning on my
> record.

The body of the speech was prefaced with her reasons for responding to the charges. She acknowledged the possibility that doing so might be perceived as dignifying them, but she stipulated that the more pressing demand was to quash any misinterpretation of her silence. Following classic debate form, the feisty congresswoman structured her argument as point-counterpoint. In other words, she meticulously attended to every charge on the sheets and soundly rebutted them with the efficiency of a master of forensics. The determined Smith reasoned inferentially, fortifying her claim with copious facts and statistics covering her eight years in Congress. Her argument was impregnable. To remind her audience that the chief intent of her message was to prove that she was morally and professionally superior to the cowardly party politicos, Smith delivered her facts with persuasive acuity. She aimed not only to defend herself but also to make her listeners aware that they, too, had been insulted. For example, she summarized the first part of her rebuttal with a scornful rhetorical question: "Who does the smear writer thinks he's fooling?" Another device she used to damage the reputation of her antagonists was to question their findings by stating them with the repetition of the introductory phrase "What he fails to point out . . ."

To respond to the claim that she was a traitor to the Republican Party, Smith presented evidence from the very party she is accused of betraying. She used testimony from reputable members to disprove the allegation. For example, she quoted favorable statements made by the highly respected Republican Speaker of the House Joseph Martin that praised her contributions to the party. Also, she compared her questionable voting record with "this imposing array of Republican leaders [who] voted the same way I did." Citing the specific pages from the *Congressional Record*, Margaret Smith listed the number of times her votes matched theirs. She concluded the argument by commenting that "[t]he ridiculous nature of his analysis is evident from the fact that in so many voting instances he picked, my vote was the same as that of top Republican leaders." By correcting the accuracy of her detractor's calculations, Margaret Chase Smith proudly proclaimed the real findings: "[T]aking those 71 in a total of at least 1500 recorded votes during my time in Congress would show that . . . I failed to vote with my party only 4.7 percent of the time — that I had voted with my party 95.3 percent of the time." With the tone of smug satisfaction, she ridiculed the sponsor of the smear sheets: "I would say that was fairly good for as I remember during my school days anything 90 percent or over was marked A and anything 95 percent or over was marked A plus. So that my Republican report card grade would be A plus."

She closed the denunciation with a comment on the folly of her opponent's efforts and the questionable nature of his character:

> If he had tried any harder, this smear writer couldn't have picked better instances to show how the Republican leaders vote the same way I do. It is no wonder that the smear writer was too ashamed and afraid to put his name on the smear sheet.

The emphasis on the word *smear* in the speech served a significant function. Lewis chose the term as the key word of Smith's campaign. Its repulsive connotation was just what Lewis wanted to communicate, causing the voters to associate that perception with the opposition. Therefore, the term is purposely repeated thirty-seven times throughout the speech: "smear tactic," "smear charges," "smear writer."[18]

The hard-hitting speech worked: The smear campaign backfired. Maine voters voiced their disgust with professional politics in favor of the fair-fighting lady. The underdog Smith, like the legendary Joan of Arc, led a valiant charge and won. To reinforce the onslaught, Lewis had "Margaret Smith's Answer" kits distributed to every city and town that had a Smith-for-Senate committee the next morning.[19] The *Portland Sunday Telegram* of June 11, 1948, printed Lewis's spin on Smith's speech: "Small fires of organized support for Smith started lighting up all over the state from Fort Kent in the north on the Canadian border to Kittery in the south on the New Hampshire border."[20] With one month to go before the primary, Smith moved the campaign into high gear.

In her forensic style argument, Margaret Smith made no specific mention of the campaign against her because she was a woman. She explained the omission in the *Portland Press Herald* the following day:

> I have avoided making an issue of being a woman in this campaign, for I truly believe that one's sex should not be a determinant in this election of public officials. But my opponents have raised the issue — and the challenge to the women of Maine — and I believe that they will accept the challenge on June 21.[21]

Nevertheless, the format, substance, and forceful delivery of the speech underscored the superior qualifications of the female challenger. Her opponent's attempts to discredit her backfired. His despicable acts cut to the very core of Maine's sense of decency. For example, one citizen wrote: "Maine people who have sensibilities at all cannot help but be ashamed of the way in which the men candidates are attempting to smear a notable record and even personal character. Maine folks just don't do things that way."[22]

Overall, Margaret Chase Smith's model served to convince voters to reconsider their position on the gender issue, as expressed by the writer of the following letter to the editor in the *Portland Press Herald*:

> The time has come to forget whether a candidate wears skirts or trousers and to judge him or her solely on the record of achievements. If some men and a few misguided women are out to knife a sincere, experienced public servant because of sex, it is time for the rest of the women to rally to her support.[23]

Lewis's strategy worked. The timing and style of the speech won tremendous support for the Smith-for-Senate campaign.

"ELECTION EVE RADIO SPEECH"

The final phase of the campaign was the "Election Eve Radio Speech." In an eleventh-hour effort to make sure that the Smith-for-Senate crusade would be the winner at the polls the next day, Margaret Chase Smith took to the airways to have the last word. Beginning with a softer, more gentle tone from "Answer to a Smear," the congresswoman delivered an impassioned plea for victory. Reaching out to her fellow Mainers and especially to "the thousands of friends and supporters who have given so much of their time and effort for me," the oration was a humble expression of gratitude. But her speech was also a powerful affirmation of her superiority as a political leader.

Her message was a rallying cry for democratic morality. Using climactic structure, she rallied her listeners to vote for her by listing reasons that appealed to them and their sense of fair play. She petitioned them to vote for her because she was the "symbol of a 'grass roots' protest against political machines, money politics, and smears." She requested that they vote for her "for the sake of those who have put so much faith in me and who have worked so hard for me." She entreated them to vote for her because "[it] will be a 'grass roots' victory that springs from the people themselves rather than from professional politicians." Smith's stance was that of the authentic representative of the people; she sought to instill the democratic notion of "government of the people, by the people, and for the people" in the electorate.

Margaret Chase Smith began the discourse by asserting that she was the better candidate for the U.S. Senate because she was the only one with congressional experience. Referring to her four-term tenure in the House of Representatives, she explained: "Those years gave me the know-how and the contacts and the seniority advantages without which I would not have been

able to get my measures through." The statement along, with her acknowledgment of the voters of the Second District and "my friends in the House who
made it possible for me" led Smith to state her thesis:

> I only hope that I shall be able to expand my service to the
> people and that my eight years of accumulated know-how,
> contact, and position in Washington may be continued to the
> future benefit of the entire State of Maine as your next
> United States Senator — with the help of divine guidance.

She begins her plea by subtly acknowledging the conventional belief
that "[t]he only effect these last-minute efforts can have is to spur the people
on a little more to go to the polls to vote for whomever they have decided
that they will support." However, she underscored that this election was not
an ordinary one. Revealing that "desperate last-minute smear sheets have
been intensely distributed against me today," she reminded the audience that
they will do the right thing:

> As a matter of fact, the sudden reappearance of these sheets
> at the last minute has given me even greater confidence that
> tomorrow will bring victory. I believe they will mean
> hundreds of more votes for me because, as they have
> incensed the fair-minded people of Maine before, they will
> rally many fair-minded people to go to the polls and register
> their repudiation of such methods by voting for me.

Hers was a call for righteousness and decency. Appealing to the
moral fortitude of the people of Maine, she defined their direct involvement:
[T]he issue of the campaign . . . has transcended personalities. . . . [It] has
grown much larger than myself or my opponents — for the people of Maine
have come to feel that there is much more at stake in this campaign than the
individual candidates themselves."
   Margaret Smith reinforced the need for the voters to become involved
in this particular election by instructing that the "candidates for United States
Senator are important only for what they symbolize." She defined herself as
"a symbol of a 'grass roots' protest against political machines, money politics,
and smears":

> [F]rom the bottom of my heart, I say to you that I want to
> win tomorrow more for the sake of those things which
> people say that I symbolize — and for the sake of those who
> have put so much faith in me and who have worked so hard
> for me.

Reaffirming her candidacy as the right choice, Smith proclaimed that the victory will not be a personal one, but an all-inclusive one, a "grass roots victory that springs from the people themselves rather than from professional politicians."

To reinforce her claim and to rally her listeners, Smith expressed her gratitude to all the "little people" throughout the state of Maine who supported her. They were her people; she was their public servant. She extended the field of common ground to all the "little people" throughout Maine. In a style akin to a rousing call to arms, Representative Smith declared her gratitude and respect for the rank and file of Maine by acknowledging fifteen representative supporters. For the purpose of intensifying her appeal, she structured her tribute in concise statements introduced with the parallel phrase "I want to win for." The repetition created a cadence that rises to crescendo pitch, resulting in a rallying effect— he kind one would hear on the battlefield or the athletic field. For example:

> I want to win for that World War Two veteran of Bangor who refused the money of one of my opponents to switch to his side — and who fought to keep my banners up when professional politicians were trying to tear them down.
> . . .
> I want to win for that Aroostook County woman farmer who courageously called the hand of those distributing the anonymous smear sheets. . . .
> I want to win for that teacher in Franklin County who refused to withdraw her support of me even though her job was threatened.

The seventeenth statement reached out to all the decent folks of Maine:

> Yes, I want to win for these typical independent Republicans . . . who have refused to sell their votes, who have courageously resisted political intimidation, who have denounced and fought smears — and who have put their hearts and souls into my campaign because they were convinced that I was their symbol of protest against such things.

On closing, Margaret Chase Smith reiterated her basic message of the need to vote, once more reminding her listeners that the issue is one of "the rank-and-file against the paid professionals": "What the voters of Maine do tomorrow will do much to either stop or perpetuate machine and money politics in Maine." She fought the good fight and admitted that she was emotionally moved by such a positive response to an underdog: "I know that you will understand and forgive me if I choke up a little when I say thank you from the bottom of my heart — believe me." The oration ends as many great orations have — by invoking the aid of the Supreme Being: "God willing, we will win because we have given the people of Maine an inspiring cause to fight for."

Margaret Chase Smith won the primary election with a record 67,786 votes, overwhelming Hildreth's 30,949, Sewall's 21,768, and Beverage's 6,399.[24] She carried sixteen of Maine's twenty-one cities, a magnificent accomplishment! Her win was the greatest victory for women in Maine since the granting of suffrage in 1920, only twenty-eight years earlier. She demonstrated what she had so often preached — that with will and determination a woman's place can be wherever she chooses. Margaret Chase Smith faced the gender issue and fractured it.

The general election, on September 13, 1948, posed no problem for the Republican candidate, as usual. Smith easily defeated her Democratic opponent, a Portland dermatologist, with a record-setting 72.8 percent of the total votes.[25]

On January 3, 1949, Margaret Chase Smith of Maine was sworn in as a U.S. Senator. She joined ninety-four male colleagues in what was heretofore considered the quintessential all-male club. At age fifty-one, the lady from Maine, neither a college graduate nor a devoted party member, took her seat among the most influential power brokers in the world. The act symbolized all that America stands for: "liberty and justice for all." According to the man whose seat she won, Wallace White, Smith's election to the Senate was "the most outstanding political event of a generation."[26]

For four terms the voters of Maine sent Smith back to the Senate, but the uphill battles continued. In her first term, for example, she won the admiration of the nation with her "Declaration of Conscience" speech, but she antagonized her party. Her accusation of McCarthy's abuse of the right of congressional privilege caused her to become the target of McCarthy's vengeance. His smear campaign against her and the efforts of the party to punish her for disloyalty made her early years as a senator very difficult.

When she sought re-election in 1954, McCarthy tried to unseat her by personally choosing her Republican opponent, Robert Jones, who assailed her with McCarthy's smears. Once more she fought to defend herself and her record, which resulted in a resounding defeat of Jones in the primary. However, the general election posed a challenge for the first time. The Democratic Party had gained much power in Maine that year, and in the general election, Margaret Smith faced a more formidable opponent, Colby College history professor Paul Fullam. His aggressive campaign— highlighted by his vicious attack on her record in the speech "Are You Proud?" — caused a bitter battle. Margaret Smith won reelection, but by a much narrower margin than in 1948.[27]

The election of 1960 was a historical one. For the first time in

American political history, two female nominees contended for a major office. Smith's challenger was a friend from the BPW, the well-educated Lucia Cormier.[28]   Edward Muskie, the first Maine Democrat elected to the Senate, in 1958, hoped to depose Smith by choosing a woman as her opponent. Smith quipped about the unusual circumstance: "I was so successful in the 1948 and 1954 elections in overcoming the campaign argument that 'the Senate is no place for a woman,' that I must have overdone it."[29]   The contest attracted national attention, with many in the media expecting a cat fight. However, both contestants "recognized that we had to guard against actions or developments that might reflect on women generally— on women in public office, women in politics."[30] Two days before the election, on November 6, 1960, both squared off in a half-hour-long televised debate. Margaret Chase Smith won by the "biggest vote in the history of Maine and the highest winning percentage of all Republican Senatorial candidates."[31] Voters confirmed Margaret Chase Smith's leadership ability.

Even since the "Declaration of Conscience" speech won Margaret Chase Smith national acclaim, talk about considering her for national leadership had become common. For example, the day after the speech, Bernard M. Baruch, the distinguished elder statesman, was quoted: "If a man had made the Declaration of Conscience, he would be the next President of the United States."[32] Two years later, in 1952, at the Republican National Convention, the Maine BPW saw the opportunity to advance women's progress by organizing a movement to nominate Senator Smith for the vice presidency.   The admirable effort proved fruitless when the presidential candidate Dwight D. Eisenhower decided that he wanted Richard M. Nixon as his running mate. Four years later, in 1956, the Maine delegation at the Republican National Convention wished to nominate Margaret as Maine's "favorite daughter" but once more, Eisenhower decided to retain Nixon as his running mate. In both situations, Senator Smith did not personally pursue the nomination. She felt honored that others held her in such high esteem. In preparation for the presidential election of 1964, rumors circulated talk about her becoming Goldwater's running mate, but Goldwater, the arch conservative, dismissed Smith for being too liberal. Nevertheless, her reputation for being a principled politician who spoke her own mind was held in high esteem. Even President John F. Kennedy, when asked about a possible Smith candidacy, replied:

> I would think that if I were a Republican candidate I would not look forward to campaigning against Margaret Chase Smith, or as a possible candidate for President. I think she is very formidable, if that is the appropriate word to use about a very fine lady. She is very formidable as a political figure.[33]

Democratic Senator Richard B. Russell was heard to comment in January 1964: "She is just ornery enough that if she were a man she would make a hell of a good President!"[34]

Margaret Chase Smith was highly respected as the exemplary public servant. She was devoted to her legislative duties as she swore never to miss a roll call or a vote and to keep in constant communication with her constituents. Besides, she was the antithesis of the professional politician, professing allegiance only to the Constitution, to her constituents, and above all, to her conscience. Margaret Smith was proud of her independence from any political bloc and of her campaign frugality. However, these two attributes tended to work against her in her pursuit of national leadership.

With the upcoming presidential election of 1964 looming on the horizon, Republicans were zealously plotting to recapture the White House. Losing such hard-won control in 1960 created an aura of hard feelings among Republicans. Richard Nixon, the Republican presidential candidate, bore the blame for losing to John F. Kennedy. The party became fractious: Conservative ideologues shouted their discontent with the liberal wing in the all-out scramble for leadership at the Republican National Convention in 1964. Several prominent Republicans vied for the opportunity to restore the party to victory — Ambassador Henry Cabot Lodge of Massachusetts, Governor George Romney of Michigan, Governor William Scranton of Pennsylvania, Governor Nelson Rockefeller of New York, and the most obsessive of all, Senator Barry M. Goldwater of Arizona, head of the ultraconservatives.

Many citizens watching this lineup of conservatives versus liberals became concerned about the threat of extremism. The voice of moderation was needed, and the best choice was Senator Margaret Chase Smith. Throughout her career, she had taken a tough stand against extremists, contending that they threaten the very core of American democracy. Letters and newspaper commentaries urged the stateswoman to cast her bid for the presidency. For example, in her book, she cites an especially complimentary editorial on her possible candidacy in the San Diego *Union* of December 1, 1963: "Whether the country or either party is ready for a woman on the presidential ticket remains to be seen. But Mrs. Smith will have her say. And just the possibility that she may run has advanced the cause of women candidates, perhaps more than most of their male opponents realize."[35]

At the age of sixty-six, she decided to consider the call seriously. The question of whether or not to run was, characteristically, Smith's independent decision. She discussed her position only with her assistant and confidant Bill Lewis. They debated the pros and cons of her situation: lack of money and organization versus offering the voters a moderate choice between liberal Nelson Rockefeller and conservative Barry Goldwater. Of course, the possibility that her candidacy may pave the way of women in politics was very appealing to her.

She gave Lewis her general ideas and asked him to draft a speech with two endings, one accepting and one declining to run. The media hounded her to disclose her decision before the speech, so that they could prepare their copy, but she refused. The television networks were informed to "take their chances on my decision and if any of them opted not to cover the speech that was their right and responsibility."[36] She did not even disclose her decision to Lewis, allowing him to speak the truth with the media. The text that Lewis distributed to the media the morning of the speech had the announcement of Smith's decision omitted. "I kept the two endings to myself."[37]

"PRESIDENTIAL CANDIDACY ANNOUNCEMENT"

Margaret Chase Smith chose to announce her decision to run for the presidency at a luncheon meeting of the Women's National Press Club on January 27, 1964. She had planned to do so earlier, on December 5, 1963, but the meeting was postponed due to the national period of mourning for President John F. Kennedy, who was assassinated on November 22, 1963.

Smith's speech follows an inductive organizational structure. After evaluating the rhetorical situation and describing her perception of it, she announced the purpose of her speech. The body consisted of a comparison of the pros and cons of her decision, followed by an honest assessment of the situation against her. After clearly demonstrating that the odds of her winning were stacked against her, the quintessential underdog declared her decision to run. Smith's deliberation was systematic, leading her listeners to conclude after each segment that she was an excellent choice for the presidency. She preferred to state her case from the point of view of the voters rather than from her personal position, reinforcing her ethos as a public servant rather than a self-serving bureaucrat. Smith's scheme was to paint an evil portrait of the effects of political extremism, therewith forcing her listeners to conclude that she, as a moderate, was the best choice.

Her strategy was based on the rhetorical impact of the element of surprise. She used a similar strategy with the "Declaration of Conscience" speech. She knew that surprise heightened curiosity, which increased interest. Not disclosing her decisions until she was ready to do so was Margaret Smith's modus operandi. No matter how hard her Senate colleagues tried to coerce her vote, she refused to be moved. Whatever the intent of the practice — whether to reaffirm her reputation as an independent, to incite attention, or simply to rankle the professional politicos, as well as the media — she enjoyed it. Her manner also demonstrated what she wanted people to admire her most for: the strength of her character.

Her announcement to run was more than newsworthy, for it was a historical event. Margaret Chase Smith would be the first woman to seek the nomination for the presidency as a major party candidate. Therefore, when the media surmised that she may enter the race for the nomination and sought confirmation, the senator, characteristically, refused to disclose her plans. No one, not even Bill Lewis, was to know her decision until she announced it herself. The media was given copies of the speech before the luncheon, but the conclusion was purposely omitted.

Margaret Chase Smith begins her speech to this favorable audience by accentuating their commonalities. She had spoken to the group before, had many good friends in it, and they shared the common interest of journalism. Reaching out to cement the lines of identification with the audience, Smith spent two paragraphs reviewing her participation in the newspaper business. She appealed to their dedication to hard work: "[I]t was when I did five columns a week nationally . . . for more than five years that I felt a greater professional kinship with you. I learned what a chore it was to produce seven hundred words almost daily."

The body of the speech began with an objective discussion of the exigency, her difficult experiences with the forces of extremism, and a reminder to the audience that she had defined herself as a moderate on a television program in December 1948 and in a speech to them in January 1949. She opened with a reference to the first time she spoke to the club — "when I had been a United States Senator for only six days." Smith described her shock at being labeled by the press as a "traitor to the cause of Republican liberalism" simply by voting for the conservative Robert Taft rather than for the liberal Henry Cabot Lodge as Chair of the Senate Republican Policy Committee. A year and a half later, she recalled being called "a traitor to the cause of conservatism" in reaction to her "Declaration of Conscience" speech. Smith reviewed her intense battle against extremist smears in her 1948 campaign for the Senate, how she had to fight the charges that she "voted 'the Marcantonio line.'" She noted that in the 1954 campaign she endured such conflicting labels as "dangerous liberal" by conservative forces in the primary and "reactionary" by liberal forces in the general election.

The second step of Smith's strategy was to address the current popular sentiment that these were the worst of times and to refute it with the claim that the sociopolitical climate of the country was better today than it was ten years ago. Smith contended that much of the distress over bigotry and hatred in the early 1960s had to do with the nation's shock from the news of the assassination of President Kennedy. Disturbed by the violence incurred from the civil rights demonstrations to destroy segregation in the South, she implies that many Americans were quick to suspect a domestic plot. However, she reminded them that "when heads began to clear and emotions cool, the truth came out — and it was not a Southern anti-negro extremist that shot President Kennedy but instead it was a Marxist, a mentally deranged Communist."

The argument contrasting the early 1960s with a decade ago offered Smith the opportunity to demonstrate that she was not out of touch with the present, as well as the chance to promote her consistent stance as the defender against extremism. First and foremost, she rekindled in the minds of her listeners her "finest hour," which was her courageous defense against McCarthyism in the "Declaration of Conscience" speech. She began her case by claiming that "our country is far freer of bigotry and hatred than it was ten years ago — or at the time of my Declaration of Conscience, when I specifically denounced Fear, Ignorance, Bigotry, and Smear." For example, Smith cited the smear campaigns of such ultraconservative groups as the John Birch Society and the Partisan Republicans of California against prominent political moderates, such as President Dwight D. Eisenhower and herself. To advance her argument as well as to fortify her image as a crusader for freedom, the Senator reviewed the abusive practices she addressed to the members of the U.S. Senate in her "Declaration of Conscience" speech by directly addressing those "who contend that hatred and bigotry is now greater than it ever was":

> I would recall . . . those days of guilt-by-association, of character assassination, of trial-by-accusation. I would recall . . . when freedom of speech was so abused by some that it was not exercised by others — when there were too many mental mutes afraid to speak their minds lest they be politically smeared as "Communists" or "Fascists" by their opponents.

The litany of dark memories growing in intensity stopped at the most egregious effect: "I would recall . . . a United States Senate . . . paralyzed by fear."

Senator Smith summarized her dramatic illustrations with a passionate recapitulation of her personal experience:

> I felt the whiplash of the hatred and the bigotry from both the extremists of the Right and the extremists of the Left — when I fought such extremism both on the Floor of the Senate and in the Federal Court — and Thank God, for common decency, when I won not only in the Senate and in the Court — but with the people at the polls.

After the fervent recollection of the moral decline of America in the 1950s, the senator completed the study in contrast by citing examples to illustrate the case of less bigotry and hatred today. She compared 1960 with 1928 when two Catholic candidates ran for the presidency. Al Smith endured vicious attacks for his religious belief; John Kennedy was elected. Smith used rhetorical questions deftly to tighten the lines of communication and to send her message home. Regarding civil rights then and now: "And who can deny that the rights of negroes are greater in 1964 than they were in 1954?" Pressing for the truth, she probed further: "Who can deny that there has been progress on civil rights in the past decade?"

The summation of her argument began with the acknowledgment of the progress to reduce hatred and bigotry made by the nation in the past decade. The venerable stateswoman comforted her younger listeners: "There is much room for improvement. But there is no need to hang our heads in shame— there is no need for us to wallow in a deep and heavy national guilt-complex."

The senator then moved to reinforce her point that the sociopolitical climate in America had improved with an enthusiastic expression of American pride. Posing one rhetorical question after the other, Smith compelled her audience to believe that their nation was the best in the world.   She challenged: "For where in the world is there a nation as free of bigotry and hate as the United States?   Where in the world is there a nation that has provided 'equality in freedom' in the degree that the United States has for its people?" Commenting on America's generosity to give financial assistance to other nations, Smith pressed her point: "Is such the record of a nation of hatred and bigotry? Is such the record of a nation torn between radicals and reactionaries— between the Far Right Extremists and the Far Left Extremists?" She answered succinctly: "No, the vast majority of Americans are not extremists."   In an effort to stimulate deep feelings of patriotism in her listeners, Smith read the inscription on the base of the Statue of Liberty as final proof that America is the best nation in the world.

Assured that her listeners were both cognitively and emotionally on her line of communication, Senator Smith addressed the question at hand: Would she run for the presidency?   She reviewed the background of the question, noting the increase of mail from all fifty states seriously urging her to do so. Admitting that the decision was not an easy one, Smith shared with the audience her analysis for and against the decision. Addressing the reasons why she should run, she first mentioned that she had more "national office experience" than any of the candidates. Her second reason was that by casting her hat into the presidential ring she would be "pioneering the way for a woman in the future," as "women before me pioneered and smoothed the way for me to be the first woman to be elected to both the House and the Senate." Doing so would enable her to "give back in return that which had been given to me."   The importance of becoming the first woman nominated for the presidency by a major political party would be "that through me for the first time the women of the United States had an opportunity to break the barrier against women being seriously considered for the Presidency of the United States." The third reason why she should declare her candidacy is "to give the voters a wider range of choice" other than conservative or liberal. By entering the race as a moderate, more voters would have the opportunity to express their will. The fourth and final reason why she was encouraged to run is that she was politically independent from big money interests and party bosses.

Smith's list of reasons not to run was a longer one. First, she cited the ever-present gender issue — the contention that a woman on the ticket would be "more of a handicap than a strength." Second, she noted that "the odds are too heavily against me for even the most remote chance of victory." The third reason also referred to the gender issue — the contention that she would not have "the physical stamina and strength to run." The fourth and fifth reason mentioned her lack of the necessary financial resources as well as the professional political organization. The sixth and final reason referred to her congressional duties. To run would take her away from Washington and "thus I would bring to an end my consecutive roll call record which is now at 1590."

Acknowledging the "reasons advanced against my running to be far more impelling," the senator reviewed the odds against her. Then, donning her favorite pose as the underdog, she faced her disappointed listeners with her surprise: "So because of these very impelling reasons against my running, I have decided that I shall enter the New Hampshire Presidential preferential primary and the Illinois primary."[38]

She explained her decision to run regardless of the obstacles against her by reminding her listeners that she was familiar with the experience. In every one of her election campaigns, she faced the same challenges and she succeeded in winning.

Indicating that she was ready to get down to the business of campaigning for the presidential nomination, the efficient Margaret Smith asserted that she regarded the New Hampshire primary as a test. Repeating the introductory clause "It will be a test of how much support will be given to a candidate who," the senator listed five factors that should measure her chances. In actuality, she set up the test as a reaffirmation of her campaign philosophy. Rather than a test to predict her success, it was a testimony of her character. The five factors she noted were those that had consistently won her the support of the voters of Maine. They were in direct contrast to the changes taking place in political campaigns, but she paid no mind. She was an old-fashioned grassroots politician who adhered to the Yankee belief that "If it ain't broke, don't fix it." Smith's factors were as follows: She sought to test her effectiveness as a candidate who will only be able to pay her own way, who depends on unpaid volunteers for campaign workers, who refuses to neglect her official duties in the Senate, who "will not purchase political time on television or radio or political advertisements in publications," and who "will campaign on a record rather than on promises."

She ended with a statement of affirmation: "I welcome the challenges and I look forward to the test."

The New Hampshire primary included Goldwater, Rockefeller, and Romney, plus Minnesota Governor Harold Stassen and two write-in candidates — Richard Nixon and Henry Cabot Lodge. Lodge, the write-in candidate, won New Hampshire. Smith's supporters recognized that with these many participants in the race she would be battling against great odds. A columnist from the *Bangor Daily News*, who covered her campaign in New Hampshire, reported that the gender issue was alive and well: The people "admired her courage in taking the big step but took the stand that the presidency was no place for Senator Smith or any other woman— at least, not yet."[39]

Smith the idealist felt that she would make a good president, but, most likely, the pragmatic Smith knew that she did not stand a chance. She was satisfied with exercising her right to bid for the office. When she explained herself as a symbol for women, a pioneer, that really was all she hoped to be. She was up against the heaviest hitters in the party. Smith received 2,812 votes to Lodge's 33,521 and Goldwater's 21,775, Rockefeller's 19,496, and Nixon's 15,752. Only Stassen received less, at 1,285.[40]

In the Illinois primary, she received a surprising 30 percent of the vote, thanks to the organized support of women. She spent only $85 on the campaign, in addition to $250 in New Hampshire. She joked, "For $335, I didn't do badly."[41] She came in fifth in the Massachusetts primary, with Lodge winning first place. She did not enter the last primary, California, but Goldwater's winning there was a sign that all the dark horse candidates did not stand a chance against him.

Margaret Chase Smith arrived at the Cow Palace in San Francisco on the eve of the convention, July 12, with only sixteen votes in hand, fourteen from the Maine delegation and the votes of South Dakota's John Rouzie and Vermont's George Aiken.[42] She refused to abide by the tradition that called for candidates to be absent during their nominating speech and stayed to hear Senator George Aiken of Vermont put her name in nomination. It must have been the moment of her lifetime. Her supporters rushed onto the convention floor to lead a rousing salute to the lady from Maine. When the final roll call began, Margaret left. She did not hear the vote cast for her by Joe Martin of Massachusetts, the two from Alaska, the three from North Dakota, one each from Ohio and Washington, the five from Vermont, or the fourteen from Maine. As the votes shifted to Goldwater, hers remained unchanged. On a technicality, she came in second.[43] She had made history. When she was asked why she wanted to run, she remarked: "There was nowhere to go but the Presidency."[44] According to her biographer Patricia L. Schmidt: "Among Republican candidates, she had more congressional experience than all of them put together. Not one had faced the odds or surmounted the obstacles she had. Her 1964 run for the Presidency was a memorial to all that she had been, and to what might have been. But it was her last hurrah."[45]

In her bid for reelection in 1966, she did not face a primary contest. She was victorious over the Democrat Elmer H. Violette, but her margin of victory was less than previous years.

The sociopolitical climate of the United States became more

pronounced as the Vietnam War developed into a contentious quagmire. President Johnson refused to run for election, and Richard Nixon, the so-called peace candidate, believed that we could end the war by extending it into Cambodia. Students reacted by demanding answers from their representatives. Summoned to "Return home and address yourself to the people whom you represent,"[46] Senator Smith, along with Senator Edward Muskie, appeared to face the angry students on the Colby College campus on May 9, 1970. She defended Nixon but, at times, appeared uninformed. But she stuck the session out, fielding their often audacious questions as honestly as she could. In retrospect, she classified the experience as "perhaps the most unpleasant experience of [her] entire public service career."[47]

The decade of the 1960s was over. The culture had changed, Margaret Smith was aging, and to put it simply, she seemed out of touch.

In 1972 she almost decided not to run, taking longer than usual to announce her candidacy. Her constant companion and confidant, Bill Lewis, had been stricken with a heart attack. She had recently undergone a second hip replacement, and she also suffered from an age-related sight impairment called macular degeneration.

Both of her opponents — in the primary and in the general election — announced their bid to contest her seat before she did. The primary opponent was Robert Monks, a thirty-nine-year-old industrialist, and the Democratic opponent was forty-eight-year-old Democratic Representative William Hathaway. The wealthy, well-educated Monks was considered a "carpetbagger" by Smith.[48] A summer resident in Maine, he resided in Massachusetts most of his life and moved to Maine only one year before declaring his candidacy. Despite Monks's outspending Smith by forty-five to one and the loss of some regular voters, Margaret won the primary with a two-to-one victory.

The campaign for the general election proved to be tougher. Hathaway appealed to voters by often duplicating the practices that Margaret Smith adhered to, for he visited every factory and shopping mall to be sure that the constituents knew that he wanted to be their representative. Smith, on the other hand, waged a quiet campaign, dispensing with a good deal of her familiar traveling. Less than two months before the election, Ralph Nader's "Citizens Look at Congress" published a disparaging report on Senator Smith, denouncing her relationship with Bill Lewis as that of a surrogate senator, questioning her lack of productivity as a legislator over her thirty-two-year tenure, and contesting, often in error, her voting record from 1966 to 1972.[49] In addition, the feminist National Organization for Women (NOW) targeted her as an enemy of the women's movement despite her advocacy for the Equal Rights Amendment. Such reports appealed to younger voters.

On election day, November 2, 1972, although in Skowhegan, she decided against going to the polls. The final tally was Smith, 197,040; Hathaway, 224,270. The heretofore indomitable Margaret Chase Smith, after thirty-two years as an elected representative to Congress, lost her first election. Even her hometown of Skowhegan voted against her. Her victor Hathaway attributed her loss simply to "Age."[50] Throughout her career the feisty Margaret Chase Smith had fought the gender issue and finally succumbed to the age issue. Apparently, she was too old a woman to hold public office.

Notes

CHAPTER 1: Margaret Chase Smith: A Great American Orator

1. "My Creed" is an excerpt from Margaret Chase Smith's personal philosophy statement made in 1953 for the radio series *This I Believe*, produced by Edward P. Morgan and starring Edward R. Murrow. That same year the statement was published in *This I Believe*, a collection of similar declarations from fifty British and American leaders, edited by Edward P. Morgan and published by Hamish Hamilton Limited, London. The following year an American edition, edited by Raymond Swing, was published by Simon and Schuster. Senator Smith often included excerpts of "This I Believe" in many of her commencement speeches and other motivational presentations. See Margaret Chase Smith Archives, Margaret Chase Smith Library Center, Skowhegan, Maine. The author has permission to reprint the Senator's papers. Also see Margaret Chase Smith, *Declaration of Conscience*, ed. William C. Lewis, Jr. (Garden City, N.Y.: Doubleday, 1972), xi.

2. Smith, 306.

3. See Karlyn Kohrs Campbell and E. Claire Jerry, "Woman and Speaker: A Conflict in Roles," in *Seeing Female: Social Roles and Personal Lives*, ed. Sharon S. Brehm (Westport, Conn.: Greenwood Press, 1988), 124-132.

4. Mary W. Graham, "Margaret Chase Smith: Presidential Campaign, 1964," *Quarterly Journal of Speech* 50 (December 1964): 390-393; Howard Schwartz, "Senator Smith Speaks on Speaking," *Communication Quarterly* 15 (February 1967): 19-22.

5. Beverly Manning, ed., *We Shall Be Heard: An Index to Speeches by American Women 1978-1985* (Metuchen, N.J.: Scarecrow Press, 1988); Patricia Scileppi Kennedy and Gloria Hartmann O'Shields, eds., *We Shall Be Heard: Women Speakers in America 1828-Present* (Dubuque, Iowa: Kendall/

Hunt Publishing Co., 1983).

6. Lois Anne Harris, "Margaret Chase Smith: An Examination of Her Public Speaking with Emphasis on the 'Declaration of Conscience, 1950,' and the 'Declaration of Conscience, 1970,'" Ph.D. thesis, Southern Illinois University, 1974. Agnes G. Doody, "A Study of Margaret Chase Smith as an Orator and of Her Senatorial Address of June 1, 1950," masters of arts thesis, Penn State, 1954.

7. For examples, see Karen A. Foss and Sonja K. Foss, "The Status of Research on Women and Communication," *Communication Quarterly* 31 (Summer 1983): 195-204 and Karlyn Kohrs Campbell and E. Claire Jerry, "Woman and Speaker: A Conflict in Roles," ed. Sharon S. Brehm *Seeing Female: Social Roles and Personal Lives* (New York: Greenwood Press, 1988), 124-132.

8. Baccalaureate Speech to Erskine Academy, Palermo, Maine, May 31, 1953, Margaret Chase Smith Archives.

9. Smith, 257.

10. Ibid.

11. Ibid., 105.

12. See, for example, "No Place for a Woman," discussed in Chapter 4 of this volume, the complete text in Part II.

13. See, for example, "Women and Leadership," discussed in Chapter 4 of this volume, the complete text in Part II.

14. See, for example, her speech to the Federation of Business and Professional Women's Clubs, 1949, in Part II of this volume.

15. See "No Place for a Woman."

16. See, for example, "Women, the Key Individual of Our Democracy," discussed in Chapter 4 of this volume, the complete text in Part II.

17. Ibid.

CHAPTER 2: "I Speak as an American"

1. Margaret Chase Smith, letter to the author July 7, 1993.

2. From "Declaration of Conscience I" speech.

3. Margaret Chase Smith, *Declaration of Conscience*, ed. William C. Lewis, Jr. (Garden City, N.Y.: Doubleday and Co., 1972), vii.

4. Smith, "Declaration of Conscience I" speech.

5. Smith, *Declaration of Conscience*, 1.

6. Smith, "Declaration of Conscience II" speech.

7. "The Communist Party in the U.S.," *Newsweek* 29 (June 2, 1947): 22-26.

8. J. Edgar Hoover, "How to Fight Communism," *Newsweek* 29 (June 9, 1947): 30.

9. William O. Douglas, "Our Political Competence," *Vital Speeches*

of the Day 14 (October 15, 1946): 645-649.

10. See David M. Oshinsky, *A Conspiracy So Immense: The World of Joe McCarthy* (New York: The Free Press, 1983), 163: "For publicity, he had a talent unmatched by any other politician of this century. Or perhaps it was an instinct."

11. Richard H. Rovere, *Senator Joe McCarthy* (New York: Harcourt, Brace and Company, 1959), 163.

12. Ibid., 105.

13. Ibid., 125.

14. Ibid.

15. Ibid., footnote, 81-82.

16. Godfrey Hodgson, *America in Our Time* (New York: Random House, 1976), 36.

17. According to George Kennan, Joseph McCarthy was not the author of McCarthyism. His name became the label for "the curious wave of political vindictiveness and mass hysteria" that flooded the American mind since the rise of Bolshevism in the 1930s — the "Red Scare." George F. Kennan, *Memoirs 1950-1963* (Boston: Little, Brown and Company, 1972), 2: 190.

18. Smith, 7.

19. Ibid.

20. Ibid.

21. Owen Lattimore, *Ordeal by Slander* (Boston: Little and Brown, 1950), 3.

22. Ibid.

23. *Congressional Record* 96 (1950): 4238.

24. Ibid., 10712.

25. Ibid., 4159.

26. Oshinsky, 162-163.

27. Ibid., 162.

28. Rovere, 82.

29. Oshinsky, 163.

30. David Halberstam, *The Fifties* (New York: Villard Books, 1993), 250.

31. See Rovere, 2.

32. *The Heart of Emerson's Journals*, ed. Bliss Terry (New York: Dover Publications, Inc., 1958), 25.

33. See Smith, 10.

34. Oshinsky, 163.

35. In 1979, the Supreme Court decided that congressional immunity did not protect a member from libel suits for allegedly defamatory statements made in press releases and newsletters, even though the material contained statements originally made on the Senate floor. (Doe v. McMillan, 412 U.S. 306, 1973; Eastland v. United States Servicemen's Fund, 421 U.S. 491, 1975;

Hutchinson v. Proxmire, 443 U.S. 111, 1979).

     36. Smith mentions four cases in her speech that serve to shed some light on McCarthy's "unproved, sensational accusations": the Amerasian case, the Hiss case, the Coplon case, and the Gold case. All dealt with espionage in the United States and the federal government. The Amerasian Case involved a grand jury probe into the handling of the case by the Justice Department. Alger Hiss, a former State Department employee, was accused of passing secret documents to Whittaker Chambers, a Communist agent. Hiss was convicted of perjury in 1950 for denying that he passed the document to Chambers, who testified against him. He served a prison sentence. Harry Gold was accused of facilitating contact between a Soviet embassy official and the Rosenbergs, who were charged with passing atomic secrets to the Soviets. His testimony against Julius and Ethel Rosenberg resulted in their execution for espionage on June 19, 1953. Coplon's espionage conviction was overturned because of lack of evidence.

     37. Smith, 11-12.

     38. Aristotle, *Politics*, Book III, Ch. 9.

     39. Margaret Chase Smith, Baccalaureate Speech, Erskine Academy, Palermo, Maine, May 31, 1953, Margaret Chase Smith Archives.

     40. It is assumed that Smith is referring to the much publicized spy trials involving Alger Hiss and the Rosenbergs.

     41. *New Republic*, 122 (June 12, 1950), 3.

     42. Oshinsky, 165.

     43. Ibid. The "powerful allies" Oshinsky refers to are listed as conservatives Robert Taft, Styles Bridges, and William Jenner.

     44. Rovere, 179.

     45. Ibid.

     46. Ibid., 180.

     47. For further information, consult James R. Andrews, "Reflection of the National Character in American Rhetoric," *The Quarterly Journal of Speech* 57 (October 1971): 316-324.

     48. Ibid., 324.

     49. Ibid.

     50. *New York Times* 2 June 1950: 11.

     51. Ibid., 14.

     52. "Speech That May Make History," *Anniston, Alabama Star* 4 June 1950: 4.

     53. *Newsweek*, 35 (June 12, 1950), 24.

     54. Smith, 21.

     55. See Oshinsky's quote from the *Congressional Record*, August 20, 1951, 216.

     56. See Oshinsky, 216.

     57. Jack Lait and Lee Mortimer, *U.S.A. Confidential* (New York: Crown Publishers, Inc., 1952), 88.

58. Smith, 38.
59. Ibid., 40-41.
60. Ibid., 45.
61. Ibid., 53.
62. See ibid., 58.
63. Ibid., 61.
64. Kennan, 146.
65. Oshinsky, 167.
66. Halberstam, 253.
67. Smith, "Declaration of Conscience II" speech.
68. Allen Nevins and Henry Steele Commager with Jeffrey Morris, *A Pocket History of the United States* (New York: Washington Square Press, 1981), 565.
69. Smith, 428. Smith notes that only ten percent of the student body were Maine residents. The student body president and signer of the telegram was also a non-Maine resident.
70. Ibid., 429.
71. Ibid., 429-430.
72. Ibid., 421.
73. Ibid., 422.
74. Ibid., 422-424.
75. Ibid., 424-425.
76. Ibid., 426.
77. Ibid., 427.
78. Ibid., 438.
79. Ibid., 440.

CHAPTER 3: "I Speak as a United States Senator"

1. See Patricia Ward Wallace, *Politics of Conscience: A Biography of Margaret Chase Smith* (Westport, Conn.: Praeger, 1995), 127-128.
2. Ibid, 128.
3. Margaret Chase Smith, ed. William C. Lewis, Jr. *Declaration of Conscience* (Garden City, N.Y.: Doubleday and Co., 1972), 261.
4. Patricia L. Schmidt, *Margaret Chase Smith: Beyond Convention* (Orono, Maine: The University of Maine Press, 1996), 255.
5. Wallace, 126.
6. Margaret Chase Smith, "On Foreign Policy," Overseas Press Club Annual Awards Dinner, New York, April 19, 1955, Margaret Chase Smith Archives.
7. Arthur M. Schlesinger, Jr., *Robert Kennedy and His Times* (Boston: Houghton Mifflin Co., 1978), 1: 449.
8. Ibid., 435.

9. Ibid., 442.

10. Ibid.

11. John F. Kennedy, "What Kind of Peace Do We Want?" *Vital Speeches of the Day* 29 (July 1, 1953): 558-561.

12. Ibid.

13. Ibid.

14. Smith, 259.

15. Ibid., 260.

16. At the Republican National Convention in 1964, Smith's name was placed in nomination for President.

17. Michael R. Beschloss, *The Crisis Years: Kennedy and Khrushchev 1960-1963* (New York: HarperCollins Publishers), 1991, 320.

18. Ibid., 320-321.

19. Smith, 273.

20. Smith, 274.

21. Ibid.

22. Ibid.

23. Ibid.

24. Ibid.

25. Ibid., 284-285.

26. Ibid., 285.

27. Beschloss, 8.

28. Ibid., 11.

29. Ibid.

30. Ibid., 451.

31. Ibid., 484.

32. Ibid.

33. Ibid., 485.

34. Smith, 285.

35. Ibid.

36. Ibid., 314.

37. Ibid., 321.

38. Ibid., 314.

39. Beschloss, 85.

40. Ibid.

41. John F. Kennedy, "What Kind of Peace Do We Want?"

42. Ibid.

43. Ibid.

44. Beschloss, 624.

45. Ibid., 625.

46. Ibid., 627.

47. Ibid.

48. Ibid., 628.

49. Smith, 313.

50. Ibid.
51. Ibid.
52. Ibid., 628.
53. Smith, 327.
54. Ibid., 332.
55. Ibid.
56. Beschloss, 636.
57. Ibid., 638.

CHAPTER 4: "I Speak as a Woman"

1. During Smith's tenure in the House (1940-1949), there were ten women who were elected, but only five were reelected.

2. For an in-depth study see Janann Sherman's "'They either need these women or they do not': Margaret Chase Smith and the Fight for Regular Status for Women in the Military," *The Journal of Military History* 54 (January 1990): 47-78.

3. In a videotaped interview I had with the Senator at her home in Skowhegan, Maine, 2 June 1992, she reaffirmed her position.

4. See Ernest G. Bormann, John F. Cragan, and Donald C. Shields, "An Expansion of the Rhetorical Vision Component of the Symbolic Convergence Theory: The Cold War Paradigm Case," *Communication Monographs* 63 (March 1996): 1-27.

5. *A History of the National Federation of Business and Professional Women's Clubs, Inc. 1914-1944* (New York: National Federation of Business and Professional Women), 1944.

6. Schmidt, Patricia L. *Margaret Chase Smith: Beyond Convention* (Orono, Maine: The University of Maine Press, 1996), 73.

7. Statements and Speeches, vol. 19, 261, Margaret Chase Smith Archives.

8. Dwight David Eisenhower, the Presidential candidate, preempted the nominating process by choosing Richard M. Nixon as his running mate in closed session.

9. Statements and Speeches, vol. 19, 266, Margaret Chase Smith Archives.

10. *Dictionary of American History* (New York: Charles Scribner's Sons, 1940), 479.

11. A version of this speech, delivered at Westbrook Junior College, in Portland, Maine, on June 7, 1953, was published under the title "Women, the Key Individual of Our Democracy: Think Well, Then Speak Your Mind," in *Vital Speeches of the Day* 19 (August 15, 1953): 657-659.

12. See Kenneth Burke, *A Rhetoric of Motives* (Englewood Cliffs, N.J.: Prentice-Hall, 1950).

CHAPTER 5: "I Speak as a Republican"

1. The popular Muskie was twice elected Governor and three times elected United States Senator, where he made no secret of wanting to unseat Margaret Chase Smith.

2. Scrapbook, vol. 6, 115, Margaret Chase Smith Archives.

3. Margaret Chase Smith, *Declaration of Conscience*, ed. William C. Lewis, Jr. (Garden City, N.Y.: Doubleday and Co., 1972), 105.

4. Ibid., 4.

5. Six women, including Hattie Caraway, Democrat from Arkansas, had preceded her in the Senate: five were appointed by their state governors to fill the unexpired terms of Senators who had died in office. Eleanor Roosevelt was offered the Democratic nomination for a New York Senate seat in 1946, a year after the death of her husband, but she turned it down. Margaret Chase Smith was the only woman who pursued the Senate seat so deliberately.

6. Smith, 4.

7. Ibid., 105.

8. Ibid.

9. Ibid.

10. Ibid., 105-106.

11. Ibid., 106-107.

12. Ibid., 108.

13. Ibid.

14. Ibid.

15. Ibid., 109.

16. Ibid.

17. Ibid.

18. The use of the term *smear* became a vital part of Smith's vocabulary for the remainder of her political career she identified herself as the enemy of smear tactics. For example, in her famous "Declaration of Conscience I" speech she attacked Senator Joseph McCarthy and his supporters with the term. In the statement of her creed regarding public service, November 11, 1953, she declared that "smears are not only to be expected but fought." (See page 1 of this volume.)

19. Patricia Ward Wallace, *Politics of Conscience: A Biography of Margaret Chase Smith* (Westport, Conn.: Praeger, 1995), 84.

20. Ibid.

21. Ibid., 187.

22. Ibid., 189.

23. See ibid., 187-188.

24. Smith, 112.

25. Schmidt, 199.

26. *Bangor Daily News* 15 September 1948, 1.

27. See the discussion concerning Fullam's "Are You Proud?" speech in *Declaration of Conscience*, 145-146.

28. For a thorough discussion of this unique contest consult the chapter "Woman vs. Woman" in *Declaration of Conscience*, 239-255.

29. Smith, 241.

30. Ibid.

31. Ibid., 254-255.

32. Ibid., 1.

33. See ibid., 361.

34. Ibid., 359.

35. Ibid., 362.

36. Ibid., 364.

37. Ibid.

38. Bill Lewis, the editor of *Declaration of Conscience*, comments in a footnote on p. 371: "When she said that she found the reasons against running to be far more impelling, a groan went up from the mostly female audience. But when she said in the next breath that because of these very impelling reasons that she *would* run, the audience roared with delight."

39. *Bangor Daily News* 15-16 February 1964, 1.

40. Ibid., 12 March 1964, 1.

41. See Schmidt, 296.

42. Smith, 380.

43. Ibid., 389.

44. *Bangor Daily News* 29 January 1964, 1.

45. Schmidt, 300.

46. Smith, 428.

47. Ibid., 429.

48. Schmidt, 321.

49. Gay Cook and Dale Pullen, "Margaret Chase Smith, Republican Senator from Maine," Ralph Nader Congressional Project: Citizens Look at Congress (New York: Grossman Publishers, 1972), 2.

50. Schmidt, 329.

PART II
COLLECTED SPEECHES

"Women and Leadership"

This convention is an example of democracy at work. It is more particularly a most impressive example of the acceptance by women of their responsibility as citizens — to think constructively and to make their thinking articulate.

Citizenship is without sex. It makes no distinction between the rights and responsibilities of men and women. Since the granting of suffrage to women the only differential between men and women as citizens has been the availability and acceptance of leadership.

Some claim that the availability of leadership to women has been unfairly limited. I have no sympathy with this view because it is only those who "make the breaks" that "get the breaks." In other words, to increase the availability of leadership, we must by our own actions create and force that increased availability. If we are to claim and win our rightful place in the sun on an equal basis with men then we must not insist upon these privileges and prerogatives identified in the past as exclusively feminine.

To some extent women have made the "breaks" for greater leadership opportunities. Especially is this the case in their superb performance in many fields during the war. Their contribution to the war was far beyond anything that anyone had even hoped for. Even the hardest cynics now acclaim their performance.

But now the challenge to women is to match their amazing wartime record with the battles for peace and the orderly reconversion to normal living. While their war records will be difficult to match, they are far better equipped for the task of winning the peace because they possess certain abilities and understanding of matters basic to peace that men do not possess.

Dirigo — "I lead" — is the motto on the official emblem of my own State of Maine. Women of this Republic could well adopt it as their motto. The question is where can they exert leadership. The answer is everywhere — (1) in the home as wives and mothers, (2) in organized civic, business and professional groups such as your own, (3) in industry and business, both management and labor, (4) in public offices, such as legislatures and schools, (5) in politics, and (6) as public citizens.

Perhaps the most lasting and basic influence of women is in the home for behind all men, great or small, are women. This might appear too obvious for mention. But it is too often that we overlook the obvious. Can the dynamic influence of Eleanor Roosevelt as a wife be denied when you compare the respectful number of women appointments in the Roosevelt Administration to the almost complete absence of such appointments in the Truman Administration? As General Jimmy Doolittle has said, "A man who underestimates the power of women is either a bachelor or a fool." You can quote this to your husbands and observe that they have but one alternative.

For lasting world peace, the wives and mothers in all nations must get together for a common understanding— in like manner of the Business and Professional Women. I am confident that the women of the world will reach a real and genuine understanding, if given the means of communication and personal exchange, far more satisfactorily than men have yet been able to.

The fight for decent conditions in communities, for improvements in food, housing, school and recreation and health facilities, must come from the women of the home— the wives and the mothers. Yes, even the critical fight against disastrous inflation, black markets and uncontrolled price rises must be led by the housewives. If necessary, they should be the leaders of a "buyers' strike"— those who have the courage to refuse to buy at unreasonable and profiteering prices.

Much, if not most, of the past leadership of women in this country has come through civic organizations and through organizations such as your own. It would be unnecessary and presumptuous for me to elaborate on this type of opportunity of leadership. Yet, I do want to take this occasion to urge you and your organization to women's leadership, and to urge you to extend your beneficial influence as widely as possible.

Women, such as you, individually can provide leadership in industry and business. You have already proved your leadership in industry and business. You have already proved your leadership ability in the field of management. But there is a discouraging dearth of women leaders in the field of labor and labor relations. Women constitute a great part of the labor force. If there is any one way that labor unions can improve themselves and members benefit, it is to have more women labor leaders, qualified for their jobs.

The Government is no more important than the Home just as the Home is no more important than the Government — both can control and influence the other, both are dependent upon each other. But in the past the women have permitted the balance to swing too heavily to the Government's influence over the Home rather than having the Home exercise its proper influence over the Government.

How can this be remedied? By taking a greater interest in our greatest investment, our biggest business— our Government— in seeking and accepting public office. In this way, women can bring the wholesome viewpoint and influence of the Home more directly into the formulation and administration of Government policy.

In the schools, as educators, women have, and will continue to instill in coming generations the very will to peace— and the very necessary guards to insure that peace.

Women fought for the right to vote. They won this battle, but they haven't followed through. They do not take the proper advantage of their voting privilege. With one-half of the population, women could easily become the most powerful single group in the electorate.

In other words, women should become more politically-minded, regardless of the party. They should be conscientious voters. They should develop the incentive and perseverance to organize politically into articulate groups that espouse their views, opinions and desires on vital issues — and independently of party affiliation.

They should be workers and officials in political parties in influencing the platforms of the parties, in getting out the maximum vote, in demanding strict administration adherence to platform promises, in stimulating women to vote and be active, and in demanding only the proper representation of women based upon population and degree of public, both political and civic, activity. They should seek public office — and their appointments to high Government positions should be vigorously advocated, supported and even forced by reorganized groups whether political or non-political like yours.

All of these phases of activity are summed up in the observation that women must give greater meaning to their role of public citizens. For the protection of the family, the basic principles for governing a wholesome family life should be emulated to a greater degree in the administration of our Government. The basic principles of our Government should stem from the home. In one sense of the word, the United States Government is really one big family— the all-American family.

American women have reason to be proud of what they have done so far in influencing greater participation by women of other nations in their governments. An American-educated woman of China, Madame Chiang Kai — Shek, has led the political emancipation of the women of China. Japanese women, under our occupation of that country, have been given the right to vote and hold office and are emulating American women by seeking and obtaining public office in Government places such as the Japanese Diet. This, in itself, is the greatest promise against future Japanese war lords. It is a shining example of how women can make the most effective contribution to the enforcement of a lasting peace by becoming leaders in their own nation and then graduating to the roles of leaders of the world.

It is regrettable that so few women have been chosen to participate in the UN, and that none sit as members of the Security Council. It is amazing when one realizes that women constitute at least one half of the world's population.

But this can be attributed to women themselves for lack of interest and aggressiveness — and the will to public careers — in this and other countries. We can't become leaders of the world until we have become leaders within our own Nation. Our influence upon others must come from within ourselves individually. In as great a measure, our influence, as a nation upon the rest of the world in creating and maintaining permanent peace, must first flow from within this country.

"No Place for a Woman"

Let me say at the outset— this is not a political talk. Nevertheless, the theme of what I have to say arises out of developments of my own candidacy for the United States Senate. The most frequent objection that has been raised to my candidacy is that "the Senate is no place for a woman."

Politics has no distinction as to the comment "no place for a woman" because for too long the many professions were said to be "no place for a woman." You, undoubtedly, have had first-hand experience with this type of negative psychology. I feel that the women of America are deeply indebted to you because you have shown that women do possess determination and the ability to overcome such barriers of negative psychology.

Your success in a profession too long regarded as the exclusive bailiwick of men has been an inspiration to the women of this country. As a matter-of-fact, those of us in politics are indebted to you because women lawyers have done more to lead the way for greater participation by women in politics than any other group.

"Where is the proper place of a woman?" is a question that I have often been asked. The quizzers have asked this question definitely, ambitiously, hopefully — and just plain inquisitively. But it has been asked so many times in so many ways and by so many types of people that, of necessity, my answer has had to transcend the normal and understandable prejudice that a woman might have.

My answer is short and simple — woman's proper place is everywhere. Individually, it is where the particular woman is happiest and best fitted. This may seem to be an over— simplification, but it is a conclusion of mine that has been repeatedly reassured by my experiences in meeting people all over the world.

I think that it is a well accepted fact that the final responsibility for wars is that of the people themselves — not of the leaders of nations. After all, the leaders have only that power which the people have granted to them.

If we are ever to achieve permanent peace, it will stem from the will of the people themselves, rather than the genius of their leaders.

I think that it is also a well-accepted fact that the United States is the most peace-loving nation in the world; that Americans are the most peace-minded of all peoples of the world; that they place the greatest value upon human life.

And what do these observations have to do with the answer to what is the proper place for women? Simply this: America, the peace leader of the world, has granted the greatest opportunity to the woman — and America's peace leadership stems directly from the influence and participation of American women in shaping the decisions of this country.

In too many places that I have visited in Europe, the Middle East, Africa, Asia and the Pacific, women are little more than slaves. They have no voice; they have no influence; they are tolerated only to bear and care for children.

The traditional belligerency of most nations is in inverse ratio to the degree of freedom and recognition that the particular nation grants to women. In other words, wherever you find the woman's voice granted even an approach to parity with that of the man's you will find a more peaceful nation.

But even in America we often hear the comment that "women are all right in their place." But what is their place? The answer of practically all men and many women is, "The Home." Some are willing to expand this concept to permit some venturing beyond the confines of the home by approving of women engaging in non-domestic activities. But this concept is restricted to fields that are considered predominantly feminine — in public life, perhaps as high as State Superintendent of Schools or Commissioner of Charities and Corrections.

You never hear the comment that "Men are all right in their place" because their place has never been restricted. They are certainly not restricted to strictly masculine fields, or more accurately stated, barred by prejudice from the normally-regarded feminine and domestic pursuits. Male chefs are honored for their culinary art although the kitchen is ordinarily considered the bailiwick of the woman. Tailors enjoy a most profitable business although the needle has come to be considered the tool of the housewife.

Yes, tailors can even be permitted the right to share their profession with services in Congress as we have at least one professional tailor in Congress at the present time. In the field of interior decorating, there are as many if not more men than women.

If there is any one proper role for women today it is that of alert and responsible citizens in the fullest sense of the word. Citizenship is without sex. It makes no distinction between the rights and responsibilities of men and women — in America. Since the granting of suffrage to women, the only differential between men and women as citizens has been the availability and acceptance of leadership.

Some claim that the availability of leadership to women has been unfairly limited. I have no sympathy with this view because it is only those who "make the breaks" that "get the breaks." In other words, to increase the availability of leadership, women must by their own actions create and force that increased availability. If women are to claim and win their rightful place in the sun on an equal basis with men then they must not insist upon those privileges and prerogatives identified in the past as exclusively feminine.

To some extent women have made the "breaks" for greater leadership opportunities. Especially is this the case in their superb performance in many fields during the war. Their contribution to the war effort was far beyond anything that anyone had even hoped for. Even the hardest cynics ultimately acclaimed their performance.

The question is where can they best serve. The answer is the same as that I have given to the question, "Where is the proper place of woman" — everywhere — (1) in the home as wives and mothers; (2) in organized civic, business and professional groups; (3) in industry and business, both management and labor; and (4) in Government and politics.

Perhaps the most lasting and basic influence of women is in the Home — for behind all men, great or small, are women. This might appear too obvious for mention. But it is too often that we overlook the obvious. The fight for decent conditions in communities for improvement in food, housing, school, health and recreational facilities must be led by the women of the Home — the wives and the mothers.

Much, if not most, of the past leadership of women in this country has come through civic organizations. The basic ingredient for this successful performance record has been the banding of women together in organized groups to give greater voice and more specific objectives to the interest and efforts of individual women.

Women have provided leadership in industry and business. This has been heavily on the Management side for there is a dearth of women leaders in the ranks of Labor. Labor unions need the balanced judgment of more women labor leaders.

If "what's sauce for the gander is sauce for the goose" why then is there a dearth of women in certain fields and why are those fields dominated by men to the almost complete exclusion of women — particularly the field of Government and politics? This is a question that must be faced and a condition that must be analyzed before an answer to the question can even be approached.

The condition is partly historical for women's suffrage is comparatively most recent. Yet, this historical fact cannot be accepted as a satisfactory answer because the ascendance of women to an equal level of acceptance with men in many respects has been extremely rapid. Women have come a long way in a very short time to increasing equality with men in the business and professional worlds.

Why is it then that they have made such little progress in the field of politics which, ironically enough, was the very arena of their emancipation — the granting of suffrage? The answer lies greatly with the women themselves. In the first place, the meteoric rise of women in the business and professional fields stems greatly from the plain fact that women had the desire for participation and success in these fields. They had sufficient determination to translate that desire into results.

A controlling factor has been the attitude of the men toward women in their respective fields. To a great extent, men have encouraged rather than opposed the participation of women in business and professions. Initially, women served their apprenticeships in secretarial jobs, but their executive abilities imperceptibly found increasing expression and opportunity as the men unconsciously began to delegate more and more of the executive duties to their women assistants.

Unknowingly, the secretarial duties expanded into executive duties and before the men realized it, they had come to rely so much upon their women assistants that they could not do without them and had to accept them in the executive field rather than let them go.

The shadings of development and promotion cannot be as subtle in politics for there is nothing subtle about being a candidate for political office. The old prejudice of men against women is given full warning for resistance. Immediately when a woman candidate announces, the male cry is that "public office" is no place for a woman or "the State is not quite ready for a woman in that office." When asked "Why" the answer is invariably that "she can't hold her own with the men" or "she can't neglect her home duties for her public office duties."

Performances disprove the negative phrase of "no place for a woman." Women have proved their effectiveness in many fields. There are many examples of women office holders who have more than held their own with men. All women in the Congress are outstanding members of most important Congressional Committees. There are plenty of examples of women public officials who have successfully maintained their homes and reared their children. A man legislator's division of his professional time as a lawyer oddly enough is never challenged.

In short, there are two reasons why women have had little past success in politics. The reasons are (1) men and (2) office — and women because they haven't stood together and exercised their power of the majority voting power.

Whether or not there is a future in politics for women depends upon the women themselves. If they have the sufficient desire and determination to hold not only public office but to organize politically and vote in blocks and elect qualified women candidates, then there is most definitely a future in women candidates, then there is most definitely a future in politics for women.

The inescapable fact is that they hold the control of the public offices with their majority voting power.

Will they exercise that power? I think that they will if they are made to realize that they hold the power. Organized women's power has been forcefully proved if the incentive is there.

Basically, the incentive and the attraction of more women in higher public office should stem from the fundamental fact that women are the governors of the home. They legislate the rules of the home; and they interpret the rules of the home. The importance of their role as governors of the home is that the home is the most fundamental form of government. Our community governments are no more than a federation of individual home governments.

The home, then, should not be severed from the government. In fact, there has been too little of the HOME in the government and too much GOVERNMENT in the home. The most obvious and natural way to reverse this trend is to put more of the HOME GOVERNORS in the government, — and that means WOMEN.

That is why there is a definite and inescapable future in politics for women. It is only a question of time — only a matter of how long the men oppose women holding public office and, more important, how long the women themselves are guilty of such political inertia as not to overcome the opposition of the men.

It is regrettable that so few women have been chosen to participate in the United Nations. It is amazing when one realizes that women constitute at least one-half of the world's population.

The dearth of women in public service can be attributed to women themselves for lack of interest and aggressiveness — and the will to public careers — in this and other countries. Women cannot become leaders of the world until they have become leaders within their own Nation. Our influence upon others must come from within ourselves individually. In as great a measure, our influence, as a Nation upon the rest of the world in creating and maintaining permanent peace, must first flow from within this country.

"Answer to a Smear"

I was in business before I entered Congress. And as a business woman, I respected the principle that real success cannot be gained by running down your competition. I have respected this principle in politics — and particularly in this campaign — and I have not made one word of criticism of my opponents. I had hoped my opponents would respect this principle.

But the campaign has reached the smear stage. My opponents have resorted to the distribution of anonymous printed lie sheets. As anyone knows, an anonymous letter is not worth the paper that it is written on. The writer of such a letter, who does not have the courage to identify himself to those charges which he cannot prove, is nothing less than contemptible. These smear sheets betray the desperation of my opponents.

But I refuse to stoop to the smear tactics that my opposition has chosen. I have refused to pursue and participate in the charges of State Administration mismanagement, of which we have all been reading so much in the papers lately, laid to Governors, past and present. I have refused to attack either Governor Hildreth or Governor Sewall or Mr. Beverage because I am campaigning on my record — not on any mistakes that they might or might not have made.

The smear charges that are being made against me, through these anonymous circulars being distributed through the State, are so ridiculous and so patently a pack of lies that they do not warrant the dignity of recognition.

But lest someone might possibly misinterpret silence on my part, I am going to answer the smears. First, let us take the smear sheet that is composed of only one page. I have been told that a relative of one of the candidates is using this sheet to try to charge that I am a puppet of the CIO [Congress of Industrial Organizations] — that is the real purpose of the distribution of the sheet.

This is easy to answer. I voted for the Taft-Hartley Bill and the CIO has called upon its members to make an all-out effort to defeat every congressman or congresswoman who voted for the Taft-Hartley Bill. In addition to this, the CIO specifically endorsed my opponent in 1944. My opponents are actually insulting your intelligence when they think that you will believe such an evident ridiculous misrepresentation that I am a tool of the CIO.

An indication of the inaccuracy of this sheet that they are putting out is that it states that Congressman Carl Vinson resigned from Congress in 1946. I know that Mr. Vinson did not resign for he was the Chairman of my committee, the House Naval Affairs Committee, and so remained throughout 1946 — and is still in Congress.

What the distributors of this smear sheet fail to tell you is that the latest CIO scoresheet on congressional voting stated that in 1947 I voted *against* the CIO ten out of twelve times.

Now let us take the second smear — Smith paper that is being circulated — it is even bigger and more impressive for it is three pages of misrepresentations — in fact it is such a masterpiece of deception that I believe its anonymous author must have had "radical" training from his evident adeptness at fabricating lies and spinning half-truths.

He saved the best for the last. So let's turn to page three of the smear paper and his punch conclusion that infers that I am un-American.

Let me answer his charges that I am un-American, first generally, and second specifically. In the first place, there have been twenty votes during the eight years that I have served in Congress that involved the House Un-American Activities Committee. Of these twenty times, I have voted to support, uphold, and continue the Un-American Activities Committee sixteen times. Only in four instances did I disagree with the committee and I offer no excuses for those four times. If you examine the *Congressional Record* you will find that there are several Republicans who have differed with that committee at times.

But after all, I supported the committee 80 percent of the time. I supported the committee on February 11, 1941, March 11, 1942, April 28, 1942, February 10, 1943, February 18, 1943, January 26, 1944, February 27, 1946, March 28, 1946, April 16, 1946, May 13, 1946, August 1, 1946, February 18, 1947, March 24, 1947, April 22, 1947, November 27, 1947, and May 14, 1948. On those occasions, Mr. Marcantonio, whom the smear writer charges I voted with "nearly 50 percent of the time," voted the opposite way from the way I voted. Who does the smear writer think he's fooling?

The smear writer points out that on June 26, 1946, I voted against the committee's proposal to bring contempt proceedings against one Corliss Lamont. But he fails to tell you that Congressman Hale of Portland voted the same way — and that not a single member of the Maine delegation voted for the committee on this issue. (See page 7600 of the *Congressional Record*.)

The smear writer states that on May 17, 1946, I voted to "attempt to prevent the Un-American Activities Committee from obtaining a $75,000,000 appropriation." This time he went a little too far in his twisted exaggerations — for $75 million is just a little too much for a congressional committee to spend. According to his figures, that would be enough to "run the business of the State of Maine for over" three years.

This statement of the smear writer is another evidence of the inaccuracies of this three-page smear sheet — for the amount sought was only one thousandth of the amount stated by the smear writer — only $75,000. I voted against the $75,000 and I have no apologies for I felt that the work that would require the $75,000 could be more effectively and efficiently done by our FBI — and certainly I don't have to make any excuses for the FBI. (See page 5224 of the *Record*.)

The smear writer points out that on January 3, 1945, I voted against making the committee a standing committee of the House. What he does not say is that many Republicans, including Congressman Clare Boothe Luce, joined me in voting this way. What he does not point out is that we voted this way because only a short time before the Congress had enacted the legislative Reorganization Act which delegated investigating functions to regular committees instead of creating special investigating committees. (See page 15 of the *Record*.)

Now let's take the smear writer's charges under the section he titles "Appropriation and Expenditure of Public Funds." In the first paragraph, he points out that on February 20, 1947, I voted against the proposed $6,000,000,000 cut in the President's proposed budget.

What he fails to point out is that the Congress never did approve the proposed budget cut — that the House and Senate never agreed on the amount of the cut — that I voted against the House proposal to cut by $6,000,000,000 because I favored the more realistic Senate cut of $4,500,000,000 — that I favored a smaller cut because I didn't want to see the Air Force funds slashed by one billion dollars as the $6,000,000,000 cut would have required.

What he fails to point out is that my view on this was vindicated recently when both the House and the Senate overwhelmingly voted to increase the funds for the Air Force — by almost one billion dollars.

In the second paragraph, the smear writer points out that on April 30, 1947, I voted against the proposed $150,000,000 cut in foreign relief. What he fails to point out is that Congressman Charles Eaton, the Republican Chairman of the House Foreign Affairs Committee, also voted against the proposed $150,000,000 cut. (See page 4420 of the *Record*.)

I offer no apologies for that vote because certainly the Chairman of the Foreign Affairs Committee is the best informed on such a matter as foreign relief — that's what we have committees for — to specialize. I talked with him before I voted and he urged me to vote the way I did.

In the third paragraph, the smear writer attacks me for voting on February 14, 1946, for an $1,854,000 appropriation for OPA [Office of Price

Administration]. What he does not tell you is that Congressman Hale voted the same way that I did— what he fails to tell you is that not a single member of the Maine delegation in the House voted differently from me. (See page 1323 of the *Record*.)

In the fourth paragraph of this section, the smear writer points out that on October 18, 1945, I voted against a recession of $52,650,000 and against the return of United States Employment Service to the States. What he fails to tell you is that Congressman Hale voted the same way that I did— that a majority of the Maine delegation in the House voted the way I did. (See page 9818 of the *Record*.)

If the fifth paragraph, the smear writer points out that on March 10, 1944, I voted against the proposed $7,500,000 cut in war housing appropriations. What he fails to tell you is that Congressman Pehr G. Holmes (Massachusetts), the then highest ranking Republican member of the Public Buildings and Grounds Committee— the committee having jurisdiction over such legislation — that Congressman Holmes voted against the cut and the same way that I did— that my vote was in keeping with that of the cognizant Republican committee leadership.

What the smear writer also fails to mention is the critical lack of housing today— 0— and how much more critical it would be if we did not have the houses that $7,500,000 built.

In the opening section of the paper, the smear writer attempts to show under the title "In Support of the Administration and in Opposition to Her Own Party" that I have been a traitor to the Republican Party. Let me answer that generally and specifically.

First, I would call the smear writer's attention to the official statement of the Honorable Joseph W. Martin, Jr., the Republic Speaker of the House, who wrote me as follows:

"Your loyalty and patriotism have made possible the building of a Republican record which I believe will restore sanity in our government."

And I would call the smear writer's attention to the statement of the House Republican Whip, Congressman Leslie C. Arends— whose job it is to round up the party votes on legislation. Of my record, he said: "Our party benefited by your ready response to every call for action."

Specifically, first the smear writer raises the question about my vote against the proposed $6,000,000,000 budget cut. I have already answered that as he raised the same question in the first paragraph of the section "Appropriation and Expenditure of Public Funds."

In the second paragraph, the smear writer points out that on January 29, 1946, I voted against returning the United States Employment Service to the States. What he fails to point out is that Congressman Richard J. Welch, then the highest ranking Republican on the House Labor Committee — the committee which had cognizance over this matter— voted the same way I did. What he fails to tell you is that my vote was in keeping with that of the cognizant Republican committee leadership. (See page 547 of the *Record*.)

In the third paragraph, the smear writer points out that on May 26, 1945, I voted for the bill to grant the president authority to declare a 50 percent tariff reduction. What he fails to tell you is that I voted with Congressmen Hale and Fellows to recommit the bill. (See page 5165 of the *Record*.)

In the fourth paragraph, the smear writer charges me with preventing political opportunism by voting on June 7, 1944, to delay the date of a congressional investigation of Pearl Harbor. What he fails to tell you is that I voted the same way that the present Republican Chairman of the House Armed Services Committee voted (Congressman W. G. Andrews) — that we along with many other Republicans felt that politics should be out during the war and that the Pearl Harbor investigation should be delayed until such time as it would not make revelations that our enemies could use to advantage — such as the working of our radar and other secret devices. (See page 5476 of the *Record*.)

In the fifth paragraph of this section, the smear writer points out that on January 25, 1944, I voted against the proposed $650,000,000 cut on the UNRRA [United Nations Relief and Rehabilitation Administration] appropriation. This he offers as evidence that I opposed my own party, the Republican Party.

This time he hit the jackpot — but for me rather than my opponents. For if I was betraying the Republican Party by my vote against the cut, so was the present Republican Speaker of the House Joseph W. Martin, Jr., for he voted the same way that I did and against the cut — so was Congressman Charles Eaton, the present Republican Chairman of the House Foreign Affairs Committee, for he voted the same way I did and against the cut — so was the greatest Republican proponent of economy and saving, Congressman John Taber, the present Republican Chairman of the House Appropriations Committee, for he voted the same way that I did and against the cut — and last but not least, so was the present Chairman of the Republican National Committee, the then Congressman B. Carroll Reece, for he voted the same way that I did and against the cut. (See page 694 of the *Record*.)

Yes, if my vote was a betrayal of the Republican Party — then the present Republican Speaker of the House, the present Republican Chairman of the House Foreign Affairs Committee, the present Republican Chairman of the House Appropriations Committee, and the present Chairman of the Republican National Committee all betrayed their party — for they all voted the same way I did.

The smear writer concludes his allegations that I have opposed my own party by pointing out that in "July, 1943" (the record voting date was July 1, 1943) I voted to continue the National Youth Administration. What he fails to tell you is that the entire Maine Congressional delegation joined me in support of this NYA vote — Congressmen Hale and Fellows (see page 6969 of the Record), and Senators White and Brewster on July 3 (see page 7089 of the Record). Yes, the entire Maine delegation voted the same way that I did for continuation of the NYA. Senator Brewster took the floor in support of the NYA. In fact, Senator White made one of the most important speeches of his entire career on the Senate Floor in favor of the NYA. (See pages 6595 and 7344 of the *Record*.)

Now for the smear writer's summary of my voting record in the 76th, 77th, 78th, 79th, and 80th Congresses. First, he says that I cast 71 votes against my party. Next, he says that I voted 107 times with Representative Marcantonio and that I am 44.2 percent with Representative Marcantonio.

In the first place, it is to be pointed out that those 71 votes he picks include those instances where the present Republican Speaker of the House; the present Republican Chairman of the House Appropriations Committee; the present Republican Chairman of the House Foreign Affairs Committee; the present Republican Chairman of the House Armed Services Committee; the present Republican Chairman of the House Public Lands Committee; the Majority Leader of the Senate, Senator Wallace White; the Junior Senator from Maine, Senator Owen Brewster; Congressman Robert Hale of the First Maine Congressional District; and Congressman Frank Fellows of the Third Maine Congressional District; and the present Chairman of the Republican National Committee when he was a member of Congress — where this imposing array of Republican leaders voted the same way that I did. Yes, in some instances where the entire Maine delegation voted the same way that I did.

In the second place, the smear writer's statistics are hard to reconcile or understand. He says a "record vote on 242 measures." So how he got only 242 record votes I can't understand for during the time that I have been in Congress from 1940 to now there have been more than 1500 record votes.

He says that I cast 71 votes — or 29.3 percent of his hand-picked 242 votes — in opposition to my party. If he were going to pick only 242 of more than 1500 recorded votes for his analysis, he should have gone all the way and picked just 1 vote so that he could say that according to his standards he could misrepresent I had voted 100 percent of the time against my party — or 1 out of 1. He could have used the NYA vote where he said I voted against the party — yes, where the entire Maine delegation voted as I did.

The ridiculous nature of his analysis is evident from the fact that in so many voting instances he picked, my vote was the same as that of top Republican leaders.

But taking his 71 hand-picked votes, which I think we can assume is the maximum number of black marks that he has against me in view of the character of his attack on me — taking those 71 in a total of at least 1500 recorded votes during my time in Congress, would show that by his own standards I failed to vote with my party only 4.7 percent of the time — that I had voted with my party 95.3 percent of the time.

I would say that was fairly good for as I remember during my school days anything 90 percent or over was marked A and anything 95 percent or over was marked A plus. So that my Republican report card grade would be A plus— and even Speaker Joseph Martin or Appropriations Chairman John Taber would not be given a grade of 100 percent by this smear writer.

The 107 times that he said that I voted the same as Marcantonio would be only 7 percent of the time— and according to the votes picked by the smear writer even Speaker Joseph Martin and Chairman John Taber occasionally vote the same as Mr. Marcantonio.

If he had tried any harder, this smear writer couldn't have picked better instances to show how the Republican leaders vote the same way I do. It is no wonder that the smear writer was too ashamed and afraid to put his name on the smear sheet.

"Election Eve Radio Speech"

Good Evening:

I look back on the 80th Congress just adjourned this morning at 6:45 with a great deal of satisfaction for during the past two years I have been able to introduce and cause the enactment of several important bills. I could not have done this without the six years of service in Congress prior to the last two years. Those years gave me the know — how and the contacts and the seniority advantages without which I would not have been able to get my measures through.

I shall never forget my service in the House of Representatives. I can sincerely say that it has been a real pleasure to serve the people of the second district — and I shall not forget my friends in the House who made it possible for me to accomplish what I have in the way of legislation because of their personal faith in me and what I proposed — I only hope that I shall be able to expand my service to the people and that my eight years of accumulated know-how, contact, and position in Washington may be continued to the future benefit of the entire State of Maine as your next United States Senator — with the help of divine guidance.

This is the eleventh hour in one of the liveliest and most interesting campaigns that Maine has ever had. You have been subjected to a last-minute barrage of campaign literature, newspaper advertising, and radio appeals.

But in my final address in the campaign I am going to report to the thousands of friends and supporters who have given so much of their time and effort for me. Friends and supporters that money can't buy.

I believe that the people of Maine have made up their minds as to how they are going to vote tomorrow and that last-minute appeals and charges cannot have any material effect upon them.

The only effect that these last-minute efforts can have is to spur the people on a little more to go to the polls to vote for whomever they have decided that they will support.

For instance, I have had several calls today from my supporters throughout the State reporting that desperate last-minute smear sheets have been intensely distributed against me today. This has not given me any concern because these smear sheets merely repeat the misrepresentations which I refuted in detail claim-by-claim weeks ago.

As a matter of fact, the sudden reappearance of these sheets at the last minute has given me even greater confidence that tomorrow will bring victory. I believe they will mean hundreds of more votes for me because, as they have incensed the fair-minded people of Maine before, they will rally many fair-minded people to go to the polls and register their repudiation of such methods by voting for me.

These sheets are actually inspiring my thousands of supporters to do even more than they already have — if that is humanly possible.

I can never express adequately my appreciation for the many, many fine things that you have done for me in this campaign. In fact, I shall probably never know what so many of you have done. This is the only regret that I have in the campaign — that I can't know how much all of you have done individually — and that I can't personally thank each and every one of you.

The only comfort I have in the physical impossibility of thanking each of you personally for what you have done for me personally is in the fact that the issue of the campaign for the Republican nomination for United States Senator has transcended personalities. The fundamental issue of this particular campaign has grown much larger than myself or my opponents — for the people of Maine have come to feel that there is much more at stake in this campaign than the individual candidates themselves.

The candidates for United States Senator are important only for what they symbolize. Each of us symbolizes something to the Maine voters. My supporters say that I am a symbol of a "grass roots" protest against political machines, money politics, and smears. They say that the issue is simple and clear — that the choice is one way or the other. And with respectful humility, I must say that they are right.

I would never attempt to deny ambition, for constructive ambition is something of which each and all of us can be proud.

But from the bottom of my heart, I say to you that I want to win tomorrow more for the sake of those things which people say that I symbolize — and for the sake of those who have put so much faith in me and who have worked so hard for me. Because the victory will not be a personal one for me — it will be a victory for them and their ideals. It will be a victory for the rank-and-file of the people of Maine. It will be a "grass roots" victory that springs from the people themselves rather than from professional politicians.

I want to win for that eighteen-year-old girl in Portland who sent me a one-dollar contribution and wrote, "I regret only two things: that this must be merely a token contribution to your senatorial campaign, and that I am not yet old enough to vote."

I want to win for that Worumbo Mill worker of Lisbon Falls who, in contributing two dollars to my campaign, reported that her job at the mill had been placed in jeopardy because she had the courage to openly support me.

I want to win for that Spanish War veteran of Norway who has contributed some of his life's earnings to my campaign and who has assured old people throughout the State that I am their real friend.

I want to win for that housewife of Bath whose integrity was openly challenged by a committeeman of one of my opponents merely because she was actively supporting my candidacy.

I want to win for that granger of York County whose position in the grange was threatened by higher grange officials merely because he was openly campaigning for me.

I want to win for that World War Two veteran of Bangor who refused the money of one of my opponents to switch to his side — and who fought to keep my banners up when professional politicians were trying to tear them down.

I want to win for that insurance man in Hancock County who defied great pressure and continued to campaign for me.

I want to win for that Aroostook County woman farmer who courageously called the hand of those distributing the anonymous smear sheets.

I want to win for those State employees in Kennebec County who had the courage to support me despite the risk that it would cause to their jobs.

I want to win for those Court House workers in Knox County who had the courage to support me in defiance of the Sheriff's machine.

I want to win for those people in Washington County who have complete confidence that as Senator I will continue to fight for Quoddy — regardless of the obstacles that others might create.

I want to win for those loyal supporters of mine in Madison who refused the money of my opposition.

I want to win for that editor in Lincoln County who denounced the smear tactics of my opponent.

I want to win for that longshoreman in Waldo County who refused to submit to an order to fight my candidacy because I voted for the Taft-Hartley Act.

I want to win for that teacher in Franklin County who refused to withdraw her support of me even though her job was threatened.

I want to win for that small businessman in Piscataquis County who refused to let one of his large customers tell him how to vote.

Yes, I want to win for these typical independent Republicans and hundreds of other rank-and-file Republicans who have refused to sell their votes, who have courageously resisted political intimidation, who have denounced and fought smears— and who have put their hearts and souls into my campaign because they were convinced that I was their symbol of protest against such things.

Our campaign has been cleanly and fairly waged. We have much to be proud of for we have given the people of Maine the opportunity to show the rest of the nation that while we like lively campaigns, we prefer that they be fair and clean.

And that is one of the principal reasons why we are going to win tomorrow. I have received reports all day from all over the State that the people are rallying to our cause — that great numbers of the former opposition are shifting over to our side and jumping on our apparently victorious bandwagon.

The only thing that we have to fear now is overconfidence— that too many of our people may feel that we have won the campaign and that their vote is not needed. We must guard against this for we cannot underestimate the highly organized and highly paid professional machines of our highly financed opponents.

The issue tomorrow is clear. It is the rank-and-file against the paid professionals. What the voters of Maine do tomorrow will do much to either stop or perpetuate machine and money politics in Maine.

That is why it is so important to get out and vote.

Tomorrow is V-Day— it is Voting Day— it is Volunteer Day— and it will be Victory Day for us if the Smith-for-Senate Volunteer nonpaid workers outwork the paid professionals of opposition and get the vote out— for the bigger the total vote the bigger our margin of victory.

I have been in campaigns for many years but never have I seen the sincerity, loyalty, and enthusiasm that you my supporters have given in this campaign. So I know that you will understand and forgive me if I choke up a little when I say thank you from the bottom of my heart — believe me. I appreciate the magnificent job that you have done. But we must carry through on that magnificent job and not let up a bit until tomorrow night. God willing, we will win because we have given the people of Maine an inspiring cause to fight for.

"Women's Progress"

I know of no higher honor than to have the approval of the Woman's Christian Temperance Union. It is an approval that is not easily gained. It is the highest tribute to one's character.

So that when I was asked to speak tonight to your annual meeting, I was most gratified and proud— but very humble. It is a privilege to be here with the very leaders of one of the greatest movements in America.

You are leading the fight for the preservation of the wholesome fundamentals that are so necessary to preserve and glorify the greatest of American traditions — the family and the home. With the courage and the determined will that so few of us possess, you are waging a relentless war on those insidious habits which can wreck our family life and our homes. You are doing it in the face of formidable opposition. Not organized opposition but rather the opposition of laxness, indifference and misguided "smartness."

War and immediate postwar times are marked with great maladjustments that stem from an intensive feeling of individual insecurity. During the war we are subjected to physical danger. After the war we have the difficult transitional period of returning from a war effort back to civilian life to try to pick up where we left off and to tie our threads of life back where they were before war interrupted them. The trouble is that we never can return to where we were before. In the first place, four or five years have intervened. Secondly, we have changed and so have others.

The overall result to many people is a feeling of frustration. And therein lies the danger. For in attempting to solve that problem of frustration, many people actually try to run away from it. Frustration, being a mental condition, makes it easy for mental escapists to turn to means of dulling their mental capacities in the false hope of forgetting or driving their frustration away.

But when they do this they make a self-attack on themselves, morally, mentally and physically. And they not only fail to conquer their frustration but rather aggravate and accelerate that frustration.

They become obsessed of living only for today— of thinking only of themselves — of developing a complete obsession of defeatism.

America is going through a most trying period now when the forces of frustration are at their peak strength. Many of the families that the war wrecked have not yet been salvaged. Juvenile delinquency and divorces are at record rates.

The thought is increasing at an alarming rate that the crime is not what one does but rather in getting caught at doing it. This means that a "wise guy" attitude of immoral cynicism has developed of do whatever you can get away with.

Not a small factor contributing to these deplorable results has been Russian communism. It has fostered aggression and aggressive threats that have left the peaceful nations of the world with great concern and fear of being attacked. They have had no choice but to concentrate their national efforts on the building of military might for their own protection. This has left them little opportunity to concentrate on the wholesome factors of peace and peacetime.

The veto tactics of Russia in the United Nations have resulted in the growing feeling of frustration within that great body on its objective of permanent peace. If that sense of frustration grows much more and becomes too great, then we might as well write the United Nations off to the same fate and demise as its predecessor, the League of Nations.

But Russian Communism has not stopped at merely creating a feeling of military insecurity. It has also made an aggressive attack on our economic security. We are carrying a record tax burden. We are pouring billions of dollars into aid for Europe in order to stop the spread of Russian Communism in Europe. In doing this, our budget is ever increasing. The more it increases, the more we approach the breaking point in our economy. And that is the very thing that the Russian Communists want — to conquer America through its economic collapse.

Yes, Russian Communism threatens our military security and our economic security. But it doesn't stop there. It threatens our moral security. It is waging a relentless war against religion and against the principles and leaders of the church. The Russian Communists and their associates in their satellite countries execute and imprison the very disciples of God. The Russian Communists are not content with executions and imprisonment of religious leaders, they campaign insidiously against the moral principles of the church by disapproving marriage.

These Russian Communist attacks upon America's, and the World's for that part, physical, economic and moral security, have undeniably created a great feeling of frustration and insecurity.

How can we combat these attacks and this feeling of frustration? Through organizations such as yours. I sincerely mean that. You have two assets that no other organization possesses — (1) you are the champions of temperance and (2) you are women.

Consequently, women's progress should be of vital importance to you because the progress of women is the progress of temperance and the progress of peace.

I would like to review some of the high points of the progress of women because they showed what can be done in the face of formidable opposition — opposition that has been almost as formidable as the opposition which you are so gallantly and effectively fighting. I think the past accomplishments of women can give you real hope.

The Charter of the United Nations has provided an encouraging guide as to what the position of women in the world should be. The preamble states that the peoples of the United Nations are determined to "reaffirm faith in fundamental human rights, in the dignity and worth of the human person, in the equal rights of men and women and of Nations large and small."

I think that the United States can be proud of the increasing recognition and equality that has been given women here. 80 years ago women held only 15 per cent of all jobs in America. Today they hold twice that amount — 30 per cent.

Today women occupy all but a few occupations. They are increasingly occupying more jobs. Being married is no longer a barrier to working, for married women constitute the largest employed group of women.

Few of us realize that one-fifth of the working women of America are heads of families.

Women have come a long way in the past century. We can best realize this when we compare their status in 1848 with that in 1948.

They were denied voting rights in 1848. Today they constitute more than 50 percent of America's total vote.

In 1848 they neither shared in lawmaking or in jury duty. Today they are in both houses of Congress and in most state legislatures. They do jury duty in 35 of the 48 states.

One hundred years ago they were not eligible to run for public office. Now they are eligible to all major elective and appointive positions.

In 1848 marriage took away a woman's legal personality and property rights. This is not the case today. Now she is responsible for her own acts instead of being in effect the ward of her husband. No longer is the husband legally authorized to restrain and punish the wife for disobedience to his commands.

Yes, we women have come a long way since 1848. But we still have quite a way to go. We must remain ever alert and vigilant to our civic responsibility from the standpoint of equality — not perpetuated feminine privileges.

All during my service in Congress I have studiously avoided being a feminist. I have been particularly conscious of, and perhaps sensitive to, the general criticism that women selfishly seek equal rights without agreeing to give up those feminine privileges and niceties which are in direct conflict with the rights sought. In other words, that we have all the rights that men have plus the feminine rights that they do not have.

I think it is a well-accepted fact that the United States is the most peace-loving nation in the world; that Americans are the most peace minded of all peoples of the world; that they place the greatest value upon human life.

The historical belligerency of most nations will be found to be in inverse ratio to the degree of freedom and recognition that the particular nation grants to women. In other words, wherever you find the woman's voice granted even an approach to parity with that of the man's, you will find a more peaceful nation.

I do not mean to imply that women have any touchstone for peace. But wars are man-made. Maybe peace should be partially woman-made. It is regrettable that so few women have been chosen to participate in the United Nations. It is amazing when one realizes that women constitute at least one-half of the world's population.

The dearth of women in state, national and international roles stems from the women's lack of will for public roles. They cannot become leaders of the world until they have become leaders within their own nation and community.

Our influence upon others must come from within ourselves individually as men and women. In as great a measure, our influence, as a nation upon the rest of the world in creating and maintaining permanent peace, must first flow from within this country.

It has been almost automatic to think of men as being the rulers of the world — at least the official rulers. But what has been overlooked is the fact that women actually do more governing of our daily lives and of shaping our future people.

Women are actually the governors of the home. They legislate the rules of the home. They execute and enforce the rules of the home. They interpret the rules of the home. They act as legislator, executive, and judge on dozens of daily home decisions. Their formula for success is simple common sense and the Golden Rule — ingredients so sorely needed by our Government and by the World.

The importance of their role as governors of the home is that the home is the most fundamental form of government. Our community governments are no more than a federation of individual home governments. The federation of our community governments makes up our State governments — and our States are federated into our Federal United States Government. That is the unbroken chain right from your home and my home to the White House.

And what bearing do these observations have on the question of women's progress? Simply this — America, the peace leader of the world, also leads the other nations of the world on opportunity granted to women. There is a definite correlation.

The greatest need of America today— and of the World today— is the total mobilization of our moral forces. We have been stressing physical force to the exclusion of moral force in our zeal for peace. Yet history shows that in the long run physical force never satisfactorily settled differences — and certainly that it never prevented wars and brought peace, but to the contrary bred wars.

That is exactly what your group is doing. We need more groups like yours.

Some might ask "What is moral force?" It is nothing more than the application of reason, common sense, and the Golden Rule. It is the will to see the other fellow's viewpoint. It is the will to give specific and concrete examples of unselfish purpose, good will and sincerity.

It is the cure for frustration and fear.

Moral force is the expression of the will to peace. It is placing the guidance of God above nationalism. It is the conscience of men and women. And you, the members of the WCTU, are our foremost soldiers in our army of moral force.

Today there is too much hate between races, creeds, colors, and even inside the groups themselves. The moral and psychological basis for world peace does not yet exist even here at home. There must be a profound change in human attitudes if we are to succeed in establishing a just and durable peace.

No longer can we afford the luxury of private indulgence in hatred, prejudice and contempt for other human beings. If the preparation of the necessary moral and psychological basis for world peace seems impossible, then world peace itself is impossible.

We all must start behaving as though we intended to live together in a world organized for peace. Cultural and industrial isolation must be ended as rapidly as possible. Organizations such as yours, our universities, churches, industries, service associations, and labor unions must be encouraged to resume contacts with similar organizations abroad.

The broad objectives of peaceful living cannot be accomplished by diplomatic and governmental contacts working alone. They must be supported by the establishment of relationships among individuals and among their cultural and commercial organizations.

It is plain that there will be no lasting peace in this world unless there is a basis for peace among the world's most powerful nations. It is plain that the leaders and the people of all nations must turn their minds to discovering what common interests may exist among them.

And it is equally plain that the mental climate for making that discovery is not the climate of prejudice and hatred, but the willingness of all the people to look and see; the desire to know, and to understand; the tolerant acceptance, on every side, of live and let live.

What we need, and what the world needs, is the simple old-fashioned neighborly goodwill to get along. We need the fearlessness to lay aside our comfortable old prejudices. We need the tolerance to let others live by their lights as we try to live by ours. We need to stop living by fear. I repeat for emphasis — we need to stop living by fear.

We need to take our eyes off the vague shapes and shifting shadows in the fateful Valley of Decision, so that we can begin to turn the light of trained intelligence upon the real objects casting those fearful shadows.

"Declaration of Conscience I"

Mr. President,

I would like to speak briefly and simply about a serious national condition. It is a national feeling of fear and frustration that could result in national suicide and the end of everything that we Americans hold dear. It is a condition that comes from the lack of effective leadership in either the Legislative Branch or the Executive Branch of our Government.

That leadership is so lacking that serious and responsible proposals are being made that national advisory commissions be appointed to provide such critically needed leadership.

I speak as briefly as possible because too much harm has already been done with irresponsible words of bitterness and selfish political opportunism. I speak as simply as possible because the issue is too great to be obscured by eloquence. I speak as a Republican. I speak as a woman. I speak as a United States Senator. I speak as an American.

The United States Senate has long enjoyed worldwide respect as the greatest deliberative body in the world. But recently that deliberative character has too often been debased to the level of a forum of hate and character assassination sheltered by the shield of congressional immunity.

It is ironical that we Senators can in debate in the Senate directly or indirectly, by any form of words, impute to any American who is not a Senator any conduct or motive unworthy or unbecoming an American — and without that non-Senator American having any legal redress against us — yet if we say the same thing in the Senate about our colleagues we can be stopped on the grounds of being out of order.

It is strange that we can verbally attack anyone else without restraint and with full protection and yet we hold ourselves above the same type of criticism here on the Senate Floor. Surely the United States Senate is big enough to take self-criticism and self-appraisal. Surely, we should be able to take the same kind of character attacks that we "dish out" to outsiders.

I think that it is high time for the United States Senate and its members to do some soul-searching— for us to weigh our consciences— on the manner in which we are performing our duty to the people of America— on the manner in which we are using or abusing our individual powers and privileges.

I think that it is high time that we remembered that we have sworn to uphold and defend the Constitution. I think that it is high time that we remembered that the Constitution, as amended, speaks not only of the freedom of speech but also of trial by jury instead of trial by accusation.

Whether it be a criminal prosecution in court or a character prosecution in the Senate, there is little practical distinction when the life of a person has been ruined.

Those of us who shout the loudest about Americanism in making character assassinations are all too frequently those who, by our own words and acts, ignore some of the basic principles of Americanism:

The right to criticize;

The right to hold unpopular beliefs;

The right to protest;

The right of independent thought.

The exercise of these rights should not cost one single American citizen his reputation or his right to livelihood merely because he happens to know someone who holds unpopular beliefs. Who of us doesn't? Otherwise none of us could call our souls our own. Otherwise thought control would have set in.

The American people are sick and tired of being afraid to speak their minds lest they be politically smeared as "Communists" or "Fascists" by their opponents. Freedom of speech is not what it used to be in America. It has been so abused by some that it is not exercised by others.

The American people are sick and tired of seeing innocent people smeared and guilty people whitewashed. But there have been enough proved cases, such as the Amerasia case, the Hiss case, the Coplon case, the Gold case, to cause nationwide distrust and strong suspicion that there may be something to the unproved, sensational accusations.

As a Republican, I say to my colleagues on this side of the aisle that the Republican Party faces a challenge today that is not unlike the challenge that it faced back in Lincoln's day. The Republican Party so successfully met that challenge that it emerged from the Civil War as the champion of a united nation— in addition to being a Party that unrelentingly fought loose spending and loose programs.

Today our country is being psychologically divided by the confusion and the suspicions that are bred in the United States Senate to spread like cancerous tentacles of "know nothing, suspect everything" attitudes. Today we have a Democratic Administration that has developed a mania for loose spending and loose programs. History is repeating itself— and the Republican Party again has the opportunity to emerge as the champion of unity and prudence.

The record of the present Democratic Administration has provided us with sufficient campaign issues without the necessity of resorting to political smears. America is rapidly losing its position as leader of the world simply because the Democratic Administration has pitifully failed to provide effective leadership.

The Democratic Administration has completely confused the American people by its daily contradictory grave warnings and optimistic assurances — that show the people that our Democratic Administration has no idea of where it is going.

The Democratic Administration has greatly lost the confidence of the American people by its complacency to the threat of communism here at home and the leak of vital secrets to Russia through key officials of the Democratic Administration. There are enough proved cases to make this point without diluting our criticism with unproved charges.

Surely these are sufficient reasons to make it clear to the American people that it is time for a change and that a Republican victory is necessary to the security of this country. Surely it is clear that this nation will continue to suffer as long as it is governed by the present ineffective Democratic Administration.

Yet to displace it with a Republican regime embracing a philosophy that lacks political integrity or intellectual honesty would prove equally disastrous to this nation. The nation sorely needs a Republican
victory. But I don't want to see the Republican Party ride to political victory on the Four Horsemen of Calumny— Fear, Ignorance, Bigotry, and Smear.

I doubt if the Republican Party could — simply because I don't believe the American people will uphold any political party that puts political exploitation above national interest. Surely we Republicans aren't that desperate for victory.

I don't want to see the Republican Party win that way. While it might be a fleeting victory for the Republican Party, it would be a more lasting defeat for the American people. Surely it would ultimately be suicide for the Republican Party and the two-party system that has protected our American liberties from the dictatorship of a one party system.

As members of the Minority Party, we do not have the primary authority to formulate the policy of our Government. But we do have the responsibility of rendering constructive criticism, of clarifying issues, of allaying fears by acting as responsible citizens.

As a woman, I wonder how the mothers, wives, sisters, and daughters feel about the way in which members of their families have been politically mangled in Senate debate — and I use the word "debate" advisedly.

As a United States Senator, I am not proud of the way in which the Senate has been made a publicity platform for irresponsible sensationalism.

I am not proud of the reckless abandon in which unproved charges have been hurled from this side of the aisle. I am not proud of the obviously staged, undignified countercharges that have been attempted in retaliation from the other side of the aisle.

I don't like the way the Senate has been made a rendezvous for vilification, for selfish political gain at the sacrifice of individual reputations and national unity. I am not proud of the way we smear outsiders from the Floor of the Senate and hide behind the cloak of congressional immunity and still place ourselves beyond criticism on the Floor of the Senate.

As an American, I am shocked at the way Republicans and Democrats alike are playing directly into the Communist design of "confuse, divide, and conquer." As an American, I don't want a Democratic Administration "whitewash" or "cover-up" any more than I want a Republican smear or witch hunt.

As an American, I condemn a Republican "Fascist" just as much as I condemn a Democrat "Communist." I condemn a Democrat "Fascist" just as much as I condemn a Republican "Communist." They are equally dangerous to you and me and to our country. As an American, I want to see our nation recapture the strength and unity it once had when we fought the enemy instead of ourselves.

It is with these thoughts that I have drafted what I call a "Declaration of Conscience." I am gratified that Senator Tobey, Senator Aiken, Senator Morse, Senator Ives, Senator Thye, and Senator Hendrickson have concurred in that declaration and have authorized me to announce their concurrence.

STATEMENT OF SEVEN REPUBLICAN SENATORS

1.   We are Republicans. But we are Americans first. It is as Americans that we express our concern with the growing confusion that threatens the security and stability of our country. Democrats and Republicans alike have contributed to that confusion.
2.   The Democratic Administration has initially created the confusion by its lack of effective leadership, by its contradictory grave warnings and optimistic assurances, by its complacency to the threat of communism here at home, by its oversensitiveness to rightful criticism, by its petty bitterness against its critics.
3.   Certain elements of the Republican Party have materially added to this confusion in the hopes of riding the Republican Party to victory through the selfish political exploitation of fear, bigotry, ignorance, and intolerance. There are enough mistakes of the Democrats for Republicans to criticize constructively without resorting to political smears.
4.   To this extent, Democrats and Republicans alike have unwittingly, but undeniably, played directly into the Communist design of "confuse,

divide, and conquer."

5.   It is high time that we stopped thinking politically as Republicans and Democrats about elections and started thinking patriotically as Americans about national security based on individual freedom. It is high time that we all stopped being tools and victims of totalitarian techniques— techniques that, if continued here unchecked, will surely end what we have come to cherish as the American way of life.

Margaret Chase Smith, Maine
Charles W. Tobey, New Hampshire
George D. Aiken, Vermont
Wayne L. Morse, Oregon
Irving M. Ives, New York
Edward J. Thye, Minnesota
Robert C. Hendrickson, New Jersey

"The Importance of Individual Thinking"

You young women are on the threshold of the finest years of your life. Make the best of those years — not only for yourselves, but for your families, your friends and your country as well. Make better use of those years than has the generation preceding you.

Give the young women who follow you a heritage of peace instead of the world of suspicion, aggression, treason, character assassination and moral deliquency that has been thrust upon you by the older generation that has preceded you.

Show them the way to think — the way to control emotions instead of being controlled by emotions. Lead them away from the emotional idolatry of personalities that so beclouds our national thinking today. Lead them away from bitter cynicism and hatred of those with whom they differ in opinion. Show them how to disagree agreeably and with constructive respect.

Help them to realize that this wonderful country of ours is greater than any individual woman or man — and that its fate, destiny and security should not be made a political football to be kicked around by clashing personalities greedy and envious of political power.

Your generation can do this. It is your destiny — the greatest challenge with which you are faced. You can meet that challenge — you can fulfill your destiny — regardless of what individual role you play in the years to come, whether in the home, in the church, in business or in public office.

There is an old slogan that you can well respect and ever keep before you. It is the slogan of "Stop, Look and Listen!" But I want to add something new to that slogan and I propose to you the slogan of "Stop, Look, Listen and THINK!" If you ever think you have been wrong and want to change your mind — do it and admit it. That's the sign of a big person.

One of the basic causes for all the trouble in the world today is that people talk too much and think too little. They act too impulsively without thinking. I always try to think before I talk.

Don't misunderstand me. I'm not advocating in the slightest that we become mutes with our voices stilled because of fear of criticism of what we might say. That is moral cowardice. And moral cowardice that keeps us from speaking our minds is as dangerous to this country as irresponsible talk. The right way is not always the popular and easy way. Standing for right when it is unpopular is a true test of moral character.

In short, I urge you to think well and deeply before you talk — but once you have made up your mind, don't hesitate to speak our mind. As long as you speak your minds, dictators and demagogues will never take control of this country.

There will always be demagogues — and there must always be people with enough moral courage to stand up and speak out against such demagogues and expose and defeat them, before they get so many unthinking people swallowing their untruthful propaganda that our country is surrendered to them because we were too lazy to do our own thinking and too cowardly to speak our minds.

Instead of making a speech to you today, I would rather think WITH you. Instead of saying just so many words in catchy phrases and consuming so much time, I would rather just "think out loud" with you, try to get my simple points across as briefly as possible and stop. I would rather say fewer words more slowly so that they can sink in mentally than to try to crowd in the maximum number of words in any lengthy speech.

And I fully acknowledge that what I say is nothing new to you nor anything that you couldn't say yourself. But it is well for all of us to review the fundamentals that are so basic and obvious that too often too many of us take them for granted.

The importance of individual thinking to the preservation of our Democracy and our freedom cannot be overemphasized. It is too often overlooked and neglected.

But when we use the word "think" just what do we mean? To "think" is to exercise the faculties of judgement, conception, or inference — to put our common sense into action. When the German people defaulted their thinking to Hitler, they surrendered their freedom. When the Russian people defaulted their thinking to Lenin and Stalin, they surrendered their freedom.

Too few people in this country realize that too many people in this country are defaulting their thinking to demagogues and that we are closer to surrendering our freedom than most of us are willing to recognize and admit. When we accept the statements and proposals of demagogues because we are too lazy to think and test their statements and proposals, we can blame no one but ourselves for subsequent events.

But thoughts, to be effective, must be disclosed. We must have confidence in our opinions and cherish the belief that they will guide others as well as ourselves. We should so proceed as to merit leadership and then not be timid about accepting it.

It is the articulate majority that rules a Democracy. But the articulate majority does not always represent the real majority. Quite often the real minority by "thinking out loud" makes itself the practical, effective articulate majority. For proof of this one need only look at the presidential election figures where he or she will find that usually the victorious candidate and party not only have small margins of victory but poll considerably less than 51% of the eligible electorate.

There is too great a tendency to regard elections as just "a lot of politics" and a popularity contest in which candidates and political parties indulge in namecalling that they themselves do not believe and forget just as soon as the election campaign is over.

Elections are more than just intense politics and popularity contests. In elections we should vote for policies on vital issues for the candidates are merely symbols and media of action.

Elections are times when we establish a policy of government for the next two or four years — a policy that public officials whom we have elected are to follow. Therein lies the importance of maximum voting for in our two party system maximum voting is the greatest possible assurance of effecting the will of the majority, of giving full vitality to Democracy.

There is a tendency to set women off separate from men when we think about these aspects. I don't like that — I don't like it simply because women are citizens just like men and have the same responsibilities of citizenship as men do. The simplest and most direct way to state my attitude is in three words — WOMEN ARE PEOPLE.

So that, I am included to accept the theme of "Woman's Role in the Defense of Democracy" with the reservation that the broad role of women in the defense of democracy is no different from that of men.

Women, just like men, have the role of voting, of thinking, of articulating — of taking a stand and expressing their beliefs. They can play that role in participating in forums and public discussions. They can organize or affiliate themselves with articulate groups that represent their views. They can help get out the vote.

The articulate action of a citizen, whether man or woman, must be constructive — must seek to improve — to build instead of tear down and destroy — must be preceded by serious and responsible thinking. Criticism unaccompanied by positive proposals of substitutes for that criticized indicates lack of informed thinking on the part of the critic.

The broader sense of the concept of the role of women in the defense of Democracy is that of the citizen doing her most for the preservation of Democracy and peace by (1) independent thinking, (2) making that thinking articulate by translating it into action at the ballot boxes, in the forums, and in everyday life, and (3) being constructive and positive in that thinking and articulation.

In the more narrow sense of the concept — the concept that makes a distinction on the basis of sex— the most important role of the woman in defense of Democracy is her traditional role as homemaker.

I wish that there were more women holding top positions in our Democracy. I wish there were more in Congress — more women in top positions in the Executive and Judicial branches of our Government.

But in that wish I regard the role of homemaker for women as being far more important than the role in public office. For surely the very backbone of our Democracy is the family and the home in which the family lives. As long as the family home structure of our nation is firm and sound our Democracy will be firm and sound and well defended.

Since woman is the homemaker— the keeper of the home— she is the key individual of our Democracy at the "grass roots" level. In that respect, woman is the primary and basic governor of our Democracy for our governing starts right in the home. Woman moulds the citizens of tomorrow in the rearing that she gives the children.

Yes, the first and original governor in our Democracy is the woman. Woman administers the home. She gets the rules. She enforces the rules. She metes out the discipline and the justice for violations of those rules.

In other words, women in their own way, like Congress, legislate the rules— in their own way, like the Executive branch, enforce and administer the rules— in their own way, like the Courts, interpret the rules— of THE HOME.

Some of you, I hope, will enter public service. I hope that more women do inject themselves into their Government for certainly our Government needs more of the HOME put into it and less of the Government in the HOME.

But whether you enter public service or not, there is no finer role that you can play in the defense of Democracy and our American way of life than that of wife, mother and homemaker. Run your homes and raise your children in the very best traditions and fundamentals of our American way of life.

But don't restrict yourself to the home to the extent of exclusion of any interest or participation in public affairs and your Government. For if you do that, your indifference to your Government and to your full citizenship will be reflected in your children who grow up imitating you.

In short, in the years that you are about to enter, you can do far more than you realize to make this a better country— to keep it the wonderful Democracy that it is— to preserve our American way of life.

You don't have to ask anybody but yourself how to do it. And there is no one who can do it for you. It is your individual responsibility. More important, it is your free and cherished right. Don't let that right die for lack of exercise.

The most precious thing that Democracy gives to us is freedom. You and I cannot escape the fact that the ultimate responsibility for freedom is personal. Our freedoms today are not so much in danger because people are consciously trying to take them away from us as they are in danger because we forget to use them.

Freedom may be an intangible, but like most everything else it can die because of lack of use. Freedom unexercised may become freedom forfeited. The preservation of freedom is in the hands of people themselves now — not the Government.

"Response to Professor Fullam's 'Are You Proud?' Speech"

Throughout this campaign I have refrained from attacking my opponent. Instead I have called him honorable, capable, likable — and not a man to stoop to pettiness and meanness.

I have said that I respected him — and that I believed the campaign should be waged on issues, not personalities — and that the basic issue was the Republican record.

To my surprise and disappointment, my opponent has become increasingly personal and erroneous in his attacks on me. When I said so the other day, he accused me of trying to keep my public record private and secret — and of not revealing and discussing my record with the people.

At the end of this address I shall give you the biggest political surprise of this campaign — so keep tuned in.

Nothing could be further from the truth. I have constantly discussed my record and votes with the people — and not just at campaign election time. Every year — not just election year — I spend a month traveling throughout the State discussing my record and my votes with the people — last year I made one hundred speeches and traveled sixty-five hundred miles through all sixteen counties.

And for practically all of the time, I have been a Senator I have given the people of Maine a daily report on my record, my actions, and my votes in the form of the daily column I wrote and which was carried by all major daily papers in Maine. In addition to that I have made a Monthly Report to the people in all of the Maine weekly newspapers.

And I call the attention of my opponent to the little primary campaign pamphlet that I distributed which gives my record explicitly and in detail.

I ask my opponent, "Who can match this in reporting and discussing one's record?"

Now as to his denial that he has made personal attacks on me — let's

look at his record. On August 4 in Portland, according to the Lewiston *Sun*,
my opponent said I was unfit to be Senator. He has accused me of "mon-
strous injustice." On television he accused me of lacking in conscience. At
Waterville on August 15 he accused me of "half-truths."

On television on August 27 he accused me of serving the interests of
the Communists — of playing right into their hands. In Lubec on August 10
he accused me of insincerity on Quoddy. In Biddeford on August 22 he
accused me of lacking understanding and being inconsistent. On September
5 in Portland he accused me of playing politics with national defense and
being trivial. On August 29 in Portland he called my record "a sorry one" in
a telecast with Massachusetts Senator Kennedy.

In Portland on a telecast later that night he said derisively that I had
done "a snow job." In Washington County he accused me of neglect.

Perhaps he reached the peak of his personal attack on me at
Rumford on September 1 with a set of questions designed to shame me
publicly. He challenged me to answer a series of "Are you proud?" questions.
Here are my answers.

In these questions he literally pointed a finger of shame at me and
made grave misrepresentations. First he asked challengingly, "Are you proud
of your State with his rising unemployment rate?" To use a harsh word, that
is a lie. The unemployment rate in Maine is not rising — the truth is that it
is falling. For the last four months it has decreased each month from 9.2
percent in May to 5.1 percent in August — in other words, it decreased 4.1
percent. If that trend of decrease continues it would drop to 1 percent by the
end of 1954.

These are authentic statistics from the Bureau of Employment
Security of the U.S. Labor Department.

Another "finger of shame" question my opponent challenged me to
answer was "Are you proud that you voted to recommit the Taft-Hartley Act
Amendments? Again this is a lie. I did not vote to recommit. I voted against
recommitting — the opposite of the way my opponent charges I did — check
page 5859 of the Congressional Record of May 7, 1954. Ironically enough, by
your question, Professor Fullam, you actually condemn all forty-eight
Democratic Senators for all of them were for to recommit.

Another "finger of shame" question my opponent challenged me to
answer was "Are you proud that you voted for Foreign Aid cuts?" Well, my
answer is this, Professor Fullam — look at pages 12495, 12496, and 13802 of
the *Congressional Record* of August 3 and 14, 1954, where the Foreign Aid
votes are recorded, and you will find that I did not vote to cut Foreign Aid
but instead that I voted all three times against cutting Foreign Aid.

You are entitled to disagree with my votes but you have no right to
misrepresent my record when I voted against the one-billion-dollar cut
proposed by Democratic Senator Long, against the 500-million-dollar cut
proposed by Democratic Senator Long, and against the 200-million-dollar cut

proposed by Democratic Senator Maybank.

Another "finger of shame" question my opponent challenged me to answer was "Are you proud that you voted for the 20-million cut for TB [tuberculosis] control?" Again this is a lie. I did not vote for any such cut. The truth is that such a cut has never been proposed or voted on since the TB control program started in 1944. The truth is that Congress this year voted two and a half million dollars more for TB control than the Budget requested. I voted for more and not less.

Another "finger of shame" question my opponent challenged me to answer was "Are you proud that you voted for the cut in the school lunch program?" Again the truth is that I did not vote for such a cut. There was no proposal to cut the school lunch program. Your shame question literally implies that I voted to take food from the mouths of our school children. Nothing could be further from the truth. In this Congress I voted for measures totaling 283 million dollars for food for children in the lunch program.

Another "finger of shame" question my opponent challenged me to answer was "Are you proud that you voted against 75 percent parity for dairy farmers and for 90 percent parity for cotton and peanut oil?" Again, Professor Fullam, you are not being truthful with such a question. There was no vote taken on the question of "75 percent parity for dairy farmers." And I did not vote "for 90 percent of parity for cotton and peanut oil."

The only other "finger of shame" question my opponent was reported by the papers to have asked me at Rumford was "Are you proud of your vote against the Kennedy Amendment?" This is the only one of your questions in which you accurately stated my vote, Professor Fullam. I voted on the Kennedy Amendment just like the Senate leaders of the Democratic Party on which ticket you are running — I voted the same way that the Senate Democratic Leader and the Senate Democratic Assistant Leader voted — against the Kennedy Amendment.

Yes, I voted the same way the overwhelming majority of the Senate Finance Committee — the expert group in the Senate on this subject matter — voted — 14 to 1 against the Kennedy Amendment. You point a finger of shame with this question not only at me but at the Democratic Leadership and the acknowledged experts, both Democrats and Republicans alike, on this Senate vote. We voted the way we did to uphold the principle set originally by a Democratic Senate that the Federal Government should not invade States' rights on this matter.

He talks sarcastically of what he calls "glamour by association." Yet, he himself has sought political advantage by association with respected people by bringing on his television program to support him a Massachusetts Senator and a most respected retired President of one of our great colleges. The interesting thing that these two telecast associates of his do not have his shame of me.

For within a week after he had the Massachusetts Senator on his telecast that very Massachusetts Senator publicly commended my actions and acts in behalf of the best interest of Maine and New England. And the greatly respected retired college President has many times praised my record and even handed me an honorary Doctor of Laws degree from his institution two years ago.

And on this point of "glamour by association" in which you attempt to ridicule me, Professor Fullam, I note that on your campaign posters you brag of your membership in the American Political Science Association. Now you may be ashamed of me — but the members of that group of which you are so proud of your association — the members of that group disagree with your shame of me — because they once took a poll in rating Senators and they rated me the Sixth Best of all of the ninety-six members of the United States Senate.

My opponent accused me of insincerity on Quoddy — he accused me of having killed Quoddy. He says that he has done more on Quoddy than I have — that he has done more by merely reading a report on Quoddy. And interestingly enough, he brings the late President Roosevelt into this campaign in talking about action for the forgotten man.

But he doesn't tell you that I have accomplished more on Quoddy legislation than President Roosevelt ever did. Even at the height of his power with his rubber-stamp Congress, President Roosevelt could not get the Senate to pass Quoddy legislation. In sharp contrast, this year I got Quoddy legislation passed unanimously by the Senate — not one vote against it. And not long ago at my request the Senate okayed and appropriated funds for a preliminary survey of Quoddy.

My opponent derides me for voting for the Maybank Amendment which proposed banning the letting of Government contracts to people who do not submit the lowest bid — thus for saving the money of the people, the taxpayers. Well, I hope you good people in Bath listen to this. The Maybank Amendment was designed to prevent such things as the loss last February by Bath of those three destroyers to Quincy, Massachusetts, even though the Quincy bid was 6.5 million dollars higher.

Is my opponent interested in Maine and Bath or in Massachusetts and Quincy? Has the Massachusetts Senator he had on his telecast completely captivated him to the cause of Massachusetts? Would my opponent be more interested in representing Massachusetts than in representing Maine?

My opponent has accused me of playing politics with national security and in effect of being an enemy of air power because last year I ultimately accepted the word of President Eisenhower whose military genius led us to victory in World War II — the word of the Secretary of Defense — the word of the Secretary of the Air Force — and the word of the Chief of Staff, the ranking General of the Air Force — on the safe size of our Air Force for National Defense.

He would have a hard time convincing members of the Air Force who watched me back in 1949 as one of a small band of nine Senators who fought for a seventy-group Air Force when the then Democratic President cut the Air Force down to forty-eight groups over the vigorous protest of the then Secretary of the Air Force. He would have a hard time convincing Secretary of Defense Wilson who thinks I am too prejudiced for the Air Force by the sharp and pointed questions I have asked him.

For your information, Professor Fullam, I am not an enemy of Air Power. Instead I have been acknowledged by such organizations as the Air Reserve Association and the Air Force Association to be a Champion for Air Power. For your information, Sir, I am a Lieutenant Colonel in the Air Force Reserve.

My opponent charges that I have played right into the hands of the Communists— in effect, that I have served the cause of the Communists. He says that I did so by introducing legislation proposing consideration of a ban on imports of the then outrageously high-priced coffee from the then Communist—controlled government of Guatemala.

Well, here in very short time, history proved the History Professor to be wrong — for the stern stand of America on the Communist-controlled government of Guatemala, as exemplified by my legislation, led to the downfall and overthrow of the Communists in Guatemala. And more than that, the price of coffee has now dropped sharply.

Thus history is against the contention made by History Professor Fullam as was the word of the specialist on the subject — the word of our top official in Guatemala — our Ambassador to Guatemala — a North Carolina Democrat— who came to me and told me that I could not possibly know how much my legislation had done to arouse the feeling of the good people of Guatemala against the Communist-controlled government and how it stirred them on to finally overthrow that Government and kick the Communists out.

My opponent would have you believe that Maine has not gotten any appreciable Federal business during my service in Congress. Well, what does he call all of the tremendous volume of shipbuilding work at Bath and Kittery — the three-destroyer contract in June to Bath, the atomic submarine to Kittery — the establishment of multimillion-dollar air bases at Limestone, Presque Isle, Bangor, and Brunswick — million of dollars for Maine potato growers?

My opponent would have you believe that I have turned my back on education and teachers. He tries to make out such a case by my votes on Tideland legislation. In the first place, I ask him to check with Democratic Senator Lister Hill, the author of the Bill "Oil for the Lamps of Learning" Amendment, who will tell him that every time that amendment has come up for a vote I have voted for it.

When the amendment has lost in spite of my vote for it, I have voted for the bill because I wanted to preserve and protect for the State of Maine all of the natural resources of its more than two-thousand-mile coast— if such could not be given to the schools — rather than turning it over to the Federal Government.

It is not entirely impossible that some day oil may be discovered off the coast of Maine as it has been in Texas, Louisiana, and California — and in such event surely we would want the millions of dollars of that oil income to be given to Maine schools and for use by Maine people rather than turned over to the Federal Government.

My opponent not only should but actually does know better than to accuse me of turning my back on schools. He knows of my unbroken support of Federal Aid to Education as I stood together with Senator Taft on this. He knows of my constant support of legislation for school construction, school lunches, and other educational measures. He knows that I am a former school teacher myself.

More than that — he has personal knowledge of how I have worked in Washington for the very school where he has so long taught — Colby College. He also knows of how I have made fund-raising speeches for his Colby College. In spite of this personal firsthand knowledge, he would have you believe that I have not extended a helping hand to the schools of Maine.

In derogation he has asked me if I am proud of my record and indicated that I should be ashamed of it and that the people of Maine should be ashamed of it. Well, the colleges of Maine are not ashamed of me— they are proud enough that his own great Colby College gave me an honorary degree of Master of Arts, Honoris Causa, in commendation of my congressional record citing me for statesmanship and devotion to duty.

Bowdoin College— the great institution once headed by a great man who appeared on one of your telecasts — was proud enough of me to award an honorary degree of Doctor of Laws, Honoris Causa, to me in 1952 citing my common sense and good judgment and expressing specifically its high regard for me — yes, and your telecast guest, who has often praised my record, handed that degree to me.

The University of Maine of which all Maine is so proud also disagrees with your shame of me, Professor Fullam — for it has expressed its pride in my record by awarding me an honorary Doctor of Laws degree with the citation calling me a conscientious leader true to my heritage.

No, Professor Fullam, you may be ashamed of my Senatorial record — but your own college is proud of my record— your own associates in your American Political Science Association are proud of my record— your own former newspaper of which you are so proud of your association with, the New York Times, has commended my record repeatedly — even the Massachusetts Senator you had on your telecast publicly commended my record within a week after that telecast— even the greatly respected retired college President that you had on a telecast has commended my record.

And now we come to you, yourself— Professor Fullam — what do you think about my record if you brush aside all the political campaign talk you have been making? Do you really believe that I am unfit to be Senator as the Lewistown Sun reported you as saying?

I can't bring myself to really believe that you mean those things you have said about my record and me. I can't believe that you really think I am unfit to be Senator— when I look at this notarized and sworn— to document I hold in my hand— sworn to on January 27, 1954. It is one of my primary nomination papers.

You signed that primary paper representing that you were a member of the Republican Party and that you were proposing my nomination for United States Senator and the nomination of no one else but Margaret Chase Smith. Yours is signature No. 32— which I point to— your own handwriting — Paul Fullam, Sidney, Maine.

Now you either misrepresented yourself as being a Republican when you signed one of my primary nomination papers— or you were a Republican at that time and because of that you couldn't even vote in the Democratic primary this past June for yourself.

You have not revealed this to the people of Maine whose vote you seek— in your campaigning throughout the State you have not revealed this to the Democratic voters or the Independent voters or the Republican voters. Yet, you have accused me of hiding my record behind generalities.

If you feel that I am unfit to be Senator then why did you sign my primary paper? If you feel that my votes — most of which predate your signing that paper — were so reprehensible then why did you propose my nomination for United States Senator? Why did you wait until after the Democratic nomination had been offered to you to attack such votes of mine and take issue with them?

You talk of the need for a strong two-party system in Maine. Is this the way to build a strong two-party system— by representing yourself to be a Republican and proposing the nomination of a person and then three months later becoming the Democratic opponent of the very person you proposed for nomination?

In closing, I ask you voters of Maine, especially you Democrats: Who has been honest with you about records, both voting and party affiliation? My opponent in his "finger of shame" attacks on my votes has actually attacked your Democratic leaders in the Senate for they voted the same way I did on so many of the votes my opponent criticizes.

You know what you are voting for when you vote for me. But do you know what you are voting for if you vote for my opponent?

I appeal to all voters — Republicans, Democrats, and Independents alike — to go to the polls tomorrow — to get your friends to the polls tomorrow— to show what you think of unfair misrepresentations and to roll up a victory for Margaret Chase Smith for United States Senator.

"Celebrating the Fortieth Anniversary"

Being with you tonight on the fortieth anniversary of the B.P.W. it is really an opportunity I appreciate. We can look back on those forty years with considerable pride and satisfaction. For in that time B.P.W. has accomplished so much for the just cause of women — and has contributed so much to the betterment of living conditions and good Government.

The results speak for themselves. For example, it was just a year after 1919 that suffrage was gained for women in 1920. That achievement would never have been realized had it not been for the valiant and effective efforts of the B.P.W.

On this fortieth anniversary, we might take a look back at 1919. This was the year after the end of World War I. It was the year of the First Session of the Sixty-sixth Congress. Woodrow Wilson was serving his sixth year as President of the United States. One of Maine's United States Senators came from this area of Maine — Senator Bert M. Fernald of West Poland. The other Senator was Frederick Hale of Portland.

The Congressman from this District was Wallace H. White, Jr., of Lewistown — who was later to become United States Senator — and who was later to be succeeded in the Senate by myself. The other Congressmen from Maine were Louis B. Goodall of Sanford, John A. Peters of Ellsworth and Ira G. heirs of Houlton.

Not only did the B.P.W. help get suffrage a year after its formation but by the time of its thirtieth anniversary in 1949 it had put a women — and more specifically one of its own members — in the United States Senate. No one should make the slightest mistake about this — for I say to you that I could never have been elected to the United State Senate without the tremendous drive that the Maine B.P.W. did for me.

And I shall never forget the B.P.W. campaign in 1952 to make me Vice President. Of course, it meant much to me personally. But it was far more important than being a personal matter. It was an advance for women generally as I was only a symbol of that advance. The real story on that B.P.W. campaign has never been revealed because there was not an open convention in 1952 on the vice presidential convention. It was closed convention as General Eisenhower decided that he desired to have Senator Nixon as his Vice Presidential running mate and so no other nominations were permitted for Vice President other than that of Senator Nixon.

Had it been an open convention on the Vice Presidential nomination — like the 1956 Democratic National Convention was an open convention when Adlai Stevenson said that he would make no choice but would leave that open to the convention — there might have been some very dramatic developments rivaling the thrilling Kefauver-Kennedy battle for the Democratic Vice Presidential nomination.

Because the 1952 vice presidential nomination was closed and not left open to the convention after General Eisenhower announced his decision that he wanted Senator Nixon on the ticket, it was never publicly revealed that the handful of B.P.W. women at the convention in the short time of a very few days at the convention had achieved the tremendous success of getting 250 delegates pledged to vote for the B.P.W. candidate for Vice President.

This was not a tribute to me. Instead it was dramatic proof of the ability of the B.P.W. to get results once the members of the B.P.W. set their minds on a specific goal. It may be several years more. But you will not be denied and some day at the B.P.W. will not only get a woman nominated for Vice President but will get that women elected Vice President.

And when that day comes that a woman is sworn in as President of the United States — and it certain to come — the only question is how soon — it will have been largely because of the determined efforts of the members of the B.P.W.

The most important role of a woman is that of wife, mother and keeper of the home. It is in that role that woman exercises the greatest influence on our country. It is mostly an unseen influence. Yes, it is mostly an influence that is not recognized or credited.

Nothing should detract in the slightest from this precious role of woman in our civilization. But recognition and respect for this role should not mean that woman should be restricted solely to the role of wife, mother and keeper of the house.

Far from it. There is a great need for woman — and her talents — outside the home and the family. What would business do without women? What would industry do without women and their special talents? Right here in Lewiston the importance of women in industry is underscored by the fact that eighty percent of the employees of the new Raytheon plant will be women.

As for the importance of women in Government, look at your own Maine State Legislature where such B.P.W. leaders as Lucia Cormier have made outstanding records of accomplishment — look at the impressive record of Marion Martin as Commissioner of Labor and Industry.

In the field of journalism note the success of Jean Gannett Williams, publisher of the Gannett papers — and Mrs. Jordan, the inspiring leader of the *Bangor Daily News* — and the women leaders of weekly newspapers such as Dorothy Roberts of Damariscotta and Lena Harvey of Fort Fairfield.

I could go down the list — business by business, profession by profession, avocation by avocation — and cite other equally inspiring success stories of demonstrated ability of women on matters outside the home. But to do so it would require all the rest of the evening and more. I wish that I could because naming just a few as I have doesn't do justice to those many, many successful women leaders that I haven't mentioned.

Is there something special about a woman— something different that makes her more proficient than men in business and professional matters? Before attempting to answer that, let me first say that, as many of you know and recognize, I am not a feminist.

I am not a feminist because I do not believe that is the best and most effective way to advance the cause of women. That's why I favor Equal Rights legislation over Equal Pay for Equal Work. That's why I say that when we, as women, asked and demanded equal rights we cannot at the same time insist upon the retention of special feminine privileges.

I have often summed this up by the very simple statement that "women are people — just as much as men are people." In other words, whether a woman is the best choice for a certain position such as the head of a business firm or a public office is to be determined strictly upon the basis of qualifications rather than the basis of sex.

That is why I say that women will not vote for a woman candidate for public office just because she is woman. Women will support only qualified women for public office. Women will not vote as a bloc for a woman they do not consider qualified for the position sought.

On the other hand, women rightly take great pride in any woman who does a good job in a prominent position. They do because creditable performance by one woman reflects great credit upon women as a whole. It proves what women can do if they are given the opportunity.

If there is any one distinction between the mental make-up of women and men it is in the temperament of women to be perfectionists. Women, generally, are not satisfied in their work unless they have done the very best possible job.

By this I do not mean that men are slack in their mental attitude toward their work or that they are content with anything less than a competent performance. To the contrary, men are just as determined as women to do a good job.

I think the difference comes on such a matter as the details. Men are inclined not to worry about the details and instead to concentrate on the overall result. In contrast, women worry about the details. They want to attend to every aspect of a problem — just like they want their house to be spic and span neat.

If anyone has the slightest doubt about this general difference between men and women, I suggest that he take a good look at how a business office is run — to see who it is that tends to the very important details that make a business run and produce the results on the most important business decisions and policies.

Is it the President or the Chairman of the Board — or is it the secretary to the President or the Chairman? The point need not be labored one bit more. The answer is obvious.

The story is told about the husband who told a pollster that he made the important and overall decisions in his home and family — and that he left the minor decisions to his wife. The pollster was a curious and persistent woman who was not content with this general answer.

So true to the characteristic of women wanting to get at the details, she probed further by asking, "What are the important decisions that you make — and what are the minor decisions that you let your wife make?"

The husband took a long puff on his cigar and with deep meditation replied, "Oh, I worry about such important things as where we stand in the space race — what is the status of our missile program — the Berlin crisis, the Chinese invasion of Tibet, Laos and India — on how we are going to settle the steel strike.

"My wife makes the decisions on such minor matters as my pay check, the paying of the grocery bill and the monthly payments on the house and the utilities, and where and how we are going to send the children to college."

Another example of how we women pay more attention to details than men do was brought home to me once when my own Assistant said to me, "Yes, Senator, you are just like the 99 men Senators in most respects. You handle the same duties. You have the same responsibilities. But there is one great
difference.

"The other 99 Senators don't worry about wearing the right clothes to the very details of matching hat, gloves, and pocketbook for each dress or suit as you do. You're just as much a Senator as the other 99 but you can't get over being a woman."

He is right. And that's the way I want it. I want to be treated equally with the other 99 Senators — without any special favors. But I don't want to forget that I am a woman — and I want to always be a lady — even if it means worrying about the details of being dressed correctly and as attractively as possible.

I want to keep the respect of both women and men — including the 99 other Senators. I want to be as thoughtful as I possibly can of everyone else and to please them as much as possible. And, in my opinion, that requires attention to details. That's why I am glad that women are naturally sticklers for details.

It is the natural temperament of women. It is an asset. But its effectiveness is only as great as is the training of that temperament for details. It is on this score that I am so grateful to the B.P.W. For nothing gave me such meticulous and valuable training on efficient tending to details as my work in the B.P.W.

The B.P.W. taught me how to work with people — and how to perform the details on getting things done for the people. So that if I have achieved any efficiency on getting things done for the people of Maine in my job in the Senate, it is greatly because of what the B.P.W. instilled in me.

"Nuclear Credibility" (1961)

Mr. President:

What I am about to say is addressed not only to the members of the United States Senate but to all Americans — and most specifically to the President of the United States.

Many times during the last decade or more we have been able to draw comfort from knowing we had strength and will that could command the world's respect and deter the Communists. But recently history is not reassuring. Ominous signs plague us.

Everywhere the Communists press forward stronger. Khrushchev, vowing to take over the world for communism, and acting with all the confidence of a winner, threatens to put an end to civilized survival for the world if we do not let him have his way.

In an effort to generate global enthusiasm for submission he has stained the sky and polluted the air with nuclear bursts.

At the dividing line in Berlin he has dared to make a frontal attack on freedom.

In speaking of the future he has embraced the risks of dire threats and ultimatums.

It is a grim spectacle such as we have never seen.

My purpose in asking your attention today is not to emphasize that this is a time of corroding fears and tensions.

— You know this as well as I do.

It is not to suggest that I have some special talent which permits me to see clearly the way out of the never-never land between high hope and deep despair, into which we have wandered.

— That would be presumptuous of me;

— But although we do not yet know a way out, I am sure the time has come *to find a way out*, and to go once again to the high ground we enjoyed just a short time ago.

My purpose is not to recite our List of Losses in the great conflict with World Communism.

— Being a long list, it is painfully evident, not only to us but to the rest of the world; and its implications are frightening.

My purpose is not to recite facts that all of us know well enough, but to pose a vital question, the answers for which none of us yet knows well enough.

— Not a question that I have composed, but which suggests itself.

— Not a question of selfish or parochial origin.

— But one far more important.

— A question of national interest.

The question for which I urge your attention is spawned from the ugly union of communism's answering ambition and its unscrupulous methods.

The implications of this question have put a chill into the hearts of millions who yearn for peace, yet it is spoken by few of us.

It now demands our attention.

While we still have time we must examine it to its deepest foundations, its remotest associations.

We must do this now.

If we fail to do it now, we may not be free to do it later on.

It is a question that challenges us to merciless objectivity and realism.

It is a challenge that is addressed not only to us who are here today. It is addressed to every American; in fact, to every free man and woman . . . and to every person who yearns to know what freedom is, or to regain a freedom wrested from him by force, or lost to him by inaction or bad advice.

What we learn from our examination, what we do about it — or *fail* to do — may be the difference for us between peace or war, win or lose, fear or freedom, and perhaps even life or death.

We must look at it against the backdrop of Khrushchev's reckless confidence, against the foul clouds of his nuclear blackmail blasts; then we can see the question I am about to pose to you as the most crucial the American people have faced since the Declaration of Independence launched us as the United States into the world of nations . . . not the strongest, not the largest; but nevertheless confident, firm, and fearing no one.

The question which is posed to all of us, the question for which we *must* find the right answers across the board — realistically and urgently — is this:

— *What has happened that permits Khrushchev to act as he does?* Let me repeat:

— *WHAT HAS* HAPPENED that lets him do it?

Understand me, please. Not what is he *doing*. We know that only too well. Our national honor bears the scars and stains of what he is doing now and has done in the past. And he has warned us, arrogantly, of what he intends to do in the future, which is even worse.

These things we know.

— But today — now — why does he feel free to do as he does? . . .
WHY?

This also we must know. And if we do not know, we are likely to lose all control over shaping our future. Worse, we may lose our future itself.

We have been exhorted to have the moral courage to live with continuing conflict. No true American will argue otherwise, nor doubt that we are equal to the rigors of our moment in history. But let us also make sure we have the courage to go straight to the reasons *why* the conflict so often runs against us and burdens us so heavily . . . why Khrushchev so often has the initiative and we are satisfied only to *react*.

I sense a tendency, strange to the American character in world affairs, to retreat from circumstances rather than to face up to them realistically and master them. I am greatly disturbed by it. I am sure we can assume that Khrushchev is greatly pleased by it.

So let us here and now make a start on our examination of the question I have posed, by asking a related question:

— Is Khrushchev free to act as he does because the Soviets have *suddenly* gained the over-all military advantage?

I say no.

The primary determinant for over-all military advantage today is the capacity for total nuclear war.

No matter how fervently Khrushchev, we, the nonaligneds, or anyone else would like to make it different, this is an inescapable fact and we must face it firmly and deal with it realistically.

No matter what the immediate objectives may be, no matter in what circumstances a critical conflict situation might develop, it is the capacity which both of us — the United States and the USSR — must put into the scales first. And until the day comes when there is much more faith and goodwill in the world than there is today, it will invariably be the weight which tips the scales one way or the other . . . for us or against us —

— Toward winning or losing;
— Toward resoluteness or retreat;
— Toward firmness or passivity;
— Toward strength or submission.

It is generally agreed that as of today the over-all military advantage rests with us and our allies. We may be sure the Soviets also recognize this fact. When they undertake to assess their risks in any venture that they contemplate— Berlin, Laos, Africa, the Middle East, Cuba— they must begin at the top, with that for which their fears are greatest and their chances smallest. It is as true for them as it is for us that they cannot hide from realism.

All of us rightly fear that the conflict may go to the ultimate level of total nuclear war. No one can say whether or not this is the destiny of our generation.   God grant that it is not.   None can doubt that we are in grave danger, but this I feel strongly:

— We are, as the President has said, engaged in a contest of will and purpose as well as force and violence.

— If today, and in the days immediately ahead, we *fail* to meet the Soviets at the ultimate levels of *will and purpose*, the danger will be greatly widened that we will have no choice later on but to meet them at the ultimate levels of *force and violence*; either that or submit to their will.   How much farther do you think Khrushchev would go today, how much faster would he move, if he was confident the over-all military advantage was on his side and not ours? . . . If he did not have to worry about the risk of acting dangerously without having the over-all military advantage?

Let me say it again:

— *The over-all military advantage is on our side.* But the day we lose sight of this fact, we are in danger of frightening ourselves . . . of being mesmerized by Khrushchev's confidence and *deterring ourselves* instead of deterring the Soviets.   While we are concerned with all that might happen to us, we must never forget that *Khrushchev also has reason to be afraid; and the main reason is plain:*

— There is a grim prospect indeed for a postwar USSR stripped of its strength and reduced to a third-or-fourth-rate nation, even though in the process of losing it he has wrought great damage on us.   This is the *choice he must face.*

To say that the Kremlin's risks are great does not make our own risks less.   But it does encourage perspective and this is important.

The risks run both ways.   This is not enough to eliminate the conflict; I believe the Communists will always go as far and as fast as we indicate we will permit them to go.   But it does create an environment in which our deterrence can be effective, if we are firm enough, if our will and purpose are equal to the test.

I am disturbed that there are some who say in effect, we can do *more* in deterring the Soviets by preparing to do *less* against them if they should provoke armed hostilities.   I refer specifically to the highly articulate and persuasive zealots who argue that increasing conventional forces is the best way to create more effective deterrence.   They believe that flexibility in the application of military force can come only from conventional forces.

— I know of nothing in political or military history which supports a thesis that it is safer to be weak than strong.

— Until the Soviets change their ways and join the society of respectable nations, I see no hope of deterring them by making the risks they must face *less fearful* for them.

— I know of no reason why we should be driven to a concept which — no matter how it is phrased — means that in order to prove our determination we would risk sacrificing the lives of men in the battle line rather than risk holding the enemy against the prospect that is most fearful to him.

That is weak choice of risks for the strongest people in the world.

What is the origin of this fear of risks? It is not part of our heritage.

The greatness of this country was not won by people who were afraid of risks. It was won for us by men and women with little physical power at their command who nevertheless were willing to submit to risks. Could it not be lost for us by people with great physical power at their command but nevertheless willing to risk submitting? I believe it could.

So may I plead once more for perspective. Nothing has happened which suddenly has transferred the power of the overall military advantage from us to the Soviets. *We can defeat the USSR at any intensity of armed conflict unless we have degraded our fighting capacity greatly by self-imposed restrictions, such as restrictions on the use of tactical nuclear weapons.*

Our words concerning early use of tactical nuclear weapons if required can be invalidated quickly if our actions demonstrate that our major efforts and investments in time of great peril, such as now, are directed mainly towards increases in conventional forces.

Mr. President, brave words are fine — but action speaks louder than words and deters Khrushchev much more.

We have the military basis for clearly demonstrating our will and purpose . . . for making deterrence work. But we will never deter the Soviets by backing away, or by offering to fight *on their terms* because we are fearful of provoking them by indicating beyond all doubt that we will fight, if fight we must, on *our terms*.

I would be the first to urge great caution; but I would also be the first to urge great firmness, and the last to cease opposing the submission of the unlimited interests of 180 million Americans to the stupidity of limited deterrence. There are other countries, once free, that have learned too late that the ultimate cost of partial security can be total defeat, or subjugation.

I repeat that it is not military *strength suddenly* acquired by the Soviets which permits Khrushchev to act as he does.

Is it then that our military strength has suddenly deteriorated?

— Have we been *suddenly* weakened?

Again I say no.

Every military authority presently responsible for our military posture will attest that our forces are stronger, not weaker; more alerted and ready, not *less* prepared.

— We cannot conclude that *this* gives Khrushchev cause for his reckless confidence. . . . He has not *won* the military advantage from us, and it has not *accrued* to him through our own military deficiencies.

So we must go further and ask yet another question:

— *Is it conceivable that Khrushchev could assess that the will of the American people has collapsed?*

— That we are ready to submit?

— That he can win with blackmail?

— That Americans, as the saying goes, would rather be RED than dead?

How do you respond to a question as impossible as this?

And yet it must be asked, for, as I have said, we must examine the fundamental question I have posed to its deepest foundations.

— *What has happened that permits Khrushchev to act as he does?*

— What gives Khrushchev his ticket to such great confidence?

— What does he assess about us that makes him so sure?

— What have we indicated to him that causes him to be so arrogant . . . to take such wide risks, in our view, in going so far?

If we hold the military advantage, why, you may well ask, is our deterrence not more effective? What's the reason it is not?

The reason is that deterrence is not a matter of forces and firepower alone. The restraints and influence are projected from the capacity to accomplish a purpose; *not just from what we have but from what we will do.*

— Deterrence cannot be regarded as an assured fact. It is a sensitive condition, always subject to proof.

Nevertheless there are influential advocates of the so-called stable deterrence.

I believe such proposals to be, at worst, demonstrably false and, at best, highly questionable.

We are dealing with military power on both sides that is infinitely complicated, composed of many critical elements. This power itself floats on a sea of uncertainty, constantly subject to the restless tides of progress and the tidal waves of great change. *To say that we can count on achieving and maintaining a balance or stability in these conditions — even if we had the Soviets' cooperation, much less their opposition — is nothing short of wishful thinking . . . a form of "nuclear escapism" to dodge the hard, cold facts.*

I am frightened by inferences that we can get rid of the nuclear peril by this device of sweeping it under the rug. I fear it would trip us and catch us off balance sooner or later.

We must examine yet another facet of this critical situation, namely, what is it that Khrushchev most likely assesses from what our spokesmen say, in the context of what we do and fail to do?

— What are the measures that we have taken to convince him, and the rest of the world, of our will and purpose?

— What kind of raw material have we provided for Khrushchev to analyze, study, assess, and use as a basis for his conclusions and actions?

I recall some of the inspiring words of the President's inaugural address, as our nation turned with high hope toward this year 1961. Specifically:

"[T]o those nations which would make themselves our adversary, we offer not a pledge but a request; that both sides begin anew the quest for peace, before the dark powers of destruction unleashed by science engulf all humanity in planned or accidental self-destruction.

"We dare not tempt them with weakness. For only when our arms are sufficient beyond doubt can we be certain beyond doubt that they will never be employed."

As I see the dark clouds that now hang low over the new frontiers of hope toward which the attention of Americans and the rest of the world was directed on that day, I wonder what it is that has tempted Castro to stoke the fires of hatred still higher in his communized Cuba and to challenge United States strength and influence throughout Latin America.

 — I do not *know* what Castro thinks,

 — But I doubt that he has been *tempted* by a *high* assessment of our *will and purpose.*

Like millions of Americans, I was deeply impressed with the President, when, in his televised press conference, he pointed to a map and eloquently explained why we had to stand firm on Laos.

The words were brave and inspiring— but only to be followed by no brave action to back up those words.

As I see the perils that press in on us, I wonder what it is that impelled Khrushchev to choose the moment of his return from his Vienna meeting with the President to fling into the face of the American people his ultimatum on a treaty with East Germany and thereafter to bring on the Berlin crisis.

 — I do not *know* what Khrushchev thinks,

 — But I cannot believe that he has been *tempted* in his Berlin gamble by a high assessment of our *will and purpose.*

Neither can we know how many others wonder about the course of events in much the same way as I do. But that there are others we do know, and I quote one now: Mr. Chalmers Roberts, in the *Washington Post* recently:

"Power and willingness to use it are fundamental to great nations. That the United States has the power is not doubted in Moscow, by every sign available here. But Khrushchev's latest actions indicate that he doubts the President's willingness to use it.

"And so it now appears that Khrushchev has decided to take the world to the brink for a test of will on the outcome of which may depend the future not only of West Berlin but the freedom of mankind."

We have a decided nuclear capability advantage over Khrushchev— and he knows it. Otherwise he wouldn't have resumed nuclear tests and would not have been deterred in the past in the slightest.

But he is confident we won't use it for he sees us turning to emphasis on conventional weapons— and ironically he has an obviously great superiority in conventional weapons and manpower over us.

We have in effect played into his hands — for the kind of warfare in which he knows he can beat us. We have restricted ourselves on the freedom of choice to use the nuclear tactical weapons which he knows would defeat him if he started war.

In short, we have the nuclear capability— and he knows and fears it. But we have practically told him we do not have the will to use that one power with which we can stop him.

In short, we have the nuclear capability— but not the nuclear credibility.

I recall some of the ringing words by the President in his address to the Nation last July.

Specifically:

"We cannot and will not permit the Communists to drive us out of Berlin, either gradually or by force."

I cannot know what Khrushchev thinks, what it is that influences him, what he looks for when he makes his judgments:

— But I fervently hope that he would not make his final assessment as to our will and purpose in Berlin on the basis of what he has seen and deduced from, for example, Laos and Cuba.

God forbid that the pattern of brave words on Laos and Cuba followed by no brave action be repeated on Berlin.

As fervently as I hope Khrushchev *would not* be influenced unduly by what he might assess from the record in Laos and Cuba, I hope with even greater fervency that he *would* recall other times and other places, where American strength and American will have prevailed in American purpose.

For example:

— Lebanon, in 1958, where we acted promptly and unequivocally to prevent the threatened overthrow of a government friendly to us.

Admittedly, no one can know what might have happened if our forces had not been sent promptly to the scene. *But everyone knows what did happen after they were sent there. The threatened trouble dissolved.*

— Or the Berlin airlift of 1948-49 through which the Soviets' first major effort to force us out of Berlin was defeated . . . admittedly under circumstances different from those we face today, but nevertheless by firm and prompt action under the same principles to which we are dedicated today.

— Or the offshore islands in the Straits of Formosa, where long ago our firmness was proved to the Communists beyond doubt.

I am thankful that we have such examples of will and purpose to balance the record in some degree at this vital time —

— When we can be sure that every indication of our determination or lack of it is submitted to the most critical of examinations in Moscow;

— When a miscalculation in this respect by Moscow could bring on the greatest calamity since the first day of the recorded history of mankind.

Last April, when the American Society of Newspaper Editors met in Washington, the President beautifully phrased his address to them. Referring to events associated with Castro's Cuba, he said he wanted the record to show that "our restraint is not inexhaustible."

I not only agree wholeheartedly with the President in this reflection of our feelings, but I urge that we apply the same thought most seriously in other vital considerations, because —

— Neither is our deterrent capacity inexhaustible. It must be revitalized appropriately with actions as well as with words and military forces.

— Neither can we afford to assume that the confidence of the American people is inexhaustible. We cannot expect the national will to overcome forever the enervating effects of repeated losses without its being revitalized by the new strength of meaningful victories.

I am confident that we *can* do better.

I believe with all my heart that we *can win* our objectives.

These are the reasons why I speak as I do today in appealing to all Americans — and especially to the President of the United States on the eve of his address to a United Nations that is threatened with collapse for lack of will and determination.

These are the reasons why I could not take myself away from the Senate Chamber and go back to the people whose trust I hold without making my concern known, without asking —

— How much longer can we afford to lose? When will we start to win?

— *Where* will we draw the line?

— If we fail to stand firm in Berlin . . . if we fail to stand there with *the best we have,* where in the world will we draw the line?

In the name of the courage, determination, and sacrifices of our forebears, *let us not be afraid to be right* at this critical time.

General de Gaulle made a statement in his press conference on September 6, 1961, which the leaders of the West could well consider because it exemplifies the realism and the determination that is so desperately needed. I place it in the *Record* at this point of my remarks and I invite your study of it.

I urge the President of the United States to consider these thoughts I have expressed before he makes his address to the United Nations assembly. While I agree with him that we should not negotiate from fear or fear to negotiate — I say we should not fear to refuse to negotiate on any matter that is not negotiable.

In these perilous hours, I fear that the American people are ahead of their leaders in realism and courage — but behind them in knowledge of the facts because the facts have not been given to them.

I would hope that every American would read what I have said today and would express themselves by direct correspondence to the President.

"The Kennedy Twist"

I shall begin tonight with a prologue — a prologue which you will not find in your printed copy of my speech. A prologue directed at the actions of last week.

As a Republican, I applaud the results of President Kennedy's use of the high office of the Presidency with all its enormous prestige and power to mold and marshal public opinion against a resented steel price rise. In United States Steel he couldn't have had a better political "patsy."

But I do not applaud other tactics that he resorted to in this matter — antics such as the threatening of criminal prosecution and the use of police state methods such as the FBI routing a reporter out of bed in the middle of the night.

Nor do I believe that price control should be effected by Presidential action solely on one industry. If price control is needed then the proper course is the enactment of legislation covering all the industries and business and covering wages.

For those who applaud the tactics of threat of criminal prosecution and the use of the FBI in police state methods, I would say — to the consumer housewife that if the President alone can set the price of steel, then he can set the wage that her husband receives — to the corner grocery store man or the corner drugstore man that if the President alone can set the price of steel, then he can tell them how much they can charge for a loaf of bread or a tube of toothpaste — to the members of the press that if the President or the Attorney General can order the FBI to rout a reporter out of bed in the middle of the night on a news story, then it can be done to you sometime on some news story you have written.

Strength, the American way, is not manifested by threats of criminal prosecution of police state methods.

Leadership is not mentioned by coercion, even against the resented.

Greatness is not manifested by unlimited pragmatism, which places such a high premium on the end justifying any means and any methods.

We are here tonight as a partisan group of a partisan meeting for a partisan purpose. There are those who decry partisanship. It does deserve condemnation if it is selfish and uninformed. But partisanship deserves praise and active support when it champions the advocacy of truth. For then it serves a real purpose in American life and it provides the best kind of politics and the most effective politics.

We of the Republican Party are in the minority. Because a Democrat occupies the White House, of necessity the Republican national record must be, for the greater part, written in Congress.

But even there we are the minority Party by almost a ratio of two to one. Since a Democratic-controlled Congress will not let Republican-sponsored bills out of committee to be voted upon by the House or the Senate, our only chance to write a Republican record — a Republican story — in Congress is by offering amendments and by challenging the actions of the Democratic President and the Democratic Majority when we disagree with their actions and proposals.

On those issues on which we stand solidly, we do write a Republican record. We Republicans don't always agree among ourselves because we simply have honest differences of opinions. I am thankful that there is nothing monolithic about us — and that we do not permit one man to tell us how to vote — that we reject political blackmail as we rejected it on the brazen attempt of the Democratic President to paint us as racial bigots on the issue of his proposed Urban Affairs Department.

But while we do have our internal differences of opinion, we are not as hopelessly split as is the Democratic Party — the Southern Conservatives pitted against the Northern Liberals — the Democratic Speaker against the Democratic President — the Secretary of Defense against the Democratic Chairman of the House Armed Services Committee.

Last year it was my privilege to lead a fight against a Democratic move in the Senate — a fight on which the Senate Republicans stood solidly together and voted solidly together. It was the fight against the Democratic Party's playing politics with National Defense on the West Virginia Political General Nomination.

We lost that fight by a vote of 45 to 37. But the manner in which the Democratic Party so brazenly and crassly played politics with National Defenses on this issue was so repugnant that eight Democrats could not swallow it and defied Democratic Party orders and voted against the confirmation.

Many Democratic Senators came to me before and after the vote and stated that the nomination was disgraceful but that their hands were tied as Party instructions had gone out that they had to uphold the political honor of the Democratic Governor of West Virginia and that they held their noses and looked the other way and voted for the nomination.

Yes, here was an instance on which the Republicans in the Senate wrote a legislative record loud and clear— a record of unanimous Republican rejection of playing politics with National Defense — a record of very clear opposition to that of the Democratic Party in its 45 to 8 record of putting the prestige of the Democratic Party — the Democratic Governor of West Virginia — ahead of the National Security interests of our country.

There are many other instances in which Republicans in Congress have been writing a legislative record of shining contrast to the record of Democrats in Congress. You know them and I need not review them with you.

The basic way in which any minority party writes a record is the traditional role of the loyal opposition. It is the hard way because it automatically brings down upon us the charge of obstructionism.

In that role we have the responsibility to be honest and reasonable. But we have just as much responsibility to scrutinize, carefully and independently, the proposals, the actions, and the record of the Democratic President — just as much as to maintain loyalty to the President in our loyalty to our country for we have a loyal responsibility to the people.

Yes, we even have the responsibility to remind the President of what he has or what he has not done on his promises and representation to the people when he was seeking their votes and on which promises and representations he got their votes. We have the responsibility to compare candidate promises with Presidential performance.

In his castigation of the Eisenhower Administration, Candidate John F. Kennedy uttered very, very strong words — and made unqualified statements. With those strong words and unqualified statements he won the Presidency. Having gained the authority he sought, he must now accept the responsibility for those words and statements by which he gained that authority.

Let us look at but a few of those strong words and unqualified statements of Candidate Kennedy and compare them with the actions of President Kennedy. First let us take the B-70- or RS-70-plane issue over which President Kennedy and his Democratic Chairman of the House Armed Services Committee were warring last month.

When seeking votes of B-70 aircraft workers, Candidate Kennedy said to them in San Diego on November 2, 1960, "I endorse wholeheartedly the B-70 manned aircraft." You will note two very important things about this statement. It was unqualified — and it was a vote seeking attack on the Eisenhower Administration's rejection of the proposed B-70 program.

But when he became President, John F. Kennedy reversed his position for in his press conference of March 7, 1962, President Kennedy said he felt that B-70 production would be "not the most judicious action" — and he clearly indicated that he was willing to battle Congress to the end on this issue.

While as Candidate Kennedy he attacked Eisenhower's position on the B-70 — when he became President Kennedy he adopted the very Eisenhower position he had opposed as Candidate Kennedy. He talked one way as a Candidate but acted the opposite as President.

Perhaps it would be appropriate to call this the "Kennedy Twist" — a rhythm in reverse action.

Next let us take the issue of Presidential Impounding of Defense funds voted by Congress. As Candidate Kennedy seeking votes before the National Convention of the Veterans of Foreign Wars, he made a scathing attack on the Eisenhower Administration on the Presidential impounding of Defense funds voted by Congress with the unqualified statement that "these funds must be unfrozen and spent."

Yet, just as soon as he got into office — as soon as he became President Kennedy— he did the very thing he had criticized as he impounded and froze Defense funds voted by Congress and refused to spend them. He did not practice what he preached. He did just the opposite. Again it was the "Kennedy Twist" — a rhythm in reverse action.

Next let us take the issue that he made as a Candidate about Federal Judge Appointments. In my home state of Maine at Bangor on September 2, 1960, Candidate Kennedy in an obvious appeal to Republican voters stated: "I must say that if I am elected President of the United States, I am not going to attempt to select men for positions of high leadership who happen to have the word Democrat after their names."

More specifically on Judicial Appointments he wrote the President of the American Bar Association decrying the fact that, in the past, appointments of Federal Judges have been made according to their political party and stated specifically, "I would hope that the paramount consideration in the appointment of a Judge would not be his political party but his qualifications for the office."

What is the record of President Kennedy on the promise of Candidate Kennedy not to appoint Federal Judges according to the political party— not to appoint just Democrats? It is a record that was condemned by the Federal Judiciary Committee of the American Bar Association, the very organization to whom he made his specific pledge— by a report on February 19, 1962, that condemned the Kennedy process and the lack of qualifications of Kennedy judicial appointees.

As of March 12, 1962, President Kennedy had made one hundred and eleven new lifetime Federal Judge appointments and of this number the score was 111 to 0 — one hundred and eleven to zero — against the Republicans with not a single Republican in this group of Kennedy appointments. Since that time he has made three or four Republican appointments.

President Kennedy did the very opposite of what he promised as Candidate Kennedy and so appointed Federal Judges on the basis of Democratic politics that his record has been condemned by the Federal

Judiciary Committee of the American Bar Association.

And significantly enough, it is a condemnation that President Kennedy must share with his 1960 Campaign Manager, brother Robert Kennedy, who became Attorney General and second only to President Kennedy on control of the Federal Judge selections and appointments.

Again it is the "Kennedy Twist" — with the additional terpsichorean movement to the "Kennedy Twist" being that this time it is a duet of the Kennedy brothers.

Next let us take the issue made by Candidate Kennedy on Presidential appointees staying on the job for the duration. Repeatedly Candidate Kennedy criticized Eisenhower appointees for leaving the positions to which they had been appointed.

In Springfield, Ohio, on October 17, 1960, Candidate Kennedy emphasized and underscored his point with the statement of "Preference in appointments will be given to those willing to commit themselves to stay on the job long enough to apply what they learn. The goal is a full-time effort for the full tenure of the Presidential term."

Yet, what happened to the first Kennedy Secretary of the Navy? Did he remain enlisted for the duration? Did he "stay on the job long enough to apply what" he had learned? Did he give "full-time effort for the full tenure of the Presidential term"? Did President Kennedy insist that he stay on the job as Secretary of the Navy?

Did the Kennedy performance and requirement as President match up with Candidate Kennedy's promise? The answer to all of these questions is "No!" For the first Secretary of the Navy left the job in less than a year — and with the full blessing of President Kennedy — and quit to run for what the two of them agreed was a higher duty than that of service to the United States on our national Defense — to run for Governor of Texas.

Yes, and now he is engaged with that other pre-eminent Democrat, Major General Edwin A. Walker, who left the National Defense effort to run for Governor of Texas. They are now engaged in mortal political combat to see who is to be the Democratic leader of Texas.

Yes, again it is the "Kennedy Twist" — this time done to the tune of "Deep in the Heart of Texas."

Now let us take the issue that Candidate Kennedy made on interest rates. On September 7, 1960, in Salem, Oregon, Candidate Kennedy made the flat and unqualified statement of "[W]e will reverse the disastrous high interest rate-tight money policies of the Republican Party."

Compare that with the *New York Times* issue of March 17, 1962, reporting a statement of Democratic Senator Albert Gore the day before with "Senator Albert Gore, Democrat of Tennessee, said today that to his 'disappointment and regret' the Treasury under the Kennedy Administration was continuing the high interest rate policies of the Eisenhower Regime."

Yes, again it is the "Kennedy Twist" with President Kennedy adopting the very interest rate policies that he had attacked as Candidate Kennedy — but this time the "Kennedy Twist" was not compatible with the square dance tempo of that noted Tennessee fiddler Albert Gore.

Next, let us turn to the subject of nepotism. With the Kennedy Administration's record on this I could talk all night. But first let me say that I do not condemn nepotism, provided the relatives really work.

After all, I am a product of nepotism — a living symbol of nepotism — for I wouldn't be in the Senate today had I not been a $3000-a-year secretary to my late husband when he was in the House — and I have a relative by marriage on my staff. We both have earned our pay.

But Candidate Kennedy condemned nepotism in strong and unqualified language on October 18, 1960, to the Washington news, which was waging an exposé crusade against nepotism, as he said, "Nepotism is dangerous to the public interest and to our national morality."

Keep your perspective on this. As a candidate he condemned nepotism unqualifiedly. But as President he acted the opposite — and it isn't necessary to run through the long list with you. Suffice is to say that it is a little more exclusive than the so-called social "400."

Yes, again it is the "Kennedy Twist" — this time instead of being just a duet of the two senior Kennedy brothers, a regular conga line has been formed that at times stretches clear around the world.

Now let us turn to the Kennedy-pressed issue of secrecy in government. Candidate Kennedy repeatedly castigated the Eisenhower Administration on what he alleged to be inexcusable secrecy in government. At Mount Clemens, Michigan, on October 26, 1960, he said, "I believe that the American people in 1960 are entitled to the truth, the truth with the bark off, the facts of the matter."

Yet on April 19, 1961, the newspaper editors of our country condemned President Kennedy for violating promises of an open-door information policy with the statement that John F. Kennedy "was on record in writing as believing in freedom of information and in his duty to see that the people are informed. To date, neither he nor his Administration has lived up to his promise."

Less than two weeks later on the April 30, 1961, "Meet the Press" television and radio program, the Democratic Chairman of the Senate Foreign Relations Committee was similarly critical of President Kennedy on his failure to live up to the promises of Candidate Kennedy.

Senator Fulbright said on that occasion, "I would hope that the President will give special attention to informing us over the television . . . to inform all of us of the nature of the conditions that we confront and what we ought to do about it . . . my principal criticism of the new Administration . . . is the failure to go through with this thought of outlining more clearly what our situation is, where we are, and then what we ought to do and where we ought to go, and I think this is very necessary."

In other words, both the American newspaper editors and his own Senate Foreign Relations Chairman took President Kennedy to task for failing to give the American people "the truth with the bark off" as he had promised as Candidate Kennedy. He was indicted of being guilty of the very thing he had alleged against President Eisenhower — of lacking in leadership on information.

Again, it was the "Kennedy Twist" — but without accompaniment by the Arkansas Traveler.

Now let us turn to the issue of prestige and prestige polls that Candidate Kennedy made in 1960. What happened when he became President? Well, with the Cuban fiasco dropping our international prestige to an all-time low under President Kennedy, his Administration ordered the prestige polls abolished as contrasted to his demands as Candidate Kennedy that they be published. This time the "Kennedy Twist" had a Cuban beat!

And of course, everyone — but everyone — recalls how Candidate Kennedy pounded away at what he called the "missile gap." Yet, less than three weeks after he became President, his Secretary of Defense revealed that there was no "missile gap." Since everyone also knows that even Jack Kennedy couldn't possibly close the alleged "missile gap" in so short a period as three weeks, it was evident that his campaign-claimed "missile gap" was only a politically expedient myth — now dumped in the boneyard of the "fall guy" CIA [Central Intelligence Agency].

Again it was the "Kennedy Twist" — and this time the rhythm in reverse action was first put into reverse by the person whom Society Columnist Betty Beale has revealed is the champion "Twister" at the White House parties, Defense Secretary McNamara. Betty says he is "terrific" when he revealed that there was no missile gap.

And you remember well how Candidate Kennedy denounced personal diplomacy and summitry — but shortly after becoming President how he engaged extensively in personal diplomacy and summitry in trips abroad.

He went to the summit with Khrushchev in Vienna where Khruschev delivered a tough ultimatum to him that he did not reveal to the American people until after Khrushchev had announced the ultimatum himself.

Again — the "Kennedy Twist" — this time to the tune of a Viennese waltz.

And to those of us in New England where the baked bean is a regional tradition and "must," we shall not forget how Candidate Kennedy downgraded the bean in the campaign, particularly in the TV-Radio debate on October 7, 1960, when he said, "[Y]ou can't tell me anyone who uses beans instead of meat . . . is well fed or adequately fed."

This from the man from the "Region of the Bean and the Cod!"

Yet, when he became President he regained his taste for beans as his Administration proudly announced on February 27 and April 27, 1961, that it was making the pea bean a "part of the effort to expand and improve the quality of food for needy persons."

Again, the "Kennedy Twist" — and even against the beans that made Boston famous even if they were Eisenhower Program beans when Candidate Kennedy denounced them. It seems that since becoming President he now knows his beans as Eisenhower did.

Next let us turn to the growth rate issue that Candidate Kennedy raised in 1960 when he repeatedly attacked the Eisenhower Administration on what he characterized as the threat of Russia overtaking us economically. At Valley Forge on October 29, 1960, Candidate Kennedy said, "That requires a rate of growth no less than 5 percent a year, and we are not growing at that rate today. Our average for the past eight years was 2.5 percent."

Richard Nixon answered this gloom and scare talk of Candidate Kennedy repeatedly with the same answer he had given to Khrushchev: "They are not going to catch us in seven or seventy years, if we remain true to the principles that have made America the richest and the best country in the world today." Dick Nixon also pointed out that the Soviet rate of growth was on a lower base.

When John F. Kennedy became President, he adopted the Nixon line on this — that Russia would not overtake us and that Russia started from a lower base — as President Kennedy stated at his June 28, 1961, press conference: "Soviet output will not reach two thirds of ours by 1970 and our rate will be easier to sustain or improve than the Soviet rate, which starts from a lower figure."

Again it is the "Kennedy Twist"— with Kennedy as President adopting the arguments of the man he argued against when he was Candidate Kennedy — in fact, I think maybe Dick Nixon could sue him for plagiarism on this point.

You may recall how Candidate Kennedy taunted President Eisenhower on the charge of failing to be a leader — of how in New York City on November 5, 1960, Candidate Kennedy said:

"I want to be a President who acts as well as reacts — who is the Chief Executive in every sense of the word — who responds to a problem not by hoping his subordinates will act, but by directing them to act — a President who is willing to take the responsibility for getting things done, and take the blame if they are not done right. . . . In short, I believe in a President who will formulate and fight for his legislative policies, and not be a casual observer of the legislative process.

"A President who will not back down under pressure, or let down his spokesmen in the Congress — a President who does not speak from the rear of the battle but who places himself in the thick of the fight."

How does President Kennedy measure up to these words of Candidate Kennedy? Well, the pro-Kennedy *Washington Post* made a measurement in its lead editorial of February 27, 1962, in which it gave just what I have quoted and then said of President Kennedy:

"Maybe it would be more apposite to wonder what sort of leadership Congress is getting from the White House. . . . The simple sending of an eloquent message to Congress can hardly be said to fill the bill. President Eisenhower sent eloquent messages to Congress . . . and Candidate Kennedy taunted him pretty roughly about his failure to do any more . . . unless a President . . . arouses the people to cross a new frontier. . . . New frontiers never get crossed . . . without leaders who really lead. . . . Without such leadership, there can be no new frontier."

In other words, the *Washington Post* condemned President Kennedy for lack of leadership — and accused him of a leadership gap!

Again it is the "Kennedy Twist" — with the pro-Kennedy *Washington Post* condemning his failure to be a leader on domestic issues and legislation — and saying in substance that the tune of "New Frontiers" had changed to that of "Lost Frontiers."

Everyone — but everyone — knows what an issue Candidate Kennedy made on Cuba against the Eisenhower Administration — of how Candidate Kennedy said, "We must attempt to strengthen the non-Batista Democratic anti-Castro forces in exile, and in Cuba itself, who offer eventual hope of overthrowing Castro. Thus far these fighters for freedom have had virtually no support from our Government."

Well, what did Jack Kennedy do, when he became President, about giving the anti-Castro forces real support — when he had a chance to back up his strong talk with action? The world knows the very tragic story of how he called off the support they needed most — the air support when they made the invasion attempt at the Bay of Pigs and how they were defeated so disastrously because of the lack of that desperately needed air support.

If anyone has the slightest doubt about this, let him or her read the Charles Murphy article "Cuba: The Record Set Straight" in the September 1961 issue of *Fortune* Magazine — or the Stewart Alsop article "The Lessons of the Cuban Disaster" in the June 24, 1961, issue of the *Saturday Evening Post*.

Why the best that Jack Kennedy, as President, could offer for that which he criticized, as Candidate Kennedy, was the pitiful and degrading "Tractors for Freedom" deal that fell through.

Again it was the "Kennedy Twist" — done in agony to a Cuban beat.

The Kennedy record on Laos is nearly as tragic. Repeatedly Candidate Kennedy called for a strong stand on Laos. Even after he became President he threatened a strong stand in his map — talk at his nationally televised press conference on March 23, 1961. He issued an ultimatum to Khrushchev to stay out of Laos and strongly indicated that we were ready to go to war if Khrushchev didn't heed the ultimatum.

Yet a year later what is the score? Khrushchev called the bluff and Kennedy did nothing. And the Communists have taken over more and more of Laos.

On May 24, 1961, Washington News Columnist Richard Starnes summed up the record this way:

"The President's ringing declaration on March 23 that Laos was worth a war . . . is now revealed as an empty statement by a man who either didn't know what he was talking about, or who was foolishly trying to run a bluff on the master bluffer of them all."

And today it is even worse than it was at the time of the Starnes column a year ago.

Again it is the "Kennedy Twist" — of talking one way and acting another way or not even acting at all — of brave, strong, and eloquent words but not to be matched by any real action.

These truths I do acknowledge — that as an American I must support the President of the United States regardless of the difference between his political party and mine — that criticism is easy to make by the person who does not have the authority and responsibility to act — just as easy for me today as it was easy for John F. Kennedy when he was a candidate in 1960 — that one should be careful and fair in indulging in that luxury of criticism — and that changing one's mind or opinion is not always a betrayal of weakness but rather often is a hallmark of courage.

While these truths may, to some extent, mitigate the instances of Kennedy reversals that I have cited to you, by no means do they excuse them or place a taboo upon discussion of them and bringing them to the attention of the American people.

It is more important for the American people to have a strong President than for either political party to win a Presidential election. It is in that spirit that I speak tonight.

I do not necessarily take exception to the stand that John F. Kennedy has taken on every issue — I do not mean for my remarks about him to be personal or to reflect any unfriendly spirit toward him.   And while I can surely be charged as speaking as a partisan, I have only cited the factual record to you as the American people are entitled to know it.

Inescapable is the fact that the image that John F. Kennedy deliberately and successfully created of himself in the 1960 campaign is far different from the actual John F. Kennedy as revealed thus far by his record as President.

The record as I have outlined it to you tonight reveals two very basic and fundamental things — first, that the record of President Kennedy is a record of repeated reversals of the campaign pledges of Candidate Kennedy — and second, that he has not been the strong President that he promised — for what strength he has displayed has been in words — eloquent, brave, and inspiring words only to be followed by no action or by timid action at best.

In the words of that distinguished *New York Times* columnist and Washington Bureau Chief, Scotty Reston:

"He has talked like Churchill and acted like Chamberlain."

And I repeat:

"He has talked like Churchill and acted like Chamberlain."

Candidate Kennedy's campaign theme was "This is a Time for Greatness"— Candidate Kennedy's campaign promise was "Leadership in the Sixties — thus far, President Kennedy has given neither greatness nor leadership— neither greatness nor leadership.

No — leadership is not manifested by coercion and police state methods.

No— greatness is not manifested by unlimited pragmatism.

"Nuclear Credibility" (1962)

One year ago on this day— impelled by concern over the fact that everywhere the Communists were pressing forward stronger — I stood in this Chamber and posed to my colleagues, to the American people, and particularly to the President of the United States, several questions which I considered to be of the utmost importance.

I asked:

How much longer can we afford to lose?

I asked:

What have *we* done (or failed to do) that permits Khrushchev to act as he does?

And:

Why is it that the Communists so often have the initiative and we are satisfied to *react*?

And:

When will we start winning?

In the year that separates us from the occasion of those remarks the course of events has been, to say the least, an unpromising one for us. The Communists, far from exploring new frontiers of friendship and cooperation, have continued the pressures of their attacks against liberty.

Not only that, but more.

Indeed, they have *increased* their efforts. And there is little in their attitude toward any problem anywhere to indicate that they intend to change for the better.

— Not in the U.N.

— Not in Berlin

— Not at Geneva

— Not in Cuba

— Not in Southeast Asia

— Not anywhere

And why should they change? Why should they, as long as they are making progress toward their goals?

The NATO Alliance, protecting an area of the non-Communist world which is of great and immediate importance to the United States, is plagued by troubles, doubts, criticisms, and uncertainties.

— More and more there is danger that Khrushchev, casting an acquisitive eye toward the Western doorstep of the Soviet Empire, will be tempted toward new challenges by military vulnerabilities that he believes exist there, or by his assessment that the Free World's will is so low as to negate its power.

A prominent, highly respected American — and very good friend of President Kennedy — recently talked at length with Khrushchev and what he reported on Khrushchev's assessment of our will made headlines on the front pages of our newspapers, on television and radio throughout the country. He reported that Khrushchev had stated that he believes that the United States will not fight to protect itself.

Certainly one of the realities that faces us today is in the form of a challenge to adopt policies and take actions which will build the confidence of NATO Europe.

— Could we possibly hope to build this confidence by demanding acceptance of U.S. policies that are not palatable to them? Would not this course be more likely to destroy their confidence than to build it?

Let us not forget that for twelve years NATO was a solid and cohesive force against Communism. In the last one and one-half years difficulty has piled upon difficulty. De Gaulle was President of France prior to this troubled period. Macmillan spoke for Great Britain, Adenauer for West Germany.

— *What has changed?*

In Laos our objective of a truly neutral and independent country is stalled by the refusal of the pro-Communist elements to comply with the peace agreement that was signed only a short time ago at Geneva.

— It makes one wonder if we based our own agreement on a concept, that the Communists are becoming more friendly and cooperative.

Do we really believe that such agreements with the Soviets will accrue to the benefit of anyone but themselves?

And do we have a basis for our actions which *does* assume an accommodation with the Soviets?

In Cuba, the Bloc countries and Castro blatantly defy the principles of the Monroe Doctrine and proceed with the Communization of that island-and in recent weeks an acceleration of transforming Cuba into a Communist arsenal.

— I ask you: Are we better off here than we were a year ago?

In Vietnam we are committing ourselves, bit by bit, to a more involved war, as the result of fashioning our responses to the patterns chosen by the enemy.

And in the realm of space the Soviets' new achievements cast the shadow of a tremendous new military potential across the whole Free World.

— Our spokesmen, calm almost to the point of placid satisfaction, enjoin us not to worry. . . . "We are far behind. But we will catch up. And meanwhile, there's no great military significance in the Soviets' feat. And Cuba really presents no threat."

Words and more words.

About the only tangible action we get is the call-up of the Reserves in which Khrushchev, in his alternating policy of first blowing hot and then blowing cold, psychologically dangles our Reservists on the end of an "on-again-off-again" line in a war of nerves — in which we react as he anticipates our reaction.

But who is really so blind as not to see that under the pressures of the last year the outlook for us has deteriorated steadily? And now it has reached such a disturbingly low level that its effects surely must be to banish the last vestige of complacency from our national attitude and to require each of us — whatever his position, whatever his responsibilities, and whatever his affiliations — to face the truth.

It is inconceivable that any amount of polished phrases — no matter how expertly put together and how adroitly presented — could longer conceal the hard facts from the American people.

— We are simply not breathing the air of success.

— In more ways than ever before within the memory of most of us our beloved country is rapidly becoming a second-rater.

No amount of contrived double-talk can longer divert the impacts of reality.

— In the eyes of the world our flag does not fly high and proudly as it once did.

And so today — impelled by the same concern that caused me to address the subject of our security and welfare a year ago — I ask again:

— *When will we start winning?*

— How much longer can we *risk* waiting?

— What can we do to turn the tide more surely in our direction?

Mr. President, it would be unwise as well as incorrect to imply that there is a short route back to the position of eminence, influence, and well-being that our country enjoyed in better days. But I have no hesitancy in asserting that there is a route back and that we had best get our feet on it, and follow it, before we lose the chance to do so.

I would not be so presumptuous as to say that I am able to see every straightaway and turning of this route all the way to its ultimate destination (which, I hope, would be a secure and peaceful community of nations), but, once again, I have no hesitancy in asserting that I can see where our *starting point* should be.

— We must start, and fashion our future progress toward an improved position, on a basis of military advantage. . . . Of this I am certain.

— Not a fancied or limited advantage in a single technique, or in a particular locale, or to react to one specific situation . . . but a realistic over-all military advantage reposing in a capability to win our objectives at any level of conflict, from the lowest to the highest.

If we are determined to have and hold the benefits of this advantage, it would be the height of folly not to take new warning from the Soviets' recent two-man orbit.

— It was a remarkable accomplishment.

— We would have been proud to claim it.

— It is unfortunate for the Free World that we could not claim it.

I deem it unfortunate because it portends physical power of indescribably greater dimensions . . . and I know of nothing in long record of aggression under the Communists to indicate that they *do not intend* to exploit, either overtly or by blackmail, any elements of physical power within their reach, if given sufficient opportunity to do so.

— Knowing how Khrushchev, Malinovsky, and others boasted of their new power after the recent space flights, who can close his eyes so tightly against the light of reality as to believe the Soviets *do not intend* to develop military power in space as fast as they are able?

Or looking toward NATO Europe:

— Knowing that the Soviets have nuclear-armed forces available, who can stray so far from the path of reality as to believe that they *do not intend* to exploit these forces if they should consider it to their advantage to do so?

— And I also ask, Mr. President:

. . . Are we trying to increase our conventional forces in NATO at the expense of our tactical nuclear forces?

. . . Are we trying to convince the people that we are conjuring up a less dangerous kind of war for them to fight?

Or looking toward the jungle area and underdeveloped regions:

— Knowing that Khrushchev has espoused "wars of liberation," who can cite valid evidence that the Communists *do not intend* to exploit the physical power and emotions of human beings in insurgency operations and other disruptive activities, whenever it suits their purpose to do so and they have sufficient opportunity?

My thesis — my reason for addressing you today — is, I feel sure, clearly evident by now; but let us accord it the emphasis that will come from additional discussion.

The President and some of his principal policy and strategy advisers have been deeply occupied with the subject of risks.

— We have been cautioned on more than one occasion that we cannot do thus-and-so because it would risk provoking the Communists;

— That, for example, we must urge NATO Europe to be satisfied with trying to defend itself by conventional means because of the stated conviction that even the highly selective use of tactical nuclear capabilities against military targets would escalate the conflict toward general war proportions.

The whole country has heard about the inhibiting effects that these risks, and other similar ones, impose upon our national policy and strategy.

It is well to be aware of these circumstances and to evaluate them carefully. But I regret to say that from the same sources I have heard comparatively little about the risks of adopting wishful thinking as a substitute for hardheaded realism in overcoming the Communists' drive for power and keeping the balance on our side.

— Can we risk the survival of our country on anyone's "opinions" as to what the Communists' *intentions* are?

I say no. It is unthinkable.

— Surely there is something better for us than gambling on a guess that the Communists *do not intend* to use every part of the military capabilities that they now have or may develop later on, if and when it suits their interests to do so.

— Or to put it another way, could we possibly risk gambling on the dangerous assumption that *their intentions will be good?*

. . . Of course not.

— Therefore, we must clearly see and clearly understand what is required of us to hold the military advantage.

What we must be prepared to do is counter the *military capabilities* that constitute a threat to us.

— We must protect ourselves against that which we know the *Communists are capable of doing.*

As you know, the concept of being prepared to counter the *military capabilities* of the Communists is generally referred to as counterforce.

The World being what it is today, you would think that no one in this country would even remotely consider taking issue with this concept.

— Who could possibly quarrel with the purpose of winning our objectives in defense of our country?

But it has become increasingly clear that there are some who, obviously failing to understand the concept, take sharp issue with it. For example, when the Secretary of Defense referred to it in a speech at Ann Arbor, Michigan, on June 16, there followed a flood of negative reaction that is still running . . . and there has even been a deep silence from the Secretary's colleagues.

I have waited for just one of them to speak out directly in support of the views he expressed. But none has — and to break his lonely position I speak out today in support of his Ann Arbor speech and say that it was the most encouraging expression to come from the Kennedy Administration since the time of my speech a year ago.

Typical of the opposition was a three-column "anti-counterforce" advertisement that ran in the *New York Times* of August 21. The signers are 175 most highly respected and patriotic faculty members of a dozen universities and colleges of recognized standing. They urged abandonment of our counterforce posture.

— Why? Because, in their view, it is provocative to the Communists;

— and it tends to promote an arms race;

— and it increases the likelihood of war.

The solution which they, in all sincerity and seriousness, recommend is to reduce our arms (even disproportionately, if necessary) for the purpose of seeking a closer approach to equality with the USSR.

With this example in mind, let us see clearly and understand fully what the most vocal and influential of the well-intentioned critics are saying. Reduced to simple terms, it is this:

— *We* are largely to blame for the Soviets' continued intransigence.

— Because we maintain the strength to counter their military capability, we give the Soviets reason to fear that we are preparing to attack them.

— They are driven to excessive secrecy and distrust by their apprehension of our strength.

In substance, these critics contend that the Soviets are bad because we make them bad. Hence, if we reduce *our* military strength, their attitude will improve, and they will become more tractable.

— Do these good and sincere people who are so critical really believe that we would be better off *without* a margin of military advantage across the board?

— Are they really willing to risk the survival of our country on their opinion of the Soviets' intentions?

— Is it conceivable that, in the present atmosphere, we would deliberately plan *not* to have more than the Soviets have?

— Is there any worthwhile evidence to cause us to see *that* way as the path toward more effective deterrence and greater security?

There are some who seem to think that deterrence is, in a manner of speaking, old-fashioned;

— that it has been overtaken by events in the forward rush of technology;

— that deterrence, as we know it today, has no future.

I disagree.

We have had effective deterrence for the majority of time over the last fifteen years. We have effective deterrence now. And I believe we can continue to have effective deterrence in the future.

— And in the future, as in the past, there is no doubt that effective deterrence will stem fundamentally from our counterforce capability;

— from our capability to win over the enemy's military forces.

    With those who favor placating the Soviets at the terrible cost of deliberately downgrading our own military advantage and settling for parity or near parity, it is unpopular to say that we can win.

    — With dangerous positiveness and shallow reasoning they say that in nuclear war there could be no winner.

    With all the emphasis at my command, I disagree.

    — We *can* win.

    I do not mean to imply that we could win cheaply. But neither do we have to manipulate ourselves into a position where we would be absolutely dead. It would not have to be a Pyrrhic victory. Winning and losing are not fundamentally questions of the intrinsic costs of damage suffered in a war. We *could lose by eroded resolve* and ultimate capitulation without suffering any physical damage at all from the enemy who defeated us. But if we are attacked, I hold with the concept that our "second-strike" force must be stronger than the force remaining to the enemy after his initial strike. If we retained this advantage we would be in a winning position.

    And what kind of reasoning, may I ask, is behind the accusation that by keeping ourselves strong in the face of a determined and capable nation, whose leaders are our avowed enemies, we are promoting an arms race?

    — Let us not surrender to this kind of self-incrimination any longer but instead set the facts straight.

    — We are *not* promoting an arms race; *not* through counterforce or *any other* means.

    The forces that we have and expect to have are not just someone's "idea." We do not get them like numbers pulled out of a hat. Far from that, our requirements are based on the most careful and complete information regarding the Communists' capabilities that it is possible for us to have.

    — And that is the way we must continue to do it, no matter what the prophets of fear and doom say.

    — For I repeat, it would be folly for us, in the present climate of relations with the USSR, *not to be able* to counter those capabilities.

    So if we are engaged in anything that resembles an arms race, let there be no mistake about who is at the bottom of the trouble: the Communists are to blame, not our concepts and strategy.

    And while we are at it, let us get rid of the fiction that our military posture indicates an intention on our part to initiate war against the Soviets by striking first.

    If this *were* our intention, would we not be stupid indeed to burden ourselves with the expense of an *aerospace defense system*, our ballistic missile *early warning* facilities, the Strategic Air Command *alert*, and other precautions of that sort? If we intended to strike *first*, could we not *forego* these things and put all of our effort and resources into *offensive* means?

    Our policy leaders stress repeatedly that we must have flexibility, a choice among alternatives. *I agree.* Certainly we want to have *several* alternatives available if we are attacked. Counterforce response against military targets is *only one* of them; but a very *desirable one*.

— Don't we want to do everything within reason to avoid needless destruction?

. . . Of course we do.

— Don't we want to provide the enemy with every possible incentive *not to attack our cities*?

. . . Of course we do.

— Do we want to subscribe to or be limited to a policy of indiscriminate devastation, which would provide an enemy with a strong incentive to attack our own cities?

. . . Of course we do not.

I do not comprehend the reasoning of those who cry for the abandonment of our counterforce posture.

— I do not understand how they believe that we can find greater safety in greater weakness.

But I am sure of this: If we *do* believe that counterforce is essential — if we *do* want to preserve it — the time has arrived for all of us . . .

— those of us here today;

— the American people everywhere;

— the President of the United States;

— not just a lonely Secretary of Defense;

— indeed, *all of us*, to do *more* to make the concept of countering the enemy's capabilities better understood and more widely accepted;

— to protect it from even those well-intentioned patriots, who through fear of imagined or real risks, or through ignorance of the facts, would destroy it and cast us adrift on the stormy seas of far greater uncertainty.

I do not intend to imply that counterforce is the answer to *everything*. *It is not*. But even in the very worst context that can be contrived without going to impossible extremes, we are still vastly better off *with* it than we could possibly be *without* it.

No one claims that it is a panacea. *No* one could say for certain that because we have a counterforce capability the future will be *easier*. But *there is* every reason to believe that if we *resolutely maintain* a counterforce capability the future will be *less difficult* than it might be otherwise. And that is a goal which, although not spectacular, we must not ignore.

"Nuclear Test Ban Treaty"

Mr. President, the vote on ratification of the nuclear test ban treaty is one of the most difficult votes that I have ever cast as a United States Senator — or even in my twenty-three years in Congress. The difficulty is not with respect to my single vote having any effect on the outcome of the final vote by the Senate. That outcome was a foregone conclusion from the very start — overwhelmingly for ratification.

During the debate I have raised several questions. I had hoped that the answers to these questions could be definite and clear — at least enough for the resolution of any doubts that I had about the treaty. But they have not been. Admittedly, the answers have been speculative.

This issue is not only dominated by speculation. It is dominated by emotions. Those who support the treaty have been called pro-Communists. They have been charged by some extremists with treason and with selling out to Khrushchev. How ridiculous can one get with these charges? The charges are so ridiculous that no sensible person would take them seriously.

They remind me of those tragic days in the early fifties when articulate coverage was almost eliminated by the techniques of "guilt by association" and "trial by accusation." The extremists of the Right did our country a great disservice by those unsubstantiated charges. The damage was irreparable. What it did to our scientists and the way that it shackled our free scientific effort was revealed in the later fifties when Russia's Sputnik revealed how tragically we were lagging behind Russia in science and technology.

I know — because I was a target of the extremists of the Right. They called me "pro-Communist" and a "fellow traveler" because of my Declaration of Conscience.

But many, many of those who back in the early fifties decried the "guilt by association" and "trial by accusation" tactics of the Extreme Right are today guilty of the same abuses and excesses on the Extreme Left of the ideological spectrum.

For too many of the Extreme Left now charge those who oppose the treaty of being "murderers" and of deliberately poisoning the milk for children with lethal doses of Strontium Ninety. At the outset of this debate, the press quoted one Senator as saying that any Senator who voted against ratification of the treaty should have his head examined.

Have we lost all sense of reasonableness? Cannot members of the United States Senate have honest differences of opinion without being charged with mental deficiency or treason or crassly poisoning milk and killing babies or being "pro Communist" by those who so emotionally disagree with them — both on the Extreme Right and on the Extreme Left?

What does the majority of the American people want? Ratification or rejection of the nuclear test ban treaty? The Gallup Poll and the Harris Poll report that an overwhelming majority of the American people want the treaty to be ratified.

But that is not what my mail shows — and it is the heaviest mail that I have ever received in all of my entire service in Congress. More than that, it is not just organized pressure mail. Instead it is individual mail in personal handwriting-not just printed or mimeographed mail — or printed cards distributed in great volume for persons just to automatically sign without thinking.

This mail is individually composed. It is highly emotional and often inflammatory— but equally so on both sides, whether for or against the treaty. Nevertheless it is clear that the people are expressing themselves with deep feeling— not just merely echoing what someone has told them to write. And the mail is from every section of the nation.

Were I to be guided by what the mail indicates is the wish of the majority of Americans, I would have to vote against the treaty. For by better than an 8 to 1 margin the senders of letters and telegrams and postal cards to me have registered vigorous opposition to the treaty.

Yet, the pattern varies when just the Maine mail is taken — for the Maine mail has favored the treaty by a 2 to 1 vote. But even with Maine the expression of feeling has changed. Prior to Labor Day and during the summer season, the Maine mail was better than 3 to 1 in favor of the treaty. But after Labor Day, the Maine mail has turned in the other direction with a majority registering opposition to the treaty. It would be difficult to conclude with any certainty what a majority of year-round Maine residents feel — since obviously a great deal of the Maine mail prior to Labor Day came from out-of-state summer visitors.

The totals of my mail run heavily in contradiction to the reports of the Gallup Poll and the Harris Poll. The only reconciliation that I can conclude is that if the Gallup Poll and the Harris Poll accurately reflect the position of a majority of Americans, then those who support the treaty apparently aren't sufficiently enthusiastic for it and won't take time or effort to write — or those who are against the treaty have such a higher degree of intensity in the opposition to the treaty that they will take the time to write and express themselves.

One thing is quite clear. Regardless of whether the majority is for or against the treaty, the degree of articulated intensity of those against the treaty is much greater than those who are for the treaty.

Another thing is clear — that the polls and the mail — and the seasonal factor in the Maine mail on this issue— are too contradictory for me to let the mail have any significant influence on my final decision.

In trying to arrive at a conscientious decision, I have considered what would happen if the Senate did reject the treaty. First, it is clear that Khrushchev would spew vitriolic propaganda charging that the United States had thus proved that it did not want peace and that we were "warmongers" intent on poisoning the air with Strontium Ninety. Even though he is guilty himself of having broken the last test ban agreement with the multi-megaton open air test nuclear explosions that Russia set off, his false propaganda would be believed by some and we would lose significant ground in the psychological war.

But Senate rejection of the treaty would not be the act that started the United States to resume open air nuclear testing. It would not for the very simple reason that President Kennedy has taken the position that the United States would refrain from open air testing as long as Russia refrained from open air testing.

Now let us face reality and the truth on this point. The Senate vote on the test ban treaty will neither stop open air testing if the treaty is ratified — nor start it if the treaty is rejected. It will not stop open air testing because it has already been stopped by President Kennedy in agreement with Khrushchev's keeping Russia from open air tests. By the same token, Senate rejection of the treaty will not start open air testing again.

I think Khrushchev feels that it is to the military advantage of Russia to keep us from resuming open air tests in the belief that Russia is significantly ahead of us in the high yield weapons and will stay ahead as long as we do not make the open air tests that are necessary if we are to close the high yield weapons gap that so heavily favors Russia.

And he doesn't need a treaty to do this. All he needs to do is to refrain from conducting such open air tests. He knows that by the simple expedient of restraint, he will stop the United States from open air testing because of the expressions made by President Kennedy. Consequently, I believe it would be most unlikely that Khrushchev would order resumption of open air testing if the Senate were to reject this treaty.

Perhaps my conclusion in this regard can be criticized as being "speculative." But it is no more speculative than the answers given to the questions that I have raised in this debate— answers that even those providing the answers have admitted were "speculative." I believe that my conclusion in this regard is far less speculative.

So that in the final analysis, my decision must rest on whether the political and psychological disadvantages stemming from rejection of the treaty would be greater than the obvious national security disadvantages stemming from ratification of the treaty. Fortunately, the political and psychological disadvantages of treaty rejection have been very ably and fully presented out in the open to the public. And no mistake about it, they are tremendously impressive arguments — almost compelling arguments.

Unfortunately, the national security disadvantages stemming from ratification of the treaty have not been as fully presented out in the open to the public. They have not because of the secrecy that has been invoked on key aspects that indicate the grave threat that the treaty can create to our national security. The public cannot be told.

But it can be told enough of the implications — implications so grave that even the enthusiastic proponents of the treaty unreservedly admit that the treaty is a calculated risk.

In the questions that I have asked in this debate, I have tried very hard to find a basis for which I could conscientiously vote for ratification of the treaty. I regret to say that the answers have not supplied such a basis.

On the other hand, it has been argued with sincerity and conviction that one could not conscientiously vote against the treaty because such a vote would be a vote against peace — or at least a first step toward peace. I cannot challenge that argument with complete certainty in my own mind. But in equal degree, I cannot challenge with complete certainty the argument made that the treaty may be a first step toward the undermining of our national security.

There have been several speeches expressing the gravest of misgivings about the treaty — only to be concluded with the announcement by the speakers that they would vote for the treaty.

I conclude my statement by saying that I have very grave misgivings about the harmful effects of rejection of the treaty— but by stating that in my opinion the jeopardy that the treaty imposes on our national security is a more compelling argument against the treaty than the political and psychological disadvantages that would stem from rejection of the treaty.

That is why I shall cast a very troubled vote against the treaty.

"Presidential Candidacy Announcement"

I always enjoy being with the members of the Women's National Press Club — even when you give members of Congress an unmerciful going over. I think that I enjoy being with you not only because of the many good friends that I have among you but also because I was a newspaperwoman myself before becoming a member of the House and Senate.

Many years ago I worked for the weekly newspaper in my home town — *The Independent Reporter* — in a succession of a variety of jobs ranging from general reporter to circulation manager and some of them concurrently performed as can be done only on a weekly paper. My only claim to fame in that effort was that in its class, while I was circulation manager, The Independent Reporter reached the seventh highest ABC rating of all weekly newspapers in the entire nation.

But it was when I did five columns a week nationally for United Feature Syndicate for more than five years that I felt a greater professional kinship with you. I learned what a chore it was to produce seven hundred words almost daily.

It has been my privilege to address your club more than once. The first time was when I had been a United States Senator for only six days. Five days before I had surprised, if not shocked, some members of the press when I voted for Robert A. Taft for Chairman of the Senate Republican Policy Committee rather than for Henry Cabot Lodge. Some even denounced me as a traitor to the cause of Republican liberalism.

And it was only a year and a half later that others in the press were calling me a traitor to the cause of conservatism because of my Declaration of Conscience made on June 1, 1950. Some even called me pro-Communist on the basis of the Declaration of Conscience.

I have often though of those instances in which I have been the target of the extremists on both the left and right. I remember how in the 1948 campaign when I first ran for the Senate an anonymous sheet was put out in the primary charging that I voted "the Marcantonio line." It failed. But the same technique was used successfully two years later against Helen Gahagan Douglas.

I remember how in the 1954 campaign I was accused in the primary of being soft on communism and a dangerous liberal — and then in the general election of being called a reactionary and an all— out effort made by the CIO to defeat me just as COPE [Committee on Political Education] did in 1960.

Yes, I have often thought of that January 8, 1949, speech that I made to this club in which I described myself as a Moderate, pointing out that I had previously given myself that label when asked a question on the "Meet the Press" program on December 10, 1948.

I have thought frequently of these things in recent months when reading the editorials and articles expressing the opinion that our nation is more rampant with bigotry and hatred than it has ever been. Many conclude that such was the cause of the assassination of President Kennedy — some even erroneously charging the assassination to racial hatred and bigotry.

In my opinion, any hatred or any bigotry— even the slightest hatred or bigotry— is too much for our nation and is to be deplored. But I cannot agree with those who contend that now there is greater hatred and bigotry than ever existed before in our country. Instead I believe that our country is far freer of bigotry and hatred than it was ten years ago — or at the time of my Declaration of Conscience, when I specifically denounced Fear, Ignorance, Bigotry, and Smear.

Let us examine a few of the contentions that bigotry and hatred are greater now than ever before. First, let us take the first claims and the first news reports on the assassination of President Kennedy. The first headlines were to the effect that President Kennedy had been shot by a Southern extreme racist, by a racial bigot. This was immediately seized upon and exploited by the Russian Communist press for propaganda purposes.

Then after the initial smoke and when heads began to clear and emotions cool, the truth came out — and it was not a Southern anti-negro extremist that shot President Kennedy but instead it was a Marxist, a mentally deranged Communist. Further, it was by accident of geography that this mentally deranged Communist was in Dallas, Texas — when it might have happened in Russia where he lived for some time or in other sections of the United States where he had lived.

No, the assassination of President Kennedy was clearly not what was first represented— the result of Southern anti-negro extremism but rather the act of a mentally deranged Communist.

Next, let us take the case of the John Birch Society and the extreme statements that it has issued against American leaders like former President Dwight D. Eisenhower. You might get the impression that never before was there an organization like the John Birch Society making such attacks.

Well, let me explode that myth by pointing out that in the early fifties there was an organization calling itself the Partisan Republicans of California that put out a smear publication charging that I was a leader of a — and I quote — "New Deal-Communist plot" to get Dwight D. Eisenhower the Republican nomination for President and to get him elected President.

To those who contend that hatred and bigotry is now greater than it ever was, I would urge a review of the conditions of the early fifties, I would recall to their memories those days of guilt-by-association, of character assassination, of trial-by-accusation. I would recall to their memories those days when freedom of speech was so abused by some that it was not exercised by others — when there were too many mental mutes afraid to speak their minds lest they be politically smeared as "Communists" or "Fascists" by their opponents.

I would recall their memories to a United States Senate that was almost paralyzed by fear — when some said that when I made the Declaration of Conscience that I had signed my political death warrant — and when that elder statesman who called one of your members and said that the Declaration of Conscience would have made Margaret Chase Smith the next President if she were a man — when such elder statesman was so clearly in the minority in his political evaluation of my speech.

Perhaps I know and feel this more strongly than some of those who evaluate and editorialize that bigotry and hatred are at their greatest heights now — because I felt the whiplash of the hatred and the bigotry from both the extremists of the Right and the extremists of the Left — when I fought such extremism both on the Floor of the Senate and in the Federal Court — and Thank God, for common decency, when I won not only in the Senate and in the Court — but with the people at the polls.

No, there is less bigotry and hate now than there was ten or fifteen years ago — and we have very impressive proof of this. The late John F. Kennedy helped prove this. After his victory in the 1960 elections, who can confidently claim that there has been more bigotry and hatred in the sixties than there was in the fifties? Who can seriously contend that there was more bigotry in 1960 than in 1928?

And who can deny that the rights of negroes are greater in 1964 than they were in 1954? Who can deny that there has been progress on civil rights in the past decade? Perhaps not as much as there should have been. But who can truthfully say that we have gone backwards and become more bigoted in 1964 on civil rights than we were in 1954?

No, I am proud of the progress that our nation and our people have made in the past decade in significantly, encouragingly — and yes, inspiringly — reducing hatred and bigotry in our nation and among our people. There is much room for improvement. But there is no need to hang our heads in shame — there is no need for us to wallow in a deep and heavy national guilt-complex.

For where in the world is there a nation as free of bigotry and hate as the United States? Where in the world is there a nation that has provided "equality in freedom" in the degree that the United States has for its people? Where in the world is there a nation that has done so much to export this concept of "freedom in equality" as has the United States in the billions of dollars that it has poured into efforts to give "equality in freedom" to the other peoples of the world? What other nation has poured out its resources and its heart to practically every other nation in the world in the past twenty-five years besides the United States — even to Russia with the multi-billion-dollar aid in World War II?

Is such the record of a nation of hatred and bigotry? Is such the record of a nation torn between radicals and reactionaries — between the Far Right Extremists and the Far Left Extremists?

I think the answers are clear. I think it is abundantly clear that the United States and its people are not hopelessly entwined in bigotry and hatred. To the contrary, I think the record shows that the American people are winning the battle against bigotry and hate — not losing it. I think the record shows that we have made significant progress in the last fifteen years.

I think it is abundantly clear that we are not a nation of extremists. To the contrary, the extremists of both the Left and the Right are very, very small minorities in size and only seem larger than they really are because they make a greater noise than the quieter non-extremists.

No, the vast majority of Americans are not extremists. They have no use for extremists of either the Far Left or the Far Right. If there be any doubter of the relative freedom of Americans from bigotry and hatred as compared to the other peoples of the world, then let him take a good long look at the Statue of Liberty and particularly those words inscribed at its base of:

"Give me your tired, your poor, your huddled masses yearning to breathe free, the wretched refuse of your teeming shore. Send these, the homeless, tempest-tossed, to me . . ."

For more than a year now I have been receiving a steady flow of mail urging me to run for President of the United States. At first my reaction was that of being pleasantly flattered with such expression of confidence in me. I was pleased but did not take the suggestion seriously for speculation prior to the past year has been limited to Vice Presidential possibilities.

And so I answered the letters by saying that I was pleased and flattered but that I was realistic enough not to take the suggestion seriously. I was sure that the trend would be short-lived and would end. But instead of fading away the mail increased and by mid-November of last year reached a new peak.

At that time one of the most persistent writers pressed hard for more than my reply of "I am pleased and flattered but know it could not possibly happen." and in response to his pressing I replied that I would give the suggestion serious consideration and make a decision within a relatively short time. My answer was picked up by the local press and some two weeks later the Associated Press queried my office quoting from the letter and asking if the quote was correct. My office confirmed the quote as being correct and then the mail began to pour in.

The mail came from all of the fifty states and to my surprise I found that the writers were taking a possible Margaret Chase Smith Presidential candidacy more seriously than I had been. Now I try to be serious without taking myself too seriously — but this mail was not what I had seriously expected. Frankly, it had its effect.

With the tragic assassination of President Kennedy came the political moratorium and the cancellation of the original date of this address. Again I anticipated that during the interim period this mail would fall off. And it did for a few days but then it started up again and now has returned to a level above that prior to the moratorium period.

In fairness to everyone, I concluded that I should make my decision before the end of January — and I have done so. It has not been an easy decision — either "yes" or "no" would be difficult. The arguments made to me that I should become a candidate have been gratifying.

First, it has been contended that I should run because I have more national office experience than any of the other announced candidates — or the unannounced candidates — with that experience going back to 1940 and predating any of the others.

Second, it has been contended that regardless of what happened to me, should I become a candidate was not really important — but that what was really important was that through me for the first time the women of the United States had an opportunity to break the barrier against women being seriously considered for the Presidency of the United States — to destroy any political bigotry against women on this score just as the late John F. Kennedy had broken the political barrier on religion and destroyed once and for all such political bigotry.

This argument contends that I would be pioneering the way for a woman in the future — to make her more acceptable — to make the way easier — for her to be elected President of the United States. Perhaps the point that has impressed me the most on this argument is that women before me pioneered and smoothed the way for me to be the first woman to be elected to both the House and the Senate — and that I should give back in return that which had been given to me.

Third, it has been contended that I should run in order to give the voters a wider range of choice — and specifically a choice other than that of Conservative or Liberal — to give those who considered themselves to be Moderates or Middle-of-the-Road advocates a chance to cast an unqualified vote instead of having to vote Conservative or Liberal. In this contention, it has been argued that this would give the voters a greater opportunity to express their will instead of being so restricted in their choice that many of them would not vote.

Fourth, it has been contended that I should run because I do not have unlimited financial resources or a tremendous political machine or backing from the party bosses— but instead have political independence for not having such resources.

There are other reasons that have been advanced but I will not take your time to discuss them. Instead let me turn to the reasons advanced as to why I should not run.

First, there are those who make the contention that no woman should ever dare to aspire to the White House — that this is a man's world and that it should be kept that way — and that a woman on the national ticket of a political party would be more of a handicap than a strength.

Second, it is contended that the odds are too heavily against me for even the most remote chance of victory — and that I should not run in the face of what most observers see as certain and crushing defeat.

Third, it is contended that as a woman I would not have the physical stamina and strength to run— and that I should not take that much out of me even for what might conceivably be a good cause, even if a losing cause.

Fourth, it is contended that I should not run because obviously I do not have the financial resources to wage the campaign that others have.

Fifth, it is contended that I should not run because I do not have the professional political organization that others have.

Sixth, it is contended that I should not run because to do so would result in necessary absence from Washington while the Senate had roll call votes— and thus that I would bring to an end my consecutive roll call record which is now at 1590.

You know of other reasons advanced as to why I should not run — and so I will not take your time to discuss them.

As gratifying as are the reasons advanced urging me to run, I find the reasons advanced against my running to be far more impelling. For were I to run, it would be under severe limitations with respect to lack of money, lack of organization, and lack of time because of the requirements to be on the job in Washington doing my elected duty instead of abandoning those duties to campaign — plus the very heavy odds against me.

So because of these very impelling reasons against my running, I have decided that I shall enter the New Hampshire Presidential preferential primary and the Illinois primary. For I accept the reasons advanced against my running as challenges— challenges which I met before in 1948 when I first ran for United States Senator from Maine, when I did not have the money that my opposition did — when I did not have the professional party organization that my opposition did— when it was said that "the Senate is no place for a woman" — when my physical strength was sapped during the campaign with a broken arm— when my conservative opponent and my liberal opponent in Maine were not restricted in campaigning by official duties in Washington such as I had — and when practically no one gave me a chance to win.

My candidacy in the New Hampshire primary will be a test in several ways.

(1) It will be a test of how much support will be given to a candidate without campaign funds and whose expense will be limited to personal and travel expense paid by the candidate.

(2) It will be a test of how much support will be given a candidate without a professional party organization of paid campaign workers but instead composed of nonpaid amateur volunteers.

(3) It will be a test of how much support will be given a candidate who refuses to absent herself from the official duties to which she has been elected and whose campaign time in New Hampshire will be limited to those times when the Senate is not in session voting on legislation.

(4) It will be a test of how much support will be given to a candidate who will not purchase political time on television or radio or political advertisements in publications.

(5) It will be a test of how much support will be given a candidate who will campaign on a record rather than on promises.

I welcome the challenges and I look forward to the test.

"Anti-ABM"

Mr. President:

I am told that this morning my amendment was attacked on the claim that it went too far, for it would adversely affect the Nike X advance development.

Let me set the record straight. This is simply untrue. The adoption of my amendment will not affect the Nike X advance development. The bill has $141 million for Nike X under a separate account. This item was approved by our committee [Armed Services Committee] and has nothing to do with the Safeguard system.

In addition to the R. and D. for Nike X advance development, the Army seeks $3 million for anti-ballistic-missile activities in research and development funds at White Sands Missile Range. This also has nothing to do with Safeguard.

Mr. President, I offer this amendment in the nature of a substitute to the Hart-Cooper Amendment because I believe that the proposed Safeguard anti-ballistic-missile system is too vulnerable and too costly and would be a waste of resources at a time when we must carefully determine our national priorities.

Even the advocates of the Hart-Cooper Amendment have at length expounded on their opposition to the Safeguard ABM system. Yet, the Hart-Cooper Amendment is a partial approval of the Safeguard ABM system in that it proposes a compromise authorization for research, development, testing, evaluation, and normal procurement incident thereto for the Safeguard ABM system.

I don't approve of such a compromise and such authorization for the Safeguard ABM system. It would be a "foot-in-the-door" authorization for a system in which I have no confidence.

Why waste funds on research and development of a system in which you have no confidence? To do so is to beg the question.

Why not face the issue directly instead of obliquely? If you have no confidence in the Safeguard ABM system, then why vote for any kind of authorization for it in any manner?

Why vote for authorization of research and development of a system in which you have no confidence? Why vote to develop a system when you are opposed to deployment of such a stem?

Mr. President, on the proposed ABM system, I find myself torn between the desire to grant to the President of the United States and the leader of my political party that which he feels is necessary but would be an unwise application of resources.

The United States is the most resourceful nation in the world. But our resources are not unlimited. We must face up to the fact that there are limits and that those limits dictate a conscientious effort to establish priorities.

As I see it, the purpose and mission of the proposed ABM basically is deterrence — to deter Russia from a miscalculation of attacking the United States because we would have sufficient defenses for our missile sites.

To the contrary, I think offensive strength is the better deterrent and as such rates national security priority over the proposed ABM system. For what really deters Russia from attacking us is our offensive arsenal.

That is what the Soviets respect the most — that is what has stayed their hand during each confrontation starting with the first Berlin crisis on through the Cuban missile crisis — that is what has preserved the peace for two and a half decades — and it is that which is most likely to cause the Soviets to engage in meaningful talks on arms limitations.

I keep hoping that arms limitations talks will ultimately be productive — that the Soviets will be reasonable, sincere, and constructive — that we can bequeath a peaceful world to succeeding generations — that we can find accommodation with honor and security for each other and for the world.

But I am like the "show me" Missourian as I have watched the Soviets achieve a power status of first-class magnitude by developing devastating weapons in complete secrecy— boastfully parading them on so-called peaceful May Day repeatedly in great surprise to our best intelligence forces — and totally rejecting inspection procedures whether it be on the limited test ban or on nonproliferation of nuclear weapons.

And, Mr. President, I am convinced that the proposed Safeguard ABM system would be woefully inadequate against a massive Soviet attack on our country should the Russians decide to attack. Make no mistake about it, if the Russians decide to attack it will be a massive attack with full utilization of all of their devastating weapons on cities as well as missile sites.

There are those who seem to think that both the United States and Russia have reached a technological plateau and in this thinking tend to doubt the probability of the development of a system superior to the proposed ABM system.

I do not share this view. I do not think that either of the two countries has reached a technological plateau. Instead I think that technology is progressing so rapidly and that the state of the art is changing so swiftly that the proposed ABM will be obsolete and outmoded before it is ever put in place.

I don't want our nation and our people to have a 40 billion or 20 billion or even a 10 billion dollar obsolete white elephant ABM system on our hands.

I am without scientific knowledge, training, or ability. I certainly cannot speak with authority. But I certainly can speak with conviction — and I am convinced that the proposed ABM would be not only a tragic waste of money but even more tragically a self-deluding Maginot Line false sense of security.

Instead, I have greater confidence and faith in the ability of our scientists to develop a far more effective and far less costly system than the proposed ABM system.

I am sure that it is no breach of security when I say that I have great hopes that before too long a sufficiently powerful laser will be developed for the defense not only of our missile sites but as well of our people and our cities.

I have been dubious about the practicability of the proposed ABM system ever since it was first proposed. Frankly, it lacked credibility to me — both the system and the rationale for it.

I don't believe that we need have any fear of a nuclear attack on this country by Red China for many, many years. Red China simply doesn't have the capability to wage nuclear war against us and won't have for many, many years.

While I think the Russian Kremlin leaders — as differentiated from the Russian common man and woman — would destroy the United States without hesitancy if they thought it was to their advantage and they could do it without any great risk to Russia, I can't see the men in the Kremlin contemplating that now.

Why? Because I am sure that the increasing defiance of law and authority in the United States by growing dissent that has degenerated into violence and the open advocacy of, and militancy for, anarchy— that this trend is increasing the confidence of the men in the Kremlin that they, and their system of communism, can complete a Communist conquest of the United States without the necessity of firing a shot.

Why then should they devastate the resources of this nation with nuclear attack? Why would they want to have the tremendous problem of rehabilitating and reconstructing a nuclear-devastated country when they are growing so confident from trends here that their own advocates among Americans will ultimately deliver this country to them?

No, Mr. President, I simply can't buy the rationale of fear of the men in the Kremlin advanced in advocacy of the proposed ABM. I simply don't find it credible. And I have so told President Nixon.

For these reasons, I do not believe that we have to precipitously rush into a most dubious ABM system for fear that Russia is on the verge of attacking us — I do not believe that there is an imminent threat of such urgency as to preclude us from trying to develop a more effective and less costly system than the proposed ABM system within not too distant a future.

Reaching the decision that I have on the ABM has not been easy. As the ranking Republican on the Armed Services Committee, it is neither pleasant nor easy to oppose the Republican President on this issue.

In the past I opposed a Democratic President when he proposed the ABM.

I opposed him on the proposed thin system — on the Sentinel system — because I felt it would be obsolete before it could be put in place — and because I felt that the claim that it was for defense against Red China was not credible.

I have felt a personal obligation as the top Republican on the Committee on Armed Services to try to see my way to supporting the Republican President on this issue — and I have listened intently in trying to find the proposed Safeguard ABM system to be sufficiently improved over the Sentinel ABM system and sufficiently credible to change and support the leader of my own political party.

But I remain unconvinced — and I cannot see my way to change my position because it is now a Republican President making the proposal instead of a Democratic President.

I respect the sincerity of those who have opposed the President on some of his selections for high federal office and have successfully blocked him on those selections. I would hope that there would be a reciprocity of respect for my own sincerity in this ABM issue. I know that there is from President Nixon.

The more I study the history of the proposal of an ABM system the more evident becomes the lack of credibility and consistency of the rationale for it.

First, a thick ABM system was proposed on the basis of defending against Russia. Then when opposition developed to the proposed thick ABM because of its great cost, the shift was made to a thin ABM system on the basis of not defending against Russia but against Red China and on the rationale of cost effectiveness.

Thus, the first shift — from thick to thin — from defense against Russia attack to defense against Red Chinese attack.

Then sites were selected and plans started on the thin ABM sites in the defense of cities and population centers.

But then another rebellious tea party broke out in Massachusetts on the part of irate citizens of the locality of a proposed site in Massachusetts — and the political fat was in the fire.

And then came another shift in the theory and rationale of the ABM — the shift from the defense of cities and population centers to defense of the missile sites.

What has not been so apparent to many is another very decided shift — for now the talk in support of the proposed thin Safeguard ABM system is not for defense against Red China but rather for defense against Russia.

Thus, the rationale for an ABM system has made the full circle in shifting on the factor of whom it is proposed to defend against, for first it was the thick system to defend against Russia, then it shifted to the thin Sentinel system to defend against Red China, and now it is back to the thin Safeguard system to defend against Russia.

This shifting on against whom to defend — first Russia then Red China and then back to Russia— coupled with the shifting on what to defend — first the cities and population centers and now missile sites— not only taxes one's credulity but even challenges one's imagination as to what the next shift will be by the advocates of the ABM.

Mr. President, I have read that retaliatory action has been taken against some of us who oppose the ABM system. I find it difficult to believe because no such action against me has even been hinted. Instead, I have found President Nixon and members of his staff to be very patient and courteous and understanding about my opposition to the ABM.

On the other hand, Mr. President, it has been charged that opposition to the ABM is being used just to try to stop President Nixon. I think that is an unfair charge. In opposing the ABM, I am certainly not trying to stop President Nixon any more than are those in his own party who have opposed some of the administrative policies of his administration.

Mr. President, let me make it crystal clear that while I don't believe in the ABM, I do believe in America.

I do believe in our form of government — but I don't believe in the ABM.

I am for our American way of life — but I don't believe in the
ABM.

The ABM is not an acid test of patriotism.

"Declaration of Conscience II"

Twenty years ago on this June First date at this same desk I spoke about the then serious national condition with a statement known as the "Declaration of Conscience." We had a national sickness then from which we recovered. We have a national sickness now from which I pray we will recover.

I would like to recall portions of that statement today because they have application now twenty years later.

I said of the then national condition, "It is a national feeling of fear and frustration that could result in national suicide and the end of everything that we American hold dear." Surely that is the situation today.

I said then, "I speak as briefly as possible because too much harm has already been done with irresponsible words of bitterness and selfish political opportunism." That is not only the situation today, but it is even worse for irresponsible words have exploded into trespass, violence, arson, and killings.

I said then, "I think that it is high time for the United States Senate and its members to do some soul-searching— for us to weigh our consciences — on the manner in which we are performing our duty to the people of the United States — on the manner in which we are using or abusing our individual powers and privileges."

That applies today. But I would add this to it— expanded application to the people themselves, whether they be students or construction workers, whether they be on or off campus.

I said then, "Those of us who shout the loudest about Americanism in making character assassinations are all too frequently those who, by our own words and acts, ignore some of the basic principles of Americanism —

The right to criticize;
The right to hold unpopular beliefs;
The right to protest;
The right to independent thought."

That applies today — and it includes the right to dissent against dissenters.

I said then, "The American people are sick and tired of being afraid to speak their minds lest they be politically smeared. . . . Freedom of speech is not what it used to be in America. It has been so abused by some that it is not exercised by others."

That applies today to both sides. It is typified by the girl student at Colby College who wrote me, "I am striking with my heart against the fighting in Cambodia but I am intimidated by those who scream protests and clench their fists and cannot listen to people who oppose their views."

I said then, "Today our country is being psychologically divided by the confusion and the suspicions that are bred in the United States Senate to spread like cancerous tentacles of 'know nothing, suspect everything' attitudes."

That applies today — but it must be expanded to the people themselves. Twenty years ago it was the anti-intellectuals who were most guilty of "know nothing" attitudes. Today too many of the militant intellectuals are equally as guilty of "hear nothing" attitudes of refusing to listen while demanding communications.

I said then, "I don't like the way the Senate has been made a rendezvous for vilification, for selfish political gain at the sacrifice of individual reputations and national unity."

That applies today. But I would add that equally I don't like the way the campus has been made a rendezvous for obscenity, for trespass, for violence, for arson, and for killing.

I said then, "I am not proud of the way we smear outsiders from the Floor of the Senate and hide behind the cloak of congressional immunity and still place ourselves beyond criticism on the Floor of the Senate."

Today I would add to that— I am not proud of the way in which too many militants resort to the illegalities of trespass, violence, and arson and, in doing so, claim for themselves a special immunity from the law with the allegation that such acts are justified because they have a political connotation with a professed cause.

I said then, "As a United States Senator, I am not proud of the way in which the Senate has been made a publicity platform for irresponsible sensationalism."

Today I would add that I am not proud of the way in which our national television networks and campuses have been made publicity platforms for irresponsible sensationalism — nor am I proud of the countercriticism against the networks and the campuses that has gone beyond the bounds of reasonableness and propriety and fanned, instead of drenching, the fires of division.

I have admired much of the candid and justified defense of our Government in reply to the news media and the militant dissenters — but some of the defense has been too extreme and unfair and too repetitive and thus impaired the effectiveness of the previous admirable and justified defense.

I said twenty years ago, "As an American, I am shocked at the way Republicans and Democrats alike are playing directly into the Communist design of 'confuse, divide, and conquer.'"

Today I am shocked at the way too many Americans are so doing.

I spoke as I did twenty years ago because of what I considered to be the great threat from the radical right — the threat of a Government of repression.

I speak today because of what I consider to be the great threat from the radical left that advocates and practices violence and defiance of the law — again, the threat of the ultimate result of a reaction of repression.

The President denies that we are in a revolution. There are many who would disagree with such appraisal. Anarchy may seem nearer to many of us than it really is.

But of one thing I am sure. The excessiveness of overreactions on both sides is a clear and present danger to American democracy.

That danger is ultimately from the political right even though it is initially spawned by the antidemocratic arrogance and nihilism from the political extreme left.

Extremism bent upon polarization of our people is increasingly forcing upon the American people the narrow choice between anarchy and repression.

And make no mistake about it, if that narrow choice has to be made, the American people, even if with reluctance and misgiving, will choose repression.

For an overwhelming majority of Americans believe that:

Trespass is trespass — whether on the campus or off. Violence is violence-whether on the campus or off. Arson is arson — whether on the campus or off. Killing is killing — whether on the campus or off.

The campus cannot degenerate into a privileged sanctuary for obscenity, trespass, violence, arson, and killing with special immunity for participants in such acts.

Criminal acts, active or by negligence, cannot be condoned or excused because of panic, whether the offender be a policeman, a national guardsman, a student, or one of us in this legislative body.

Ironically, the excess of dissent on the extreme left can result in repression of dissent. For repression is preferable to anarchy and nihilism to most Americans.

Yet, excesses on the extreme right, such as those twenty years ago, can mute our national conscience.

As was the case twenty years ago when the Senate was silenced and politically intimidated by one of its members, so today many Americans are intimidated and made mute by the emotional violence of the extreme left. Constructive discussion on the subject is becoming increasingly difficult of attainment.

It is time that the great center of our people, those who reject the violence and unreasonableness of both the extreme right and the extreme left, searched their consciences, mustered their moral and physical courage, shed their intimidated silence, and declared their consciences.

It is time that with dignity, firmness and friendliness, they reason with, rather than capitulate to, the extremists on both sides — at all levels — and caution that their patience ends at the border of violence and anarchy that threatens our American democracy.

"I Speak as a Woman"

Throughout my years in the United States Senate wherever I went I was asked if, as the only woman, I was treated equally and fairly by the men Senators. I was— but not because of any application of Equal Rights but rather because of the operation of the seniority system. The seniority system was the greatest guarantee of Equal rights to me, whether it be selection of office suites, garage parking spaces, or committee assignments.

On the goal of the Equal Rights Amendment, which I sponsored throughout my years in Congress, the most effective champion has been Representative Martha Griffiths of Michigan. She has done a brilliant and most intelligently effective job and in a very gracious and ladylike manner.

Once seemingly well on its way to ratification by the states, the Equal Rights Amendment is now on the verge of being rejected. The last count was that only two more states had to reject it in order for it to be killed.

Why the rapid reversal? Individual opinions and evaluations vary. Mine is only one of many. It may have some significance in view of the fact that I have so long been a sponsor of the Equal Rights Amendment and for many years the only woman in the United States Senate. I leave the validity of my opinion to your judgment.

I think there are two basic reasons. One could be termed a long term, strategic, fundamental and ideological weakness. The other could be considered a short term, tactical, superficial and practical weakness.

The long term, strategic, fundamental and ideological weakness is that too many of the militant, overly vociferous advocates of the Equal Rights Amendment have really wanted more than Equal Rights. They have, in effect, want to be more Equal than men. They have wanted to have their cake and eat it too. For with their demand for Equal Rights they have insisted on retaining their special feminine privileges. And that clearly is not Equal Rights.

The result is that their credibility has been seriously impaired. A selfishness has been exposed. They have been caught in an apparent inconsistency that has made their seriousness and sense of fairness suspect. This is the external aspect of their long term, strategic, fundamental and ideological weakness that impairs their effectiveness in attempting to persuade support for the Equal Rights Amendment.

But more important and serious is the internal aspect of this weakness. For the apparent inconsistency of clinging to special feminine privileges while crusading for Equal Rights is bound to have its toll on the mental effectiveness of the Equal Rights Amendment advocates. For if they cannot convince themselves to give up special feminine privileges and reject all qualifications on the concept of Equal Rights, how then do they think that they can convince others? Thus, a basic weakness in what they think.

The second weakness — the short term, tactical, superficial, and practical weakness — has been in what they do — and especially since the congressional passage of the Equal Rights Amendment. It has been
in the overapplication of the "hard sell" on the Equal Rights Amendment.

It was the intelligent, persuasive strategy and tactic as led and personified by Michigan Representative Martha Griffiths that produced the great success on the Equal Rights Amendment. I don't think it could be accurately described as a "soft sell" but it certainly was not a "hard sell" of offensive and officious proportions.

The "hard sell" that has backfired to undermine the heretofore success on the Equal Rights Amendment passage has come in forms of questionable pressure, exhibitionism, and name calling. And very frankly, this intense pressure — as contrasted to respectful persuasion — exhibitionism, and name calling has turned a lot of people off from support of the Equal Rights Amendment.

An example of the "hard sell" of name calling has been characterizing any man who would not readily and immediately support the Equal Rights Amendment to be a despicable "male chauvinist." This has not only alienated those who have so been characterized but it has, as well, alienated many possible converts to the cause — the real potentials for support of the Equal Rights Amendment. They have been turned off and lost because they consider it anything but fair play.

An example of the exhibitionism of the "hard sell" is the "bra burning." The reaction of disgust to this needs no elaboration. Suffice it to say that few want to associate themselves with sensational "bra burning" exhibitionists. Few find them hardly credible and truly serious. Most are turned off with their taste of expression.

As an example of the "hard sell" of pressure is that pressure that has publicly been put on members of state legislatures with demands of immediate ratification. Too often it has backfired. Just put yourself in the shoes of an uncommitted member of a state legislature. What would be your reaction if any lobbying group tried to put you on the spot publicly with pressure?

Chances are that you would resent it deeply because of the implication to the public that any lobbying group could assume that it could control your vote by the means of public pressure or by any other form of pressure. Chances are good that you would vote the opposite to prove to the public that they didn't control you.

While such "hard sell" tactics of "male chauvinist" name calling and "bra burning" exhibitionism have backfired in a reaction of increasing disgust and resentment, that has been relatively latent despite its quiet growth, it is the "hard sell" tactic of pressure made publicly in recent weeks that has been the most damaging to the cause of the Equal Rights Amendment.

State legislators who resent and resist the attempted pressure of putting them publicly on the spot are now finding support from the heretofore latent disgust and resentment of so many quiet people to the "bra burning" and shouts of "male chauvinism." The end result is that they are receiving quiet and private expression of opposition from the public to such extremism in tactics.

So if the Equal Rights Amendment is to have a chance, we had better quickly return to the Martha Griffith's way of friendly, but firm, persuasion in face-to-face talks or personal letters to state legislators — rather than talking to them through the news media with public pressure news releases.

At the outset, I spoke of the questions asked me about my experience of being the only woman in the United States Senate for many years. A broader and more challenging question that has been asked me is that of "Where is the proper place for a woman?" It has been asked of me wherever I have gone both
here in the United States and in many foreign countries.

It has been asked defiantly, ambitiously, hopefully — and just plainly inquisitively. But it has been asked so many times in so many ways and by so many types of people that, of necessity, my answer has had ways and by so many types of people that, of necessity, my answer has had to transcend the normal and understandable prejudice that a woman might have.

The answer is short and simple — woman's proper place is everywhere. Individually, it is where the particular woman is happiest and best fitted. It is, first, in the home as wives and mothers; second, in organized civic, business and professional groups like yours; third, in industry and business, both management and labor; and, fourth, in Government and politics.

Perhaps the most lasting and basic influence of women is in the Home — for behind all men, great or small, are women. This might appear too obvious for mention. But it is too often that we overlook the obvious. The fight for decent conditions in communities, for improvement in food, housing, school, health, and recreational facilities has been led by the women of the home — the wives and the mothers.

Basically, the incentive and the attraction of more women in higher public office should stem from the fundamental fact that women are the governors of the home. They legislate the rules of the home; they execute and enforce the rules of the home; and they interpret the rules of the home.

The importance of their role as governors of the home is that the home is the most fundamental form of government. Our community governments are no more than a federation of individual home governments.

Much, if not most, of the past leadership of women in this country has come through civic organizations such as yours. The basic ingredient for this successful performance record has been the banding of women together in organized groups, such as you have done, to give greater voice and more specific objectives to the interests and efforts of individual women.

Let me conclude with some remarks on a subject on which I am sure some of you would like to make some expression— on the so-called women's liberation.

Women are more emancipated today— even though the Equal Rights Amendment has not yet been ratified — than ever before. Less and less are they dependent upon men for their sustenance and their survival. This is greatly because of their own doing and group leadership action. I speak of the economic and financial independence which has been gradual and evolutionary and achieved only after years and years of a very hard struggle. Women earned this kind of independence.

But now through the achievement of medical science, women also have physical and biological security and freedom— suddenly and explosively given them and with it a female revolution.

I don't propose to evaluate the pill in terms of moral standards. I leave that to others to do— to others who are far more competent on either moralizing or demoralizing.

Instead I speak of the pill objectively— and at the risk of a pun— as an inescapable, even if suddenly new, fact of life. Some of its consequences are bluntly clear — as clear as the "see-through" dresses and as revealing as the micro-mini skirts. Adam's rib simply isn't the sedate sanctum it once was. Eve's pill has changed all that.

Yes, women are now in an age of unprecedented power in which they are more openly, more candidly, and more honestly pursuing rather than pretending to be pursued — in which they are more openly, candidly, and honestly pursuing whether it be for economic security, personal achievement, or a mate.

They are doing it with twin authoritative powers of economic security and biological security. But my caution to those of my own sex is that with such authority goes serious responsibility and that such power should be very carefully exercised lest it ultimately be the self-destruction of woman and her rightful and responsible place in civilization rather than "mankind."

In closing, I want to commend you on your banquet theme of "Respect, Reverence and Responsibility" and your state theme of "A Woman's

Influence" within that context.

I join you in respect for the Flag. I voted for legislation that would make destruction and desecration of the Flag a crime. The man who defeated me was one of a handful in the House that voted against it.

I join you in respect for our beloved country and in defending it against those radicals here at home that derogate it.

I join you in reverence for God. In my "this I Believe" statement featured by the late Edward R. Murrow in his radio program and book, I said that "I must believe in God — if life is to have any meaning." In fact, these were the concluding words of my book *Declaration of Conscience* at page 448, as they are the concluding words in this address to you.

Chronology of Significant
Speaking Events

The purpose of this chronology is to help the reader gain greater understanding of the speeches delivered by Margaret Chase Smith during her long career. As with all successful speakers, she addressed the occasion of the speech event, the time and the place, as well as the audience. These basic demands of public communication, viewed through the perceptual filter of the speaker's unique experiential world, determine the verbal and nonverbal codes selected for the particular speaking event. Her choice of words and expressions discloses a great deal about the character of the speaker and her attitude toward the speaking situation.

The texts of the addresses listed below can be found in Part II. Twelve of the speeches are the subjects for analysis in Part I; the remaining five are alluded to in those chapters.

1946

| July 8 | National Federation of Business and Professional Women's Clubs, Cleveland, Ohio | "Women and Leadership" |

1948

| Jan. 20 | Women's Bar Association, Washington, D.C. | "No Place for a Woman" |
| May 21 | Somerset County Republican Club, Skowhegan, Maine | "Answer to a Smear" |

| June 20 | Maine | "Election Eve Radio Speech" |

1949

| Aug. 20 | Woman's Christian Temperance Union, Philadelphia, PA | "Women's Progress" |

1950

| June 1 | U.S. Senate, Washington, D.C. | "Declaration of Conscience I" |

1951

| April 21 | Hood College, Frederick, Maryland | "The Importance of Individual Thinking" |

1954

| Sept. 12 | Senate Election Campaign (televised address) | "Response to Professor Fullam's 'Are You Proud?' Speech" |

1959

| Oct. 24 | Federation of Business and Professional Women's Clubs Convention, Lewiston, Maine | "Celebrating the Fortieth Anniversary" |

1961

| Sept. 21 | U.S. Senate, Washington, D.C. | "Nuclear Credibility" |

1962

| April 16 | National Republican Women's Conference Banquet, Washington, D.C. | "The Kennedy Twist" |

| Sept. 21 | U.S. Senate,
Washington, D.C. | "Nuclear Credibility" |

1963

| Sept. 24 | U.S. Senate,
Washington, D.C. | "Nuclear Test Ban Treaty" |

1964

| Jan. 27 | Women's National Press
Club, Washington, D.C. | "Presidential Candidacy
Announcement" |

1969

| Aug. 6 | U. S. Senate,
Washington, D.C. | "Anti-ABM" |

1970

| June 1 | U.S. Senate,
Washington, D.C. | "Declaration of Conscience II" |

1973

| April 25 | Ohio Federation of
Women's Clubs, Columbus | "I Speak as a Woman" |

Bibliography

PRIMARY SOURCES

The most complete collection of Margaret Chase Smith's papers, documents, and political memorabilia can be found at the Northwood University Margaret Chase Smith Library, built adjacent to, and including, her home overlooking the Kennebec River in Skowhegan, Maine. The library's archival holdings consist of more than ninety file cabinets, containing over 300,000 documents, 500 scrapbooks, over 5,000 photographs, and numerous audio and video recordings from Senator Smith's thirty-two-year political career. The scrapbooks thoroughly document her career as seen in newspaper accounts and periodical literature. They also contain the newspaper column, "Washington and You," written by Senator Smith between 1941 and 1954 (syndicated nationally from 1949-1954). The collection holds forty-three volumes of Senator Smith's speeches in Congress, her public pronouncements, and reports to her constituents. Also included are the Clyde Smith Papers and the William C. Lewis, Jr. Papers, correspondence between Senator Smith and leading policymakers and government officials, constituent correspondence, and government hearings.

Margaret Chase Smith Archives

Scrapbooks (500)
Statements and Speeches (43 vols.)

Interviews and Correspondence with the Author

Smith, Margaret Chase. Interview with the author. June 2, 1992, Skowhegan, Maine.

———. Interview with the author. 1993.
———. Correspondence with the author. 1992-1995.

Documents

U.S. Congress. House. *Congressional Record*. 1937-1948.
U.S. Congress. Senate. *Congressional Record*. 1949-1972.

SECONDARY SOURCES

Books on Margaret Chase Smith

Agger, Lee. *Women of Maine*. Portland, Maine: Guy Gannett, 1982.
Fleming, Alice. *The Senator from Maine*. New York: Thomas Y. Crowell Co.,
    1969.
Gould, Alberta. *First Lady of the Senate — A Life of Margaret Chase Smith*.
    Mt. Desert, Maine: Windswept House Publishers, 1990.
Graham, Frank, Jr. *Margaret Chase Smith: Woman of Courage*. New York:
    John Day Co., 1964.
Lamson, Peggy. *Few Are Chosen: American Women in Political Life Today*.
    Boston: Houghton Mifflin, 1968.
Schmidt, Patricia L. *Margaret Chase Smith: Beyond Convention*. Orono: The
    University of Maine Press, 1996.
Smith, Margaret Chase. *Declaration of Conscience*. Ed. William C. Lewis, Jr.
    Garden City, New York: Doubleday, 1972.
Wallace, Patricia Ward. *Politics of Conscience: A Biography of Margaret Chase
    Smith*. Westport, Conn.: Praeger Publishers, 1995.

Articles on Margaret Chase Smith

Cook, Gay, and Dale Pullen. "Margaret Chase Smith, Republican Senator
    from Maine." In *Ralph Nader Congressional Project: Citizens Look at
    Congress*. New York: Grossman Publishers, 1972.
Doody, Agnes G. "A Study of Margaret Chase Smith as an Orator and of
    Her Senatorial Address of June 1, 1950." Master's thesis, Pennsylvania
    State University, 1954.
Gallant, Gregory P. "Margaret Chase Smith: McCarthyism and the Drive for
    Political Purification." Ph.D. dissertation, University of Maine, 1992.
Goodyear, Sarah. "A Singular Act of Courage." *Down East* 41 (January 1995):
    28-31, 60-62.
Graham, Mary W. "Margaret Chase Smith: Presidential Campaign, 1964."
    Quarterly Journal of Speech 50 (December 1964): 390-393.
Harris, Lois Anne. "Margaret Chase Smith: An Examination of Her Public

Speaking with Emphasis on the 'Declaration of Conscience, 1950' and the 'Declaration of Conscience, 1970.'" Ph.D. dissertation, Southern Illinois University, 1974.

Schwartz, Howard. "Senator Smith Speaks on Speaking." *Communication Quarterly* 15 (February 1967): 19-22.

"Senator Smith: A Woman Vice-President?" *Newsweek* 35 (June 12, 1950): 24.

Sherman, Janann. "'They Either Need These Women or They Do Not': Margaret Chase Smith and the Fight for Regular Status for Women in the Military." *Journal of Military History* 54 (January 1990): 47-78.

Smith, Margaret Chase. "Woman, the Key Individual of Our Democracy: Think Well, Then Speak Your Mind." *Vital Speeches of the Day* 19 (August 15, 1953): 657-659.

——— . "Impatience and Generosity: Comments on European and Asian Trips." *Vital Speeches of the Day* 21 (May 15, 1955): 1230-1233.

Vallin, Marlene Boyd. "Margaret Chase Smith: The Spirit of Conviction." In *Courage of Conviction: Women's Words, Women's Wisdom,* eds., Linda A.M. Perry and Patricia Geist. Mountain View, California: Mayfield Publishing Co., 1997. 87-99.

HISTORICAL SOURCES

Books

Aristotle.   *The Politics.*   Ed. Stephen Everson. New York: Cambridge University Press, 1988.

Beschloss, Michael R. *The Crisis Years: Kennedy and Khrushchev 1960-1963*. New York: HarperCollins, 1991.

A Congressional Quarterly Guide to Congress. 4th ed. Washington, D.C., Congressional Quarterly, 1991.

Dictionary of American History. New York: Charles Scribner's Sons, 1940.

Encyclopedia of American Political History: Studies of the Principal Movements and Ideas. Ed. Jack P. Greene. New York: Charles Scribner's Sons, 1984.

Goldwater, Barry, with Jack Casserly. *Goldwater*. Garden City, New York: Doubleday, 1988.

Halberstam, David. *The Fifties*. New York: Villard Books, 1993.

The Heart of Emerson's Journals. Ed. Terry Bliss. New York: Dover Publications, Inc., 1958.

A History of the National Federation of Business and Professional Women's Clubs, Inc. 1914-1944. New York: National Federation of Business and Professional Women, 1944.

Hodgson, Godfrey. *America in Our Time*. New York: Random House, 1976.

Kennan, George F. *Memoirs 1950-1963*. Boston: Little, Brown, 1972.

Khrushchev Remembers: The Last Testament. Trans. and Strobe Talbott. Boston: Little, Brown, 1974.

Lait, Jack, and Lee Mortimer. *U.S.A. Confidential.* New York: Crown Publishers, 1952.

Lattimore, Owen. *Ordeal by Slander.* Boston: Little, Brown, 1950.

Leeman, Richard W. *"Do Everything" Reform: The Oratory of Frances E. Willard.* New York: Greenwood Press, 1992.

Nevins, Allan, and Henry Steele Commager, with Jeffrey Morris. *A Pocket History of the United States.* New York: Washington Square Press, 1981.

Oshinsky, David M. *A Conspiracy So Immense: The World of Joe McCarthy* New York: Free Press, 1983.

Pullen, John J. *Patriotism in America.* New York: American Heritage Press, 1971.

Rovere, Richard H. *Senator Joe McCarthy.* New York: Harcourt, Brace and Company, 1959.

Schlesinger, Arthur M., Jr. *Robert Kennedy and His Times.* Vol. 1. Boston: Houghton Mifflin, 1978.

Weatherford, Doris. *American Women's History.* New York: Prentice-Hall, 1994.

White, Theodore H. *Breach of Faith: The Fall of Richard Nixon.* New York: Atheneum Publishers/Reader's Digest Press, 1975.

Articles

"The Communist Party in the U.S." *Newsweek* 29 (June 2, 1947): 22-26.

Douglas, William O. "Our Political Competence." *Vital Speeches of the Day* 14 (August 15, 1948): 645-649.

Editorial. *New Republic* 122 (June 12, 1950): 3.

Hoover, J. Edgar. "How to Fight Communism." *Newsweek* 29 (June 9, 1947): 30.

Kennedy, John F. "What Kind of Peace Do We Want?" *Vital Speeches of the Day* 29 (July 1, 1953): 558-561.

Newspapers

Anniston, Alabama Star. June 4, 1950.
Bangor Daily News. September 15, 1948.
——— . January 29, 1964.
——— . February 15-16, 1964.
——— . March 12, 1964.
Huntsville Times. June 4, 1950.
New York Times. June 2, 1950.
New York Times. June 3, 1950.

CRITICAL STUDIES

Books

Burke, Kenneth. *A Rhetoric of Motives*. Englewood Cliffs, New Jersey: Prentice-Hall, 1950.

Edelman, Murray. *Political Language: Words That Succeed and Policies That Fail*. New York: Academic Press, 1977.

Hinds, Lynn Boyd, and Theodore Otto Windt, Jr. *The Cold War as Rhetoric: The Beginnings, 1945-1950*. New York: Praeger, 1991.

Kennedy, Patricia Scileppi, and Gloria Hartmann O'Shields, eds. *We Shall Be Heard: Women Speakers in America 1828-Present*. Dubuque, Iowa: Kendall/Hunt Publishing Co., 1983.

Manning, Beverly, ed. *We Shall Be Heard: An Index to Speeches by American Women 1978-1985*. Metuchen, N.J.: Scarecrow Press, 1988.

Perelman, Chaim, and L. Olbrechts-Tyteca. *The New Rhetoric: A Treatise on Argumentation*. Notre Dame, Ind.: Notre Dame University Press, 1969.

Smith, Craig Allen. *Political Communication*. San Diego: Harcourt Brace Jovanovich, 1990.

Windt, Theodore Otto, Jr. *Presidents and Protesters: Political Rhetoric in the 1960s*. Tuscaloosa: University of Alabama Press, 1990.

Articles

James R. Andrews. "Reflections of the National Character in American Rhetoric." *Quarterly Journal of Speech* 57 (October 1971): 316-324.

Blankenship, Jane, and Deborah C. Robson. "A 'Feminine Style' in Women's Political Discourse: An Exploratory Essay." *Communication Quarterly* 43 (Summer 1995): 353-365.

Bormann, Ernest G., John F. Cragan, and Donald C. Shields. "An Expansion of the Rhetorical Vision Component of the Symbolic Convergence Theory: The Cold War Paradigm Case." Communication Monographs 63 (March 1996): 1-27.

Campbell, Karlyn Kohrs, and E. Claire Jerry. "Woman and Speaker: A Conflict in Roles." In *Seeing Female: Social Roles and Personal Lives*, ed. Sharon S. Brehm. Westport, Conn.: Greenwood Press, 1988. 124-132.

———. "Hearing Women's Voices." *Communication Education* 40 (January 1991): 33-47.

Foss, Karen A. and Sonja K. Foss. "The Status of Research on Women and Communication." *Communication Quarterly* 31 (Summer 1983): 195-204.

Hart, Rodererick P. "A Commentary on Popular Assumptions about Political Communication." *Human Communication Research* 8 (Summer 1982): 366-389.

———. "Contemporary Scholarship in Public Address: A Research Editorial."

Western Journal of Speech Communication 50 (Summer 1986): 286-295.

Kramer, Cheris. "Women's Speech: Separate But Unequal?" *Quarterly Journal of Speech* 60 (Summer 1974): 14-24.

Logue, Cal M., and Eugene F. Miller. "Rhetorical Status: A Study of Its Origins, Function, and Consequences." *Quarterly Journal of Speech* 81 (1995): 20-47.

Lucas, Stephen E. "The Renaissance of American Public Address: Text and Context in Rhetorical Criticism." *Quarterly Journal of Speech* 74 (1988): 241-260.

Videorecordings

Burton-Norris, Judith. *Personhood of Margaret Chase Smith*. Videocassette.

Debate between Senator Margaret Chase Smith and Mrs. Eleanor Roosevelt. *Face the Nation*. November 4, 1956.

King, Angus. A Conversation in Maine with Margaret Chase Smith. WCBB-TV. August 18, 1988. Videocassette.

Murrow, Edward R. Senator Margaret Chase Smith and Mr. Robert Jones. On *See It Now*. 1954. Videocassette.

Wiggins, Patsy. *Margaret Chase Smith: A Woman of Courage*. Maine Broadcasting System. December 11, 1987. Videocassette.

Index

Aiken, George, 3, 11, 22, 111
Americanism
  basic principles, 7, 25, 31
  Smith, defender of, 11, 30, 41
  threat to, 14, 35, 36.
  See also "Declaration of
  Conscience I"
"Answer to a Smear," 95-100,
  136-142
"Anti-ABM," 214-218

Baruch, Bernard, 13
Beverage, Albion, 96, 98, 103
Business and Profession Women
  [BPW]
  advancement of women's rights,
  76, 104
  purpose, 74, 76-77, 79
  support of MCS, 4, 5, 9, 76, 79,
  97, 104.
  See also "Celebrating the Fortieth"; "Women and Leadership"

Caraway, Hattie, 9
"Celebrating the Fortieth Anniversary," 170-174
citizenship

value of, 24, 42
women's rights, 85, 90.
See also "Declaration of Conscience II"
Colby College, 38, 41, 48, 103,
  112
Cold War
  definition, 5, 15, 45, 75
  nuclear arms control, 8, 67
  rhetoric, 75
  sentiment, American, 67
  superpowers, 45, 59, 64.
  See also "Anti-ABM"; "Declaration of Conscience I"; "Nuclear Credibility"(1961); "Nuclear Credibility" (1962); "Nuclear Test Ban Treaty"
Commencement speeches, 9, 10,
  74, 91.
  See also "Importance of Individual Thinking, The"
Common sense, 3, 81, 82, 84, 89
Communism
  emergence, 15
  fear of, 16, 34, 46
  spread of, 46, 75.
  See also Vietnam War
Cormier, Lucia, 104
Craig, May, 95

"Declaration of Conscience I," 14-35, 153-157
"Declaration of Conscience II," 35-44, 219-222
Democratic administration
   criticism of, 14, 21, 24, 25, 28
   support of, 93, 94, 96
democratic principles, 15, 24, 26, 28, 36
   morality, 10, 100
   values, 6, 7, 8, 89
   virtues, 84.
   See also Americanism

Eisenhower, Dwight D.
   foreign policy, 37, 47, 49, 50, 58
   Nixon, choice for v.p., 104
election (1940), House of Repre-sentatives, 7
election (1948), Senate
   gender issue, 48, 95
   primary opponents, 96
   results, 103.
   See also smear campaigns
election (1954), Senate
   McCarthy's candidate, 103
   Democratic opponent, 48.
   See also "Response to 'Are You Proud'"
election (1960), Senate, 104
election (1966), Senate, 111
election (1972), Senate, 112
   age issue, 113
   general, 112-113
   Nader Report, 112
   primary, 112
   results, 113
"Election Eve Radio Address," 100-103, 143-146
equality for women
   Nineteenth Amendment, 5, 10
   suffrage, 77, 79, 80, 85, 86, 103
ethos, use of

   for general appeal, 68
   as model Senator, 27-30
   as model woman, 9, 75
   as public servant, 106
   as representative American, 7, 55-57

feminism
   Smith's view, 10, 74, 77, 81, 90.
   See also "I Speak as a Woman"
Fullam, Paul (Professor), 48, 103.
   See also "Response to 'Are You Proud'"

gender issue, 9, 73-74, 91
   primary (1948), 95, 100, 103, 110-111.
   See also "Answer to a Smear"; "No Place for a Woman"
Goldwater, Barry, 4, 104, 105, 111
grassroots politics, 93, 102, 110.
   See also "Election Eve Radio Address"

Hathaway, William, 112-113
Hildreth, Horace, 96, 98, 103
House of Representatives
   armed services committees, 10, 47, 74
   gender issue, 73
   public servant, 24
   tenure, 7, 95, 100

identification, use of, 6, 7
   common ground, 52, 79, 84, 97, 102, 107
"Importance of Individual Thinking, The," 87-91, 158-162
"I Speak as a Woman," 223-227

Johnson, Lydon B., 5, 37
Jones, Robert, 103

Kennedy, John F., 8, 37, 71
  foreign policy, 8, 48-53, 57-60,
    66, 67.
  See also "Kennedy Twist, The,";
    "Nuclear Credibility" (1961);
    "Nuclear Credibility" (1962);
    "Nuclear Test Ban Treaty"
"Kennedy Twist, The," 184-194
Khrushchev, Mrs.
  view of Margaret Chase Smith,
    8
Khrushchev, Nikita
  and JFK, 51-58, 64, 66
  Margaret Chase Smith's dis-
    trust of, 60, 69, 70
  view of Margaret Chase Smith,
    8

Language
  choice, 38
  power of, 54
  style, 6, 29, 30, 52, 54
Lewis, William C. (Bill), 4, 5, 13,
  22-24, 39
  military man, 47-48
  political strategist, 96-100, 105-
    107
Lodge, Henry Cabot, 110, 111

Maine voters, 9,11, 24, 91, 93.
  See also "Election Eve Radio
    Address"
Marcantonio, Vito, 16, 96, 107.
  See also "Answer to a Smear"
McCarthy, Joseph, 7, 10, 14, 16-
  24, 34-35.
  See also "Declaration of Con-
    science I"

McCarthyism, 7, 18, 35, 89, 108.
  See also political extremism
Monks, Robert, 112
moral code, 12, 29, 75
moral courage, 9, 10, 30, 83, 88,
  91
moral cowardice, 10, 15, 30, 51
moral force, 82
Muskie, Edmund, 93, 104, 112

National Organization for Wom-
  en [NOW], 112
national security, 48-50, 52, 55,
  60, 68, 70.
  See also "Nuclear Credibility"
    (1961); "Nuclear Credibility"
    (1962)
Nixon, Richard, 4, 5, 8
  presidential candidate (1964),
    110-112
  vice president, 104-105.
  See also Vietnam War
"No Place for a Woman," 84-87,
  131-135
nuclear arms race, 16, 46
  Nuclear Test Ban Treaty, 71.
  See also "Anti-ABM"; "Nuclear
    Test Ban Treaty"
"Nuclear Credibility" (1961), 50-
  58, 175-183
"Nuclear Credibility" (1962), 58-
  64, 195-202
"Nuclear Test Ban Treaty," 64-71,
  203-206
nuclear warfare, 47-54, 56-58, 68-
  71
  American superiority, 8.
  See also "Nuclear Credibility"
    (1961); "Nuclear Credibility"
    (1962)

oratorical style, 6

oratory, 6, 28, 51

personal philosophy, 7, 9, 115
political extremism, 8, 14, 42, 68,
    108-109
  Left, 14, 35, 36, 38, 40-43
  Right, 13, 35, 40-42.
  See also "Declaration of Con-
    science II"
political machine, 100-101
political philosophy, 7, 13, 14, 29,
    48.
  See also Americanism, moral
    code
presidential campaign, 4.
  See also "Presidential Candida-
    cy Announcement"
"Presidential Candidacy An-
    nouncement," 106-111, 207-213

Republican National Convention
    (1964), 3, 20, 32, 79, 95, 104,
    105, 120
Republican Party
  conservatives, 21, 105
  moderates, 21, 32, 41, 108
"Response to 'Are You Proud,'"
    163-169
rhetoric, type of
  deliberative, 6, 51
  epideictic, 6, 26, 87
  forensic, 6, 85, 98, 99
rhetorical stance, 7-10, 57, 85, 87,
    100, 107.
  See also ethos
rhetorical strategy, 6, 30-31, 41,
    52.
  See also ethos; rhetorical stance
Roosevelt, Franklin D., 5
  New Deal, 21

Sewall, Sumner, 96, 98, 103
smear campaigns
  Margaret Chase Smith's re-
    sponse, 96-99, 100-103
  Margaret Chase Smith's, view
    of, 14, 25-26, 30
  McCarthy, 13, 20, 23, 34
  Senate primary (1948), 96
  U.S.A. Confidential, 34.
  See also "Answer to a Smear";
    "Declaration of Conscience I"
Smith, Clyde, 4, 47
Smith, Margaret Chase
  age issue, 105, 113
  awards and honors, 11
  background, 4
  ERA, support of, 10, 112
  "no place for a woman," 8, 104
  rose, 8
  world tour, 47
Somerset County Republican
    Women's Club, 95
Soviet Union [USSR]
  aggression, 45, 46, 65-66
  expansionism, 15, 46
  nuclear arms race, 16, 51-52
  space race, 46.
  See also Khrushchev, Nikita

Truman, Harry, 5, 17

Vietnam War
  anti-war protests, 8, 37-40, 112
  Smith's view, 60
  U.S. involvement, 5, 37, 43-44,
    47
Violette, Elmer H., 111

White, Wallace, 103
women, in politics
  research, 5-6

"Women and Leadership," 76-79,
  127-130
Women's Bar Association
  gender issue, 84
Woman's Christian Temperance
  Union [WCTU], 80.
  See also "Women's Progress"
women's equality.
  See citizenship; gender issue;
  "No Place for a Woman"; "Wo-
  men and Leadership"; Women's
  Progress"
Women's National Press Club,
  106
"Women's Progress," 79-84, 147-
  152
women's status in military, 74
women's traditional role.
  See "Importance of Individual
    Thinking"; "Women's Prog-
    ress"
World War II
  aftermath, 45, 75

About the Author

MARLENE BOYD VALLIN is Associate Professor of Speech Communication at Pennsylvania State University, Berks-Lehigh Valley College. She is the author of another volume in the Great American Orators series: *Mark Twain: Protaganist for the Popular Culture* (Greenwood, 1992).

Great American Orators

"Do Everything" Reform: The Oratory of Frances E. Willard
Richard W. Leeman

Abraham Lincoln the Orator: Penetrating the Lincoln Legend
Lois J. Einhorn

Mark Twain: Protagonist for the Popular Culture
Marlene Boyd Vallin

Delightful Conviction: Jonathan Edwards and the Rhetoric of Conversion
Stephen R. Yarbrough and John C. Adams

Harry S. Truman: Presidential Rhetoric
Halford R. Ryan

Dwight D. Eisenhower: Strategic Communicator
Martin J. Medhurst

Ralph Waldo Emerson: Preacher and Lecturer
Lloyd Rohler

"In a Perilous Hour": The Public Address of John F. Kennedy
Steven R. Goldzwig and George N. Dionisopoulos

Douglas MacArthur: Warrior as Wordsmith
Bernard K. Duffy and Ronald H. Carpenter

Sojourner Truth as Orator: Wit, Story, and Song
Suzanne Pullon Fitch and Roseann M. Mandziuk

Frederick Douglass: Oratory from Slavery
David B. Chesebrough

Father Charles E. Coughlin: Surrogate Spokesperson for the Disaffected
Ronald H. Carpenter

ISBN 0-313-29163-2

90000>

EAN

9 780313 291630

HARDCOVER BAR CODE